EXPLORING
GREEK
MYTH

This book is dedicated to the memory
of my sister, Miranda Smith

EXPLORING
GREEK
MYTH

MATTHEW
CLARK

WILEY-BLACKWELL

A John Wiley & Sons, Ltd., Publication

This edition first published 2012
© 2012 Matthew Clark

Blackwell Publishing was acquired by John Wiley & Sons in February 2007. Blackwell's
publishing program has been merged with Wiley's global Scientific, Technical, and Medical
business to form Wiley-Blackwell.

Registered Office
John Wiley & Sons Ltd, The Atrium, Southern Gate, Chichester, West Sussex, PO19 8SQ, UK

Editorial Offices
350 Main Street, Malden, MA 02148-5020, USA
9600 Garsington Road, Oxford, OX4 2DQ, UK
The Atrium, Southern Gate, Chichester, West Sussex, PO19 8SQ, UK

For details of our global editorial offices, for customer services, and for information about
how to apply for permission to reuse the copyright material in this book please see our website
at www.wiley.com/wiley-blackwell.

The right of Matthew Clark to be identified as the author of this work has been asserted in
accordance with the UK Copyright, Designs and Patents Act 1988.

Wiley also publishes its books in a variety of electronic formats. Some content that appears
in print may not be available in electronic books.

Designations used by companies to distinguish their products are often claimed as trademarks.
All brand names and product names used in this book are trade names, service marks,
trademarks or registered trademarks of their respective owners. The publisher is not associated
with any product or vendor mentioned in this book. This publication is designed to provide
accurate and authoritative information in regard to the subject matter covered. It is sold on the
understanding that the publisher is not engaged in rendering professional services.
If professional advice or other expert assistance is required, the services of a competent
professional should be sought.

Library of Congress Cataloging-in-Publication Data
Clark, Matthew, 1948-
  Exploring Greek myth / Matthew Clark.
      p. cm.
  Includes bibliographical references (p.   ) and index.
  ISBN 978-1-4051-9456-3 (hardcover : alk. paper) – ISBN 978-1-4051-9455-6 (pbk. : alk. paper)
1. Mythology, Greek. I. Title.
  BL783.C53 2012
  292.1'3–dc23

                                   2011038291
A catalogue record for this book is available from the British Library.

This book is published in the following electronic formats: ePDFs 9781444362121;
ePub 9781444362138; Mobi 9781444362145

Set in 10/13pt Minion by Thomson Digital, Noida, India

1   2012

Contents

List of Illustrations

Preface

Introductory courses in ancient Greek myth are taught in many colleges and universities throughout North America. In my own university, our full-year introductory course ("Myth and Imagination in Ancient Greece and Rome") regularly attracts about 400 students. There are also many popular books about Greek myth for the general reading public. Clearly Greek myth retains its interest for a wide public, both inside schools and out.

An introductory course, however, can only begin to suggest the richness and complexity of Greek myth. The introductory textbooks and popular accounts of myth quite rightly concentrate on telling the major myths, those that were widely known in ancient Greece and adapted in later Western art and literature, such as the myths of Demeter, Persephone and Hades; Oedipus; Jason and Medea; the Trojan War; and so on. But there are many other Greek myths, not so well known, that deserve study, both because they are great stories in themselves and also because they have something to tell us about the culture of the ancient Greeks. The textbooks and general introductions also present some discussion of cultural context and theoretical approaches to myth, but again there is much more to be said, both about the way these myths fit into the social practices of their times and also the way they were used as tools for thinking about important ideas, such as fate, justice, or the nature of divinity.

This book, then, is intended for students (and those in the general reading public) who have some background in Greek myth but want to know more. There is a huge body of scholarship on the topic, but much of this scholarly discussion is not easy for students, especially for those who don't read Greek or Latin. This book tries to bridge the gap between the introductory books and the scholarly studies, to present some of the research that has accumulated over the past decades in a way that is accessible for those who are not yet scholars in the field.

The primary goal of this book is to ask why the ancient Greeks told themselves the stories that we call the Greek myths. (They told themselves other kinds of stories, stories that can't be considered myths, but it is impossible in a book this size to take these into account as well.) In order to grapple with this question a reasonable knowledge of the variety of mythic stories is necessary. The Panhellenic myths – the myths that were told over all or most of the ancient Greek world – are a good start, but a number of local myths will have to be examined as well. These may give a rather different and broader sense of the place and function of myths in ancient Greek society.

Myths can be studied in many different ways. Some scholars have argued that myths give explanations for the creation and nature of the physical world, including the weather and features of the landscape. Other scholars believe that myths provide charters for social structures and practices, such as the division of people into nations or tribes, or the rules of sacrifice. (Myths that serve as explanations are called aetiological myths; both myths of nature and charter myths can be considered aetiological, since they both give explanations, whether of natural phenomena or social practices.) Comparison of myths from different cultures has suggested that some myths have spread widely, through a process known as diffusion, or perhaps that some myths represent fundamental psychological structures, mythic archetypes. Some myths may contain traces of historical events, such as the myths of the Trojan War. Myths can be interpreted as the narrative manifestation of abstract codes, fundamental patterns of thought. Myths may be used to express and attempt to resolve tensions within society.

All of these ways of interpreting myth have contributed to our understanding, and none has the exclusive key to the meaning of myth. The topics chosen for discussion here were not selected in order to promote any particular theory or approach, but rather to examine some fundamental questions (such as how myth is to be defined or characterized, or how Greek myth is related to Greek religion) and to explore some of the most important areas of recent research in the study of myth (such as comparative myth, myth and gender, or structuralist approaches to myth). The reader should not expect, therefore, a single argument about ancient Greek myth, but rather a series of different views from different angles and perspectives. Some themes, however, do recur, such as the role of myth in relation to ancient Greek social practices and even to the ancient Greek understanding of the landscape, the difference between Panhellenic myth and local myth and the importance of both for the study of myth, and the various ways that myth has meaning, both in its own time and throughout the Western tradition.

The investigation of these questions will not be simple or direct, and the course of the discussion will involve various aspects of ancient Greek myth. Each chapter is organized around a particular topic or problem or question. Chapter One introduces some definitions and characteristics of myth. Chapter Two deals with the relationship between Greek myth and Greek religion, and Chapter Three examines the web of traditions which we can deduce might have been known to the ancient Greeks. Chapter Four asks about the sources for our knowledge of Greek myth, and Chapter Five considers the question of the meaning of myths, including some brief account of modern theories of myth. Chapter Six concerns hero cult, an important aspect of Greek ritual practice, with close connections to myth. Chapter Seven discusses myths about the foundation of cities, including cities on the mainland of Greece, such as Athens and Corinth, and some of the Greek colonies, such as Cyrene. Chapter Eight considers the methods of comparative mythology, as Greek myths are studied in the light of myths from other cultures, and Chapter Nine is concerned with myth and gender. Chapter Ten asks about the relationship between myth and history, Chapter Eleven considers myth as a way of thought, and Chapter Twelve looks at myth and philosophy, particularly in the works of Plato. The primary focus of the discussion will be on the ancient myths in their ancient context, but from time to time there will be some consideration of the continuing use of myths in the Western tradition. Each chapter will also include suggestions for further reading, limited to works in English, including of course translations from other languages, and brief suggestions for further explorations in the form of essays or research projects.

Readers will probably already know some of the myths discussed here, but not all, and in any case it is easy to forget details in all these stories. Narrating all the myths mentioned would expand this text beyond any reasonable limit. Some myths, especially those that are little known, will be told in detail, but others will appear only in summary, either in the body of the text or in boxes, and sometimes only the points that are important for the discussion will be mentioned. Readers may find it useful to have on hand a good encyclopedia of myth for reference and for exploration of the many Greek myths which have not found a place in this discussion.

The Greek myths are fascinating stories in themselves. They are also important evidence for how the ancient Greeks thought and how they lived. And since they retain their interest for us today, they tell us something about ourselves as well. If this book leads students on to further exploration of the myths and of the scholars who study the myths, it will have served its purpose.

The following short forms have been used for three ancient sources referred to frequently in the text:

Library = Apollodorus, *The Library of Greek Mythology* (the final section is preserved in an epitome, referred to as *Epit.*)
Guide = Pausanias, *Guide to Greece*
Met. = Ovid, *Metamorphoses*

NOTE ON SPELLING

The spelling of Greek names in English is a problem. The older practice was to use more or less Latinized versions of names (Aeschylus, Oedipus, Aegisthus, Lycus), where, for example, the Greek diphthongs "oi" and "ai" are represented as "oe" and "ae", the Greek kappa is represented by "c", and the nominative ending "-os" is represented by "-us", but the recent trend has been to stick closer to transliteration of the Greek (Aiskhylos, Oidipous, Aigisthos, Lykos). The name of the mythic founder of the Aeolian Greeks can be spelled three different ways: some scholars use the Latinized form "Aeolus," some prefer "Aiolos," and some prefer a mixed form, "Aeolos," which is the form adopted here. The problem becomes worse if both Greek and Latin sources are cited: the name of the young hunter killed by his own hounds would be spelled "Aktaion" in a Greek source but "Actaeon" in Ovid's *Metamorphoses*. Probably no solution is perfect. Here Greek names are generally preferred to their Latin counterparts ("Demeter" rather than "Ceres"). Familiar names are spelled in their most familiar way, usually Latinized, but less familiar names are kept in spellings closer to the Greek.

FURTHER READING

There are several good introductions to Greek myth, such as Graf 1993, Kirk 1970, Strenski 1987, Dowden 1992, and Lincoln 1999. The three most used introductory textbooks are Powell 2008, Harris and Platzner 2011, and Morford *et al.* 2011. Buxton 1994 is good on the social and cultural contexts within which myths were told. Bremmer 1988 is a collection of scholarly articles. The best ancient handbook is Apollodorus' *The Library of Greek Mythology*; available in a Loeb translation by J. G. Frazer. The most complete modern encyclopedia is *Early Greek Myth*, by Timothy Gantz (1993). Robert Graves' *Greek Myths* is generally reliable when he is simply telling the story, but his interpretations should be regarded with caution at best.

Acknowledgments

These explorations would never have happened without the help of many people. I begin by thanking those teachers, colleagues, and friends with whom I have discussed myth over the years, in particular Eric Csapo and Gregory Nagy. Special thanks also to those with whom I have shared the teaching of Humanities 1105, "Myth and Imagination in Ancient Greece and Rome": James Rives, Laurence Broadhurst, and Clifford Ando; this course is now in the able hands of Rob Tordoff. The wonderful editorial group at Wiley-Blackwell has been helpful and encouraging from beginning to end; Haze Humbert (who got the whole thing going), Galen Young, Allison Medoff, Nik Prowse, and Michael Coultas, as well as the anonymous readers. Thanks also to Ann Lau for the indexing. And thanks to the many students over the years who have allowed me to ramble on about the wonders of Greek myth.

Chapter One

THE KNIFE DID IT
*Definitions and Characteristics
for the Study of Myth*

This chapter introduces definitions and concepts necessary for the exploration of Greek myth. Myth is not easy to define, and there is no definition which would receive universal approval, but an approximate definition is presented in Section I. Section II continues with a few characteristics of Greek myth not covered by the definition, including time in Greek myth, and the interconnected web of stories which make up the mythic tradition. Section III asks if the Greek themselves had a concept of Greek Myth. Sections IV and V introduce an important distinction between Panhellenic myths – myths which were widely known throughout the Greek world – and local myths – myths which were of primary interest to those resident in a particular city or region of Greece. Section IV uses the myth of the abduction of Persephone as an example of Panhellenic myth, and Section V presents the story of the Athenian festival of the Bouphonia as an example of local myth.

I. WHAT IS A MYTH?

It is easy to give examples of Greek myths – the Abduction of Persephone, for instance, or the Labors of Herakles – but surprisingly difficult to say exactly what a Greek myth is. Scholars generally agree that myth is a slippery category. According to G. S. Kirk, "There is no one definition of myth" (1970: 7). Walter Burkert asks, "What is myth?", and he answers, "A simple definition will not do" (1979: 1). Eric Csapo warns that "Definition is never the innocent first step in a process of empirical discovery . . .; it is rather always the final precipitate of an already elaborate theory", and he continues, "If I begin with a discussion of the problems of defining myth, it is to urge suspicion" (2005: 1). Despite these warnings, it seems appropriate to attempt a provisional definition, so that the reader will have an idea of what will count as a Greek myth in this book, and then to indicate some of the problems such a definition may raise.

Exploring Greek Myth. First Edition. Matthew Clark.
© 2012 Matthew Clark. Published 2012 by Blackwell Publishing Ltd.

As an approximate definition, then, *a myth is a traditional story that speaks to important issues in the culture in which it is told*. This definition is not perfect, as further discussion will show, but it marks off at least a central area that everyone would consider myth. This definition should not be used too rigidly, however; the edges of the category are fuzzy, and myths that are atypical by this definition should not be excluded from consideration.

According to this definition a myth is a story, that is, a connected account of a series of events and actions, a narrative. Thus a character is not a myth: Herakles, for example, is not a mythic character until he takes part in some mythic story. Some theorists of myth, particularly the psychologist Carl Jung and his followers, have been particularly interested in so-called archetypal characters, such as the Hero or the Divine Child. According to the definition of myth used here, these archetypal characters are not in themselves myths, and they are part of the study of myth only insofar as they can be found in the kinds of stories called myths.

There are, however, a few myths that do not seem to be narratives, strictly speaking. One of the most important is the Myth of the Five Ages in Hesiod's *Works and Days*. According to this myth, the world has gone through a succession of Ages: the Golden Age, the Silver Age, the Bronze Age, the Age of Heroes, and the Iron Age. There are no characters here and really no events, just a series of descriptions. This account, as well as some parts of Hesiod's *Theogony* that are not narrative, have been called myths for so long that it would seem perverse not to include them in the category. Nonetheless, they are not typical of myth simply because they are not stories, and it is worthwhile making some kind of distinction, whether they are included or not.

Myths, according to the proposed definition, are traditional, that is, they are told and retold, and they can change in the process of retelling. There is no such thing as the only correct version of a myth. In this regard, myth is fundamentally different from most other kinds of literature (if we can count myth as a kind of literature at all). Most literary scholarship depends on a particular text by a particular author. Scholars studying Jane Austen's *Pride and Prejudice* will want to have exactly the words that Austen wrote, and their interpretations will work from this text. Sometimes there is no single correct literary text, if, say, the writer wrote more than one version (as there are two versions of many of the novels of Henry James) or because the text was produced in more than one version (as many of the plays of Shakespeare were printed in more than one version). But still the ideal of a single correct text lies behind most literary scholarship.

The study of myth, on the other hand, is based on the idea, stated clearly by the French anthropologist Claude Lévi-Strauss, that a myth consists of all of its versions. Rather than trying to prune away variant texts to get at the single correct version, scholars collect as many versions of a myth as possible in order to find the range of differences the tradition provides. Sometimes the variations seem unimportant – for example, according to Homer, the mother and wife of Oedipus was named Epikaste, while Sophocles calls her Jokasta – but sometimes they are fundamental. According to some stories, including Euripides' play *Helen*, Helen of Troy never went to Troy at all, but stayed in Egypt, where Menelaos found her after the war. (Variants of myth will be discussed further in Chapter Five.)

Even a traditional story had to have a first telling, though its beginning may now be lost beyond recovery. A story is not traditional the first time it is told, or the second or the third, and so a story is not a myth until it becomes accepted as a myth by the tradition, that is, by generations of tellings and retellings. In the process of telling and retelling, the original author loses control of the story, as elements are added or changed or deleted. It is almost possible to say that a myth is a story that has escaped from its author.

Of course some particular author may tell a traditional story, a myth, in a form that can be considered literature. Indeed, many of the important texts for the study of Greek myth are also works of literature, such as the Homeric epics or the tragedies of Aeschylus, Sophocles, and Euripides. These texts can be studied as literature or as myth, and what scholars say about them will be somewhat different depending on which approach they take. This book will concentrate on these stories as myth, but it will not exclude literary analysis. Each approach illuminates the other. But some myths were never told in a literary form; these can be found in the writings of historians or philosophers or travel writers; a few we know only from visual sources, such as paintings on vases. A study of myth that is restricted to literary versions will omit some important stories.

According to the proposed definition, myth has a certain kind of importance for the society in which it is told. This part of the definition is certainly too vague to be useful as it stands. What kind of importance should a myth have? Probably every story told has some kind of importance. The point here is what kinds of stories are excluded. For instance, many jokes are traditional stories, but most scholars would not include jokes in the study of myth. Jokes clearly have a kind of cultural importance, but it is not the kind of importance that myths have. Fables, such as the fables attributed to Aesop, are traditional stories, and these often have a serious point, but again most scholars do not think of fables as myths. Folktales, such as Jack and the Beanstalk or Jack the Giant Killer, present a more difficult problem. Many myths, such as the story of Perseus or the story of the Cyclops in the *Odyssey*, have elements of folktales, and many of the methods and concepts used in the study of folktales can be very useful in the study of myths. Perhaps the best we can do is to say that myths were taken seriously in a way that folktales were not. The question of how Greek society thought about their myths will be a continuing topic throughout this book.

There is one item missing from my proposed definition which might have been expected, and that is the gods. In many cultures the myths, or the stories that scholars choose to call myths, largely or exclusively concern the gods, and some definitions of myth insist that mythical stories tell about the deeds of the gods. There are certainly Greek myths about the gods – the myth of divine succession in Hesiod, for example – but in many Greek myths the gods are secondary and in some they are merely mentioned along the way. In Sophocles' version of the story of Oedipus, the Oracle at Delphi plays a role, but otherwise the gods are absent. Many Greek myths concern the deeds and sufferings of mortal heroes rather than gods (though the word hero may have only a circular definition: a hero is the kind of character who plays a part in the myths; there is much more to be said about heroes, and I will return to the topic in Chapter Five).

One last point concerns the truth of myths. In ordinary English usage, the word "myth" is often applied to a story that is false, perhaps in order to counter a claim that the story is true. We often distinguish "myths" from the stories of religion or history that we claim are "true" stories. Clearly most people today would not think that Ikaros actually flew too close to the sun or that Persephone was abducted by Hades. It is also clear that not all Greeks believed all the stories (see Chapter Twelve for discussion of ancient skepticism), and no Greek myth had the kind of claim to truth that "true" stories of religion or history have. But it is not generally useful to think of the Greek myths as "false" stories, since what matters most now, and what mattered most then, was something other than "truth" as it is understood in modern times. The myths were important stories, even for those who did not believe in them, because they provided fundamental ways of thinking about the world.

The result of this discussion is not a clear definition which precisely includes everything scholars want to call a myth and precisely excludes everything that they don't, but a certain lack of precision is no fault, and perhaps even a virtue. There is a set of stories that are central to the idea of a myth, and then other stories which are less clearly myths but still interesting to discuss. And that rough definition of myth may be all that is necessary.

II. FURTHER CHARACTERISTICS OF GREEK MYTH

In many cultures mythic stories seem to occur in a time disconnected from historical time, perhaps a time before history. Mircea Eliade, an important historian of religion, used the Latin phrase *in illo tempore* ("in that time") to designate this mythic time, the time of origins. According to Eliade, the function of many myths and religious rituals is to bring about a kind of return to the experience of mythic time. Some Greek myths do indeed seem to occur in a time before history, or at least a time which is hard to bring into relationship with historical events. Some myths are connected to rituals in Greek religion, and these rituals may bring the participants into a kind of return of primordial events. In this sense, Greek myth can refer to events *in illo tempore*. But many Greek myths on the contrary seem to be closely linked to history, either through a chronological connection to historical events or through the effects of historical events on the shape of the mythic story, although the modern understanding of historical events may not match ancient Greek ideas. Some scholars would say that traditional stories with a basis in historical events are legends rather than myths. Such a distinction would exclude many stories that have traditionally been considered Greek myths: the stories of the Trojan War, for example. Some may distinguish myths and legends, but it is characteristic of ancient Greek culture that divine myths were not sharply divided from legends. (For more about myth and history see Chapter Ten.)

Greek myths tend to be connected to each other. A quick examination of one intricate web of interconnected stories makes this point clear. It is not important to remember all of the details of this web, but rather to get a general impression of how these various stories are tied together. This web begins with Niobe, who was the mother of many children (different versions of the story give her different numbers of children; according to Homer there were six boys and six girls). She was very proud of her children and she boasted that she was a better mother than the goddess Leto, who had only two children, Apollo and Artemis. In order to punish Niobe for her presumption, Apollo and Artemis killed all of her children. This story is found as early as Homer's *Iliad*, and in one form or another it was widely told.

In some versions of the story Niobe is the daughter of Tantalos; her brother, then, was Pelops. According to some stories, Tantalos was a great friend of the gods, who allowed him to feast with them. In order to test them, he chopped up his son, Pelops, boiled the child and served him up to the gods. All of the gods realized what they were being served, except for Demeter, who was perhaps distracted because of her grief over the abduction of Persephone; in any case, Demeter ate Pelops' shoulder. The gods put Pelops back together and replaced his shoulder with a piece of shining ivory. Tantalos was punished for this and other crimes; Odysseus sees him in the Land of the Dead. Pelops went on to marry Hippodameia and found the Olympic Games; he was the father of Thyestes and Atreus and thus the grandfather of Agamemnon and Menelaos.

Niobe, the daughter of Tantalos and sister of Pelops, was married to Amphion. Amphion and his twin brother Zethus were the children of Zeus and the mortal woman Antiope. The story of Antiope is somewhat complicated. She was the daughter of Nykteus, who in turn was the brother of Lykos, the king of Thebes. According to the ancient mythographer Apollodorus, Lykos ruled in Thebes after the death of Pentheus, who was killed by his mother, Agave. When Antiope became pregnant, her father Nykteus threatened her, and she ran away and married a mortal man named Epopeus. Meanwhile, Antiope's father Nykteus died, but Lykos waged a war against Epopeus, killed him, and took Antiope prisoner. On the way back to Thebes Antiope gave birth to the twins, Amphion and Zethus; she exposed them, but they were saved and brought up by a cowherd. Amphion was a great musician, perhaps the first mortal to play the lyre; Zethus was a hunter and herdsman.

Years later Antiope managed to escape; she happened to meet up with her sons, now grown up, and they took revenge against Lykos and his wife Dirke for their mistreatment of Antiope. Amphion and Zethus then built walls for the city of Thebes; according to some versions, while Zethus struggled to carry stones for the wall, Amphion was able to move them by the power of his music. In a lost play by Euripides, *Antiope*, the two sons debate about the merits of the active or the quiet life; Plato mentions this play in his dialogue *Gorgias* (485d; 506b).

The myth of Niobe is thus connected to the myth of Tantalos and the myth of Pelops, and through Pelops to the myths of Thyestes and Atreus and the myths of Agamemnon and Menelaos, as well as to the myth of Antiope and the myth of Amphion and Zethus. It would be easy to extend this web of stories even further. This kind of web is very characteristic of Greek myth, but it is not at all characteristic of fictional stories, such as novels, which are usually sealed off from each other: Elizabeth Bennet from *Pride and Prejudice* is not related to Heathcliff from *Wuthering Heights* or Pip from *Great Expectations*.

III. DID THE GREEKS HAVE GREEK MYTHS?

The definition proposed above, though imperfect, gives at least an approximate idea of what will count as Greek myth in this book. Does this category, rough as it is, correspond to any category in ancient Greek thought or culture? Did the Greeks have Greek myths? The answer is yes and no. A number of scholars have demonstrated that the word "muthos" in ancient Greek did not necessarily mean what the word "myth" means today.[1] A traditional story might be called a "muthos", but it might also be called an "epos" (the source of the modern word "epic") or even a "logos" (the source of the modern word "logic"). The Greeks did not always clearly distinguish what scholars today call myth from other kinds of stories, including folklore and history and philosophical tales.

On the other hand, the Greeks did have a set of stories that were particularly appropriate to be told in tragedy, and almost every tragedy produced in Athens in the fifth century BCE told a story that would today be called a myth.[2] In addition, in the fifth century BCE the lyric poet Pindar wrote a series of poems celebrating victorious athletes, and almost all of these include references to one or more stories of myth; likewise the lyric poet Bacchylides. So it seems that the playwrights and the lyric poets recognized a set of stories that largely overlaps with the stories that today are considered Greek myths.

One should not assume, however, that the ancient Greeks thought about these stories the way they are thought about today. The myths played a role in ancient Greek society that may be quite different from the role they play in modern culture. These stories, then, were not myths in the modern sense of the word myth. One of the goals of this book is to explore some of the ways the Greeks used and thought about their myths.

IV. PANHELLENIC MYTH

The Panhellenic myths are those myths that were widely known in the ancient Greek world, such as the stories of the Trojan War, the Theban myths, the myths of the Athenian tragedies, and so on. Most of the stories told and discussed in introductory textbooks and also in popular accounts of Greek myth are Panhellenic, and these Panhellenic myths have also been the focus of much scholarly work. This scholarly interest in Panhellenic myth is parallel to scholarly study of the development of other Panhellenic institutions in the Archaic period, such as the Olympic Games, the Delphic Oracle, and Panhellenic epic.[3]

The story of the abduction of Persephone, for example, was very widely known in the ancient world, and indeed it is still widely known today. The primary source for this myth is the so-called "Homeric Hymn to Demeter".

The story of Persephone, as told in the "Homeric Hymn to Demeter"

Persephone, the daughter of Zeus and Demeter, is abducted by her uncle, Hades, who takes her to the Underworld to be his queen. Demeter realizes that Persephone has been kidnapped and goes in search of her. While on her travels she comes to the city of Eleusis, where (in the disguise of a mortal) she takes the job of nurse to Demophoön, the son of the King and Queen. She tries to make Demophoön immortal by placing him in a fire, but when the Queen sees her child in the fire she cries out. Demeter takes Demophoön out of the fire and explains that because of the Queen's interference he will remain mortal; he will, however, receive the honors of a hero. She orders that a temple be built outside the city for her and she says that she will establish the rituals to be carried out there.

Now Demeter, still grieving for Persephone, brings a famine on the earth; the human race is in danger of destruction, and no offerings can be made to the gods. Zeus sends various gods to Demeter to ask her to relieve the famine, but she refuses so long as Persephone is in the Underworld. Zeus finally sends a messenger to get Persephone back from Hades. Hades agrees, but he has tricked Persephone into eating a pomegranate seed, and therefore she must stay in the Underworld for one third of the year. Nonetheless Demeter is appeased, and plants begin to grow again. She returns to Eleusis and teaches the rituals to be carried out in her temple.

The Hymn itself was probably composed sometime between 650 and 550 BCE, but it has survived in a single damaged manuscript, discovered in Moscow in 1777, which was probably copied out in the early 1400s CE. This Hymn is one of 33 hymns attributed to Homer, but Homer was certainly not the author, as many even in the ancient world knew.

Even though only this single manuscript of the Hymn survives, other evidence shows that the story was widely known. Homer, who is perhaps the earliest of the Greek poets, does not tell the story, but he knows that Persephone is Queen of the Land of the Dead (*Odyssey* 10.534, 10.564, 11.633–35, etc.). Hesiod, the other poet of the earliest phase of Greek literature, has a brief but clear reference to the story: "And [Zeus] came to the bed of all-nourishing Demeter, and she bore white-armed Persephone whom Hades carried off from her mother; but wise Zeus gave her to him" (*Theogony* 912–14).

Euripides includes a version of the story in his play *Helen*, 1301–61; this version tells about the abduction, but it entirely omits the events of the middle section of the Hymn, the story of Demophoön and the foundation of the rituals at the temple in Eleusis. The Athenian orator Isocrates (436–338 BCE) mentions the abduction of Persephone in his famous speech the *Panegyrikos*, sections 28–29: because of the hospitality the people of Attica showed Demeter when she was searching for Persephone, the goddess first gave agriculture to the human race and also revealed the sacred mysteries. The story is also told in the so-called Orphic Hymns, a group of anonymous poems ascribed to the legendary poet Orpheus, who is supposed to predate Homer, but the earliest of these poems probably date from the sixth century BCE.

Post-classical Greek works which tell or refer to the story of the abduction include a Hymn to Demeter by the Hellenistic poet Callimachus, who was active in the third century BCE; the *Library of Greek History* written in the first century BCE by Diodorus Siculus (sections 5.3–8; 5.68–69.3); and the *Library of Greek Mythology*, which dates from the first or second century CE and is ascribed to Apollodorus, though we don't really know who this person was. Pausanias, the travel writer who wrote a *Guide to Greece* in the second century CE, refers to the story several times; he specifically mentions the "Homeric Hymn to Demeter", though his version of the Hymn seems to be somewhat different from the surviving version. He also mentions a version of the story by a poet named Pamphos, who is supposed to predate Homer (1.38.3 and 8.37.9), but no other information about this poet or his works is known. Then in the late fourth or early fifth century CE the Greek poet Nonnus included the story in his enormous epic poem, the *Dionysiaca*.

The story was also well known in the Latin world. (In the Latin versions, by and large, Latin names are used: Ceres for Demeter, Proserpina for Persephone, and Pluto or Dis for Hades.) Cicero mentions the story in his speech *Against Verres* (2.4:106–08) and also in *On the Nature of the Gods*. The Latin writer Hyginus told the story very briefly in his book of fables (*Fabulae* 146), and there are references to the story in Vergil's *Georgics* 1.39, in Lucan's epic poem *Civil War* (6.698–700 and 739–42) and in Statius' epic the *Thebaid* (12.270). Ovid tells the story at some length twice, in the *Metamophoses* (5.385–661) and in the *Fasti* (4.417–620). Much later, in the late fourth century CE, the Latin poet Claudian wrote three books of an unfinished epic about Persephone (*De raptu Proserpinae*).

In addition to these literary sources, there are also some visual representations of the story: a fifth-century BCE red-figure vase from Attica shows Hades pursuing Persephone; a fourth-century BCE red-figure vase from Apulia in southern Italy shows Hades and

Persephone in a chariot, while Demeter seems to be pursuing them, carrying a torch, as several other figures look on; a fourth-century krater shows Hades, accompanied by Hermes and Hekate, returning Persephone to the upper world; another red-figure krater shows Persephone rising out of the ground, illuminated by Hekate carrying torches, as Demeter and Hermes look on (see Figure 1.1); and a tomb at Vergina, in Macedonia, has a remarkable fresco from the fourth century BCE showing Hades in a chariot carrying off Persephone, who is clearly trying to get away, as one of her companions looks on in dismay.[4]

The story was also closely connected to the Eleusinian Mysteries, a cult which flourished for a thousand years, from the Archaic period until the late fourth century CE. Essential parts of the cult ritual were secret and have never been revealed, but all of the many thousands who were initiated into this cult must have known the story, which was probably recounted in some form during the rituals.[5]

It is clear from this list that the story of the abduction of Persephone was known in many places and over a long period, from Athens to Macedonia to southern Italy to Rome and Egypt, from Homer's time to late antiquity.

Figure 1.1 Persephone rising out of the earth from the Underworld. Persephone Painter (ca. 440 BCE). Attic bell krater (bowl for mixing wine and water), obverse. H. 41 cm; D. of mouth 45.4 cm. The Metropolitan Museum of Art, New York, NY, USA. Fletcher Fund, 1928. 28.57.23. Copyright © The Metropolitan Museum of Art/Art Resource, NY

Persephone in Western tradition

The story of Persephone has continued to fascinate writers and artists in the Western tradition. The Moscow manuscript of the *Homeric Hymn to Demeter* was discovered only in 1777, but the story was known from other sources, especially Ovid; both Edmund Spenser ("The Garden of Proserpina", in *The Faerie Queen*, and John Milton (*Paradise Lost* 4.268–71) refer to it. Shakespeare mentions the abduction of Proserpina in *The Winter's Tale* (IV.iv.116–18), and some critics have argued that the story provides an important theme of the play. In the nineteenth century Mary Shelley, author of *Frankenstein*, wrote a verse play for children based on the myth, and poems based on the story were written by Alfred Lord Tennyson, George Meredith, and Algernon Swinburne. The myth has been very popular in the twentieth century. Twentieth-century poets who have written about Demeter and Persephone include Ezra Pound, H.D. (Hilda Doolittle), Edgar Lee Masters, Edna St. Vincent Millay, Robert Lowell, Sylvia Plath, and Margaret Atwood. The story has been particularly important for feminist writers and thinkers; see the section on Further Reading at the end of the chapter.

Some of the ancient versions of this myth are quite short and therefore not very detailed, but some are extensive, and they are hardly identical. For example, in the *Homeric Hymn*, Zeus is responsible for the decision to marry Persephone off to Hades, but in Ovid's version in the *Metamorphoses* (in which the Latin names for the gods were used), it is Venus who contrived the plan to make Dis fall in love with Proserpine; Jupiter had nothing to do with it. In some versions, the abduction occurred in Sicily, but in others it occurred near Athens.

According to the travel writer Pausanias, when Demeter was searching for Persephone, she was followed by Poseidon, who was intent on having sex with her. She turned herself into a mare, but Poseidon turned himself into a stallion and mated with her. Demeter bore him two children: one was a daughter whose name cannot be mentioned, and the other was a stallion named Areion (*Guide* 8.25.5). Some part of this story was known also to the second-century CE mythographer Apollodorus (3.6.8), but it is not widely told; it was probably part of a local tradition and therefore not Panhellenic.

Many versions of the myth either omit the episode of Demophoön or change it in some way. As noted above, Euripides leaves it out. Likewise the version in Ovid's *Metamorphoses*; in his version of the story in the *Fasti* he does include this episode, but changes some of the details, and also changes the name of the baby, who is called Triptolemos. A person named Triptolemos is mentioned briefly near the end of the *Homeric Hymn*, at line 474, but there he is called one of the kings, and he is definitely not the child nursed by Demeter. In some versions a character named Triptolemos plays a very important role: after Demeter became reconciled to Zeus, she gave grain to Triptolemos and told him to instruct everyone in agriculture. This story is told by Apollodorus (*Library* 1.5.2), by Callimachus (*Hymn 6 to Demeter* 17ff.), by Diodorus Siculus (*Library of History* 5.68.1), by Hyginus (*Fabulae* 147, 277;

Further explorations on Demeter

Demeter is best known in her role in the story of the abduction of Persephone, as narrated in the *Homeric Hymn to Demeter*, and in her connection to the Eleusinian Mysteries, but there were other stories about Demeter and other rituals in which she played an important role. There is especially rich evidence for Demeter in Pausanias' *Guide*. Using the index to the *Guide*, write an essay about Demeter as she is portrayed there. Pay particular attention to events not mentioned in the *Homeric Hymn* and to Demeter's role in cult outside of Eleusis.

Astronomia 2.14), and by Ovid (*Met.* 5.645–61). Pausanias mentions the story several times (*Guide* 1.14.2; 7.18.2; 8.4.1); he says that there was a shrine to Triptolemos in Eleusis (1.38.4) and he also mentions a threshing-floor and altar to Triptolemos (1.38.7). There are also many visual representations of Triptolemos with Demeter and Persephone, far more than representations of Hades and Persephone. The story of Triptolemos itself counts as a Panhellenic myth (see Figure 1.2).

Each of these versions deserves its own interpretation. For example, those versions in which Triptolemos plays a major role are concerned with the beginning of agriculture, whereas the *Homeric Hymn* clearly states that agriculture already existed before the story begins. According to Jenny Strauss Clay 1989, the *Homeric Hymn* shows the role of Demeter among the gods, since at the end of the story she has become the patron goddess of the Eleusinian Mysteries. In addition, the story of Demophoön in the *Homeric Hymn* can be interpreted as a demonstration of the distinction between human mortality and divine immortality.

Figure 1.2   Triptolemos in his winged chariot setting out to teach agriculture, the gift of Demeter. Attributed to the Triptolemos Painter (5th century BCE). Attic red-figure stamnos. H. 53.5 cm. Louvre, Paris, France. Inv. G 187. Photo: Hervé Lewandowski. Copyright © Réunion des Musées Nationaux/Art Resource, NY

V. LOCAL MYTH

The story of the abduction of Persephone was Panhellenic because it was known very widely over the Greek world for a very long time. (Moreover, it was known to the Romans and it has continued to be retold and reinterpreted in modern times as well). Most of the famous myths – the myth of Oedipus, the myth of Jason and the Golden Fleece, the myth of the Trojan War – were also Panhellenic, and these stories remain familiar today. But many other stories were not so widely known. These stories were interesting to the people who lived in a particular place but for one reason or another they were not so interesting to people elsewhere, and so they were not told throughout the Greek world, they were not passed on to the Roman writers, and they are not widely known today. Stories that were primarily of interest in only a small region are called *local* or *epichoric* myths (*epichoric* derives from the Greek "epi", meaning "at" or "on", and "chôra", meaning "a place"). Local myths can be very interesting and important because they often preserve details of local rituals, customs, and beliefs which are not preserved in Panhellenic myths, which tended to include only those elements of the stories that appealed to a wide audience from many different places.

The Athenian story of the Bouphonia is an example of a local myth. Long ago, in the days of Erechtheus (a mythical early king of Athens), in the days when people gave only grain offerings to the gods, before people began to eat meat and perform animal sacrifice, a man named Sopatros (or perhaps Diomon) moved to Attica (perhaps from Crete). One day he had set out an offering of oil, honey, and grain, but an ox came up and ate his offering from the altar. Sopatros became angry; he picked up an axe and killed the offending animal. When his anger subsided, he realized that he had committed sacrilege by killing an animal at the altar. He secretly buried the ox and ran away to Crete.

A great drought now afflicted Athens and all of Attica and brought on a famine. The Athenians consulted the Oracle at Delphi; the response, like many oracular responses, is not entirely clear, or perhaps it has become somewhat garbled, but the gist seems to be that the fugitive should be found and the murderer should be punished and the dead ox in some way should be resurrected in the place it had been killed.

As the story continues, the Athenians found Sopatros, who decided that the guilt for the killing should be shared by having everyone take part in future sacrifices and by having everyone eat some of the meat. The Athenians then established a formal procedure, in which a number of oxen were paraded around an altar until one of them ate the grain placed there. The offending ox was killed, and the person who killed it ran away. A trial was then held to determine responsibility for the killing. All the participants in turn were absolved: the young girls who had brought the water for sharpening the axe and the knife, those who sharpened the axe and the knife, and so on. Finally, the axe (or perhaps the knife) was convicted and thrown into the sea. In addition, the skin of the ox was stuffed and placed in front of a plow, so that the victim was in a sense resurrected. This, more or less, is the story as it was told by Porphyry, a Greek philosopher of the third century CE in a book titled *On Abstinence*, an argument in favor of vegetarianism.[6]

The story of Sopatros and the ox may have been designed to explain a particular Athenian ritual, the "Bouphonia", which means "the murder of the ox". This ritual was performed on the fourteenth of the month called Skirophorian, in the middle of the summer, and it seems to have taken more or less the form explained in the myth, a ritual sacrifice of an ox followed by a trial and the condemning of the knife. The travel writer Pausanias describes the sacrifice, which was evidently still being performed when he visited Athens in the second century CE (*Guide* 1.24.4 and 1.28.11). The comic playwright Aristophanes mentions the ritual very briefly in the *Clouds* (984–85), which was produced in the late fifth century BCE. There are a few other scattered references, and there are vase paintings which probably illustrate the ritual (one of these may be seen in Burkert 1983: plate 6). But this is not much compared to the wealth of sources for the story of the abduction of Persephone. There is no known ancient Greek literary treatment of the Bouphonia in any hymn or in any tragedy. Moreover, this story did not attract the attention of Ovid or any other Roman writer, and it has inspired no modern retellings.[7] This story was local rather than Panhellenic.

Some readers might wonder if this story really should count as a myth. One might argue, for instance, that this story is really a legend. But many Greek myths, including the very important stories of the Trojan War, are legends at least as much as this story. Or one might argue that there are no gods involved, except as the recipient of the sacrifice and the author of the oracle. But the role of the gods in Sophocles' *Oedipus Tyrannos* is no greater, and that story is always counted as a myth. This story fulfills one of the typical roles of myth: it is a charter, that is, a story which explains the origin of some ritual or custom (just as the *Homeric Hymn to Demeter* is at least in part a charter of the Eleusinian Mysteries). Thus this story makes a fundamental statement about the way human beings should relate to the gods. Before Sopatros, so the story says, people ate only grain and gave only grain offerings to the gods, but now people kill animals, give meat offerings to the gods, and eat meat. This story belongs to mythic time, the time of origins, and the myth and ritual are designed to repeat the events of that time.

Of course this myth is not an accurate historical account of the origins of animal sacrifice, which must have begun in a time long before the traditions can recount, most likely before the development of agriculture. The point of the story is not historical, but religious, and perhaps social and even psychological. According to some scholars, this myth attempts to deal with the guilt people might feel about killing the animal. First, the murder of the ox was not deliberate, but an act of passion, and the murderer was not even a native Athenian; in a sense the ox was really to blame, since it ate the grain that was consecrated to the gods; then the guilt is distributed to the whole community, and finally it is displaced onto objects, the knife and the axe.

This explanation seems plausible, up to a point, but there is perhaps some danger in reading too much into this myth and ritual. A modern analogue might be the annual ritual in which the President of the United States gives a pardon to one turkey on Thanksgiving Day. In the distant future scholars looking back at this ritual might suppose that everyone in the United States feels deeply guilty about killing and eating turkeys. Perhaps the ritual does reflect the awareness in our society that in order to eat meat we have to kill an animal, and no doubt some people do feel guilty, and some people don't eat meat, but I do not believe there is a widespread anxiety about eating meat throughout the United States.

Likewise, the myth and the ritual of the Bouphonia probably reflected the awareness among Athenians that they had to kill animals in order to eat meat, but I am not convinced that most people in ancient Greece were terribly upset about it. As early as the time of Aristophanes, in the fifth century BCE, the ritual of the Bouphonia was regarded as old fashioned, and the evidence does not suggest that it was taken very seriously. Nonetheless, the ritual was performed in Athens every year from well before the fifth century BCE until at least the second century CE. It must have meant something to Athenians, if only as a tradition. Sacrifice was a frequent and important part of ancient Greek life, and there are several other charter myths about sacrifice. If we are trying to build up a picture of what ancient Greeks thought and did, then these myths have their place, along with many others that can be recovered sometimes only from obscure sources.

The Panhellenic myths show what the ancient Greeks in general thought about, and often these myths provide stories for the Western tradition to continue to think about. The study of Greek myth quite properly begins from the Panhellenic myths, but it should not stop there. But precisely because these Panhellenic myths had to appeal to a general Greek public from many times and places, they lost the detail and specificity found in the local myths, a kind of detail that reveals aspects of life and thought in the various Greek cities that are not found in the Panhellenic myths.

The distinction between the Panhellenic and the local, however, is a matter of degree. A myth may be more or less Panhellenic, and a Panhellenic myth may include local elements and variants. Presumably many Panhellenic myths began as local myths and only gradually attracted attention throughout Greece. Some local myths were known beyond the borders of their home cities or regions, without achieving a Panhellenic status. Most of the myths which became important in the later Western tradition were Panhellenic, but some Panhellenic myths were more or less forgotten, and a few local myths managed to attract the attention of later writers. None of these distinctions and correlations is absolute.

CONCLUSION

This chapter has presented some fundamental concepts necessary for the study of myth. A provisional definition was suggested – myths are narrative; they are traditional, and therefore they typically have variant forms rather than one correct text; they express ideas and problems which have a certain importance for the society in which they are told – and some of the limitations of this definition were noted. Some other typical characteristics of myth in general were discussed, though these may apply less strictly to Greek myth than to myth in other traditions: myths often concern the actions of gods, but in many Greek myths the gods are secondary or even absent; and many myths take place in a time outside of history, but many Greek myths are connected to the Greek sense of historical time. The stories of the Greek mythological tradition tend to be interwoven with one another in complex webs, which are often expressed as genealogical relationships. Although there is no specific word in ancient Greek which means what we mean by the word myth, there is some reason to believe that the ancient Greeks did have a special regard for the stories we call Greek myths. This chapter also made a distinction between Panhellenic myths – which were known very widely throughout Greece – and local myths – which were of primary interest to a particular locality; the Panhellenic myths more likely represent what was of general interest to all Greeks, while the local myths often show a kind of specificity and detail of ritual and belief lost in the Panhellenic myths. All of these ideas and concepts will be continuing themes in later chapters. Chapter Two will explore the very important question of the relationship between Greek myth and Greek religion.

FURTHER READING

For discussion of the problems involved in defining myth, see Kirk 1970, Bremmer 1988, Calame 2003, and Csapo 2005. Richardson 1974 is a scholarly commentary on the *Homeric Hymn to Demeter*. Foley 1994 has a translation of the Hymn with a short commentary and a collection of recent articles. See also the chapter on the Hymn in Clay 1989. Hayes 1994 discusses the use of the myth of Persephone in modern literature. On the Bouphonia, see Burkert 1983: 136–43, and Tyrell and Brown 1991.

Chapter Two

SIX HUNDRED GODS
Greek Myth and Greek Religion

Greek myth and Greek religion are not the same, but they are closely connected. The gods play a large role in the stories of myth; they are also the focus of Greek ritual practice. Some myths are closely connected to ritual, but other myths present the gods in ways that have no clear relation to ritual and are sometimes hard to reconcile with the role of gods in ritual. The myths were certainly not scripture, and they did not provide the basis for Greek religious thought in the way that the Bible or the Koran provide the basis for Judaism, Christianity or Islam. The question of the relationship between Greek myth and Greek religion is complicated, moreover, by problems of definition. Some of the difficulties involved in defining myth were discussed in Chapter One; religion is, if anything, even harder to define. This chapter will concentrate on two aspects of Greek religion: first, ritual practices performed by the ancient Greeks, such as sacrifices and festivals, and second, what one might call theological speculation, that is, speculation about the nature of the gods and their relationship to mortals.

The chapter begins with a brief account of the gods in Hesiod's *Theogony*, and then a closer look at Kronos and Hestia in myth and ritual. Next there is a discussion of personified abstractions as divine figures, in Hesiod and in Greek religion generally. The following section examines some divinities not included in Hesiod's account. The next two sections explore myths which serve as aetiologies for ritual and then the place of some of these rituals in Greek society. The final section shows the importance of myth and ritual in a literary work, Aeschylus' *Oresteia*. The question of this chapter, then, is: How does Greek myth connect to Greek ritual practices and theological speculation?

I. ANCIENT GREEK POLYTHEISM AND HESIOD'S *THEOGONY*

Ancient Greek religion, as every student knows, was polytheistic. The dominant religions of the Western world – Judaism, Christianity, and Islam – are monotheistic, though of course

Exploring Greek Myth. First Edition. Matthew Clark.
© 2012 Matthew Clark. Published 2012 by Blackwell Publishing Ltd.

there are modern polytheistic religions, such as Hinduism and Shinto. Even in the dominant Western monotheistic religions there are elements which complicate the picture. To an outsider, the Christian Trinity may not seem like a single god, and in all three Western religions there are angels and other spiritual beings, entities which are not divine but not mortal. On the other hand, some ancient Greeks thought that divinity was really a single thing, and the gods were only manifestations of that single divinity (Price 1999: 138). The great majority of ancient Greeks, however, thought of the gods as separate entities and worshiped them individually. So, with a few qualifications, it is not misleading to make a basic distinction between the polytheism of ancient Greece and the monotheism of the dominant modern Western religions.

The God of the monotheistic religions is usually thought of as eternal: there was never a time when God did not exist, and perhaps God exists in some way outside of time. The Greek gods were thought of as immortal, they would never die, but they were not eternal, they were born in time, and some, such as Dionysos and Herakles, had a human parent. The monotheistic God is outside of nature, but the Greek gods are part of nature. The Greek gods were neither omniscient nor omnipotent; they were subject to *moira*, which is something like fate, though often it is not quite so restrictive. (For more about *moira* see Chapter Ten.) The God of the monotheistic religions is usually thought of as the guardian of morality, but the Greek gods were not necessarily good. Zeus was the guardian of some moral principles, such as hospitality and the keeping of oaths, but in other areas his own morals were not exemplary, at least in myth.

In general Greek religion did not have any sacred books, like the Bible or the Koran, and there was no dogma, no set of required beliefs. (Some marginal sects did have sacred writings, such as the Orphic writings, discussed briefly below.) Religious practice, especially in the form of regular sacrifice, was more important than belief, though it would be wrong to suggest that the ancient Greeks did not have religious beliefs and religious feelings. Many Greeks acted as if they believed in the gods and believed that the gods were very powerful.

It is not easy to determine exactly how many gods there were in the Greek system, partly because the concept of god was not entirely clear. The first generations of divine figures, including Gaia (Earth) and Ouranos (Sky), and the Titans, including Prometheus, were clearly among the immortals, but only a few of these received any ritual (see below for discussion of rituals for Kronos). The familiar Olympian gods, such as Zeus, Hera, Apollo, Athena, and so on, were at the center of both myth and ritual. In addition, there were many other figures who were more or less divine. Nymphs, for example, were certainly not human, but they were probably not gods, though some were more godlike than others, and some nymphs were worshiped. Heroes were mortal, but they received honors as well. (For more on heroes, see Chapter Six.)

The most important ancient catalogue of Greek gods is Hesiod's *Theogony*, a long poem which details the births of the various gods and recounts a few divine myths along the way. The *Theogony* is one of the basic texts for anyone interested in Greek myth or Greek religion. It is well described in the introductory studies of myth, but students should read the poem itself (as well as Hesiod's other poem, the *Works and Days*).[1]

Hesiod organized his poem roughly according to the generations of the gods, in three broad groupings: the period from Chaos to the castration of Ouranos; the period of the rule of Kronos; and the period of the rule of Zeus. Literally hundreds of gods are listed in the course of the catalogue: more than 600 are named, and others are mentioned without names, such as the 3000 Okeanids, daughters of Okeanos and Tethys. Most of the gods are organized in families, and these family relationships often make some kind of conceptual sense; thus Night is the mother of Doom and Bane and Death and Sleep and Dreams, among others.

The divine powers include the major gods, that is, the Olympians and a few others. Hesiod also includes less important divinities, such as the sea gods Nereus and Doris and their 50 daughters, each one given a name (243–62); also divinities connected to aspects of nature, such as Ouranos (Sky), Helios (Sun), Selene (Moon); divine monsters, such as Geryon, Echidna, Khimaira; and finally there are gods that might be considered divinized abstractions, such as Dikê (Justice), Eirene (Peace), Prometheus (Foresight).

In addition to the list of names, the *Theogony* includes several important stories. The most important of these is the Myth of Succession: Ouranos, the first king of the gods, is deposed by his son, Kronos, who in turn is deposed by his son, Zeus. Prometheus, who is one of the Titans, and thus a divinity of the second generation, plays a major role in two stories, the sacrifice at Mekone and the theft of fire, and these lead to the story of the creation of the first woman. The Titans as a group figure in another Hesiodic myth, the War of the Titans and the gods, but no single Titan other than Prometheus stands out as an individual character. This story is in a way a continuation of the Myth of Succession, but with a difference, since the result is not a change in rulers, but the continuation of the rule of Zeus. Zeus' position as king is further confirmed by his victory over Typhoeus, and then the final threat to his rule is overcome when he swallows his first wife, Metis, and gives birth himself to Athena.

The Olympians

The Olympian gods are usually Zeus, Hera, Apollo, Artemis, Athena, Ares, Aphrodite, Demeter, Hephaistos, Hermes, Poseidon, and Dionysos. Even though Hades is the brother of Zeus and Poseidon, he is not usually thought of as an Olympian, since he stays in the Underworld. Persephone is not considered an Olympian, though she was the daughter of two Olympians. Hestia was a sister of Zeus, but she is not considered an Olympian because she is associated with the household and the hearth. Herakles was taken up among the Olympians after his death. The Muses live on Olympus, but they are not numbered among the Olympians.

The Myth of Succession (153–210, 453–506)

Gaia (Earth) bore many children to Ouranos (Heaven), but Ouranos hated them and even kept some of them confined inside Gaia. Gaia gave a sickle to her son Kronos, who castrated his father Ouranos and succeeded him as ruler of the gods. (Aphrodite was born from the severed genitals.) The goddess Rhea then bore Kronos many children, but he had learned that one of his sons would overthrow him, so he swallowed all his children when they were born. When Zeus was born, Rhea hid him and gave Kronos a stone, which he swallowed instead of Zeus (see Figure 3.) When Zeus grew up he overthrew Kronos and managed to make Kronos disgorge the children he had swallowed. From that time on Zeus was the king of the gods.

The Myth of the Sacrifice at Mekone (534–69)

When the gods and mortals were dividing an ox at Mekone, Prometheus attempted to deceive Zeus. He took the good parts of the meat and hid them in the stomach of the ox, and he hid the bones in shining fat. Zeus was not deceived, but he took the bones and fat nonetheless. And ever since men burn the bones as a sacrifice to the gods.

The Theft of Fire, the First Woman, and the Punishment of Prometheus (570–616)

In his anger at men, Zeus withheld fire, but Prometheus stole fire and gave it to men. Zeus then ordered Hephaistos to make a woman, presumably the first woman, a lovely curse for men. This first woman becomes the wife of Epimetheus, the brother of Prometheus. (In the *Theogony*, this woman is not given a name, but in the *Works and Days*, she is named Pandora. The story of Pandora's jar is also told in the *Works and Days*.) Zeus ordered that Prometheus be bound in chains; every day

an eagle would come and eat his liver, which would then grow back over night. Eventually Prometheus was freed by Herakles.

The War of the Gods; the Battle against Typhoeus; and the Birth of Athena (629–725; 820–68; 886–900)

The Titans, children of Ouranos, fought against the children of Kronos, led by Zeus. He managed to bring over to his side Kottos, Gyes, and Briareus, who each had 100 arms. After a mighty battle the Titans were defeated and sent to Tartarus, far below the earth. Gaia and Tartarus then had a child, the monster Typhoeus, but Zeus defeated him as well. Zeus then married Metis, the wisest of all gods. He was warned by Gaia and Ouranos, however, that the son of Metis would overthrow him. He swallowed Metis and gave birth to Athena.

The lists in the *Theogony* show what kinds of beings populate the world of the divine, and the myths explain how that divine world is organized. Hesiod's cosmos is full of divine powers, hundreds of them, of various kinds, gods, monsters, aspects of nature, personified abstractions. Hesiod's polytheism, and Greek polytheism in general, assumes a world that is teeming with gods and the power of the sacred, almost everywhere. But among all this profusion of divine powers, Zeus stands out as the dominant power in the cosmos, the king of the gods, at least by the end of the story. Thus there is a kind of balance between a world full of gods and the single god who rules them. But Hesiod's cosmos is not static: Zeus was not always the king of the gods, and he had to fight to gain his position. In general the divine cosmos in the *Theogony* has improved through the generations, and the final generation of gods, with Zeus as its king, is better than the first or the second generation.

Hesiod presents a view of the gods that would have been understood and accepted by most people of the ancient Greek world, at least in its broad outlines. According to the historian Herodotus, Hesiod and Homer were the first to describe the lineage of the gods, give them their names, apportion their various honors and powers, and describe their outward forms (*Histories* 2.53).[2] Herodotus exaggerates the influence of these two writers; certainly the names and the power of many gods were established much earlier. But his comment does suggest that Hesiod's catalogue held an important place in ancient Greek culture.

The *Theogony* was Panhellenic in its influence, and the divine world as described by Hesiod provides a fundamental background to ancient Greek thought and religion, even for those who did not agree with it. In one of the Platonic dialogues, Socrates learns that his acquaintance Euthyphro has accused his own father of murder. Socrates is rather surprised, and Euthyphro admits that all of his relatives think that he is wrong to take his father to court. But Euthyphro appeals to divine precedent: "Does not mankind believe that Zeus is the most excellent and just among the gods? And these same men admit that Zeus shackled his own father for swallowing his sons unjustly, and that Kronos in turn had gelded his father for like reasons. But now they are enraged at me when I proceed against my father for wrongdoing, and so they contradict themselves in what they say about the gods and what they say of me" (*Euthyphro* 6a). Socrates replies that he rejects these immoral stories about the gods, and that's why he is now being prosecuted himself. Socrates may not believe the Hesiodic Myth of Succession, but the story still serves as the background for this discussion of piety.

II. KRONOS AND HESTIA IN MYTH AND RITUAL

These myths were not just words and stories for the ancient Greeks, they were also represented in temples, rituals, vase illustrations, and even in the landscape. Most of the rituals of Greek religion were associated with one or another of the Olympian gods: for example, the Eleusinian Mysteries were associated with Demeter, the Dipolieia was associated with Zeus, the Panathenaia was associated with Athena, and the Dionysia (where the Athenian dramas were performed) was associated with Dionysos.[3] (A number of such rituals will be discussed in later chapters.)

Ritual was not restricted, however, to the major Olympian gods. Kronos, for example, the second ruler of the gods, deposed by his son Zeus, was honored by the Athenians at a festival called the Kronia, on the twelfth of the month Hecatombaion, the first month of their year, in midsummer (Parke 1977: 39–40; Parker 2005: 202–03). Very little is known about this festival, but it may have been a harvest festival, and it perhaps involved a measure of license for slaves, as did the Latin Saturnalia; in one account masters served their slaves at a banquet that day (Versnel 1988: 130). Probably some sort of ritual was performed at the temple of Kronos and Rhea in Athens (*Guide* 1.18.7). Two Athenian vases, both from the mid-fifth century BCE, have illustrations of Rhea giving Kronos a rock wrapped in swaddling clothes: a vase attributed to the Nausicaä Painter in the Metropolitan Museum in New York (06.1021.144) and an Athenian red-figure vase of the mid-fifth century in the Louvre in Paris (G 366) (see Figure 2.1; this may also be seen in Carpenter 1991, figure 94).

There is evidence for ancient Greek interest in Kronos outside of Athens as well. In the second century CE, the traveler Pausanias visited a headland in Achaia where, he was told, Kronos threw the reaping hook into the sea after he had castrated his father Ouranos (*Guide* 7.23.3). Pausanias also visited Mount Marvelous in Arcadia, where it was said that Rhea gave Kronos the stone to swallow instead of Zeus. Near the top of the mountain there was a cave dedicated to Rhea, and only women consecrated to Rhea were allowed to enter it (*Guide* 8.36.8). But the Boiotians claimed that Rhea tricked Kronos into swallowing the rock on a crag near the city of Khaironeia (*Guide* 9.41.3). And in Delphi Pausanias saw the very stone which Kronos swallowed. The people there poured oil on the rock every day, and in festivals they would make offerings to it of unspun wool (*Guide* 10.24.5). In Eleia, according to

Figure 2.1   Rhea deceives Kronos by giving him a stone to swallow instead of the baby Zeus. Group of the First Mannerists (ca. 460 BCE). Attic red-figure crater. Louvre, Paris, France. Inv. G 366. Photo: Hervé Lewandowski. Copyright © Réunion des Musées Nationaux/Art Resource, NY

Pausanias, some people say that Zeus wrestled Kronos there and that this was the beginning of the Olympic Games, but others say that Zeus founded the games to celebrate his victory over Kronos (*Guide* 5.7.7). On the peak of Mount Kronion in Eleia priests called the Kings offered sacrifice to Kronos at the spring equinox (*Guide* 6.20.1). In a temple of Hera in the city of Plataia in Boiotia, Pausanias saw a sculpture of Rhea bringing a rock in swaddling clothes to Kronos (*Guide* 9.2.5). In a temple of Zeus by the river Herkyna near the Boiotian city of Lebadeia, he saw statues of Kronos, Hera, and Zeus (*Guide* 9.39.3).

In Arcadia Pausanias heard a local myth that is not included in Hesiod's *Theogony*: when Rheia gave birth to Poseidon, she hid him in a sheepfold. She told Kronos that she had given birth to a horse and she gave him a foal to swallow. Pausanias saw a fountain there called Arne, which means Lamb, named in honor of this event (*Guide* 8.8.2). This story is clearly based on the familiar story about Zeus and the stone, and perhaps it serves to give Poseidon a position of importance in the Succession Myth. We can also note Poseidon's connection to the horse; in Chapter One we noticed another Arcadian myth in which Poseidon in the form of a stallion rapes Demeter in the form of a mare.

Kronos was not a major god, and not one of the Olympians. He was a god of the second generation, and he no longer had power, since had been deposed by Zeus. His role in ritual can be linked to his role in myth: he is particularly suited to be the patron of the Kronion, when masters served their slaves, precisely because he is the god without power, the god in chains (Versnel 1988: 146-47).

The goddess Hestia, the goddess of the hearth (which was also called "hestia"), was one of several household deities, and she received frequent offerings, perhaps daily, in every house. New brides were brought to the hearth, and newborn children were symbolically accepted into the family by being carried around the hearth (Parker 2005: 13–15). In Athens there was also a city cult to Hestia, which in effect made all the citizens members of a single family. In Olympia there was a public altar for Hestia, and there she received the first sacrifice, while the second sacrifice went to Olympian Zeus (*Guide* 5.14.4). Hestia was an important part of Greek ritual, but she has relatively little myth; myth alone is thus an incomplete and misleading source for the understanding of Greek religious practice.[4]

Further explorations on Hera

The goddess Hera is an important character in Homer's *Iliad*, where she is depicted as a supporter of the Greeks and also as an argumentative wife who is suspicious of her husband Zeus and acts to oppose his plans. She plays the role of the suspicious and jealous wife in other myths, such as the myth of Io or the myth of Herakles. Hera was also important as a civic goddess and there were a number of rituals associated with her. Write an essay in which you discuss the relationship between Hera in myth and Hera in religious ritual. Sources for your research could include Homer's *Iliad* and other myths in which Hera appears as well as secondary sources, such as Burkert 1985: 131–35, O'Brien 1993, Clark 1998, and Larson 2007. You may note that these scholars use the same evidence to come to somewhat different conclusions; how do they justify their interpretations? Is there one interpretation which you find most persuasive?

III. PERSONIFIED ABSTRACTIONS AS DIVINITIES

Hesiod's personified abstractions probably present the greatest difficulties for modern readers. The major gods are familiar, and it is perhaps not hard to understand the gods – some of them, at least – as rulers over certain aspects of nature or over other forces, such as erotic passion. But personifications such as Memory or Sleep or Strife or Work or Forgetfulness seem rather abstract, and it may be hard to believe that Hesiod or the ancient Greeks really thought that these abstractions were divine.

The personified abstractions in Hesiod cannot be clearly distinguished from the other kinds of divine forces. Eros, for instance, is clearly a god; he has at least a minor role in many myths, he is the primary subject of Plato's *Symposium*, he appears in many vase illustrations, there was an altar to Eros in Athens near the Academy, and he received sacrifice, for instance in the Athenian Panathenaia, but his name simply means Love or Desire, and so he also counts as a personification. Hebe was the daughter of Hera and eventually the wife of

Prometheus

Prometheus was a particularly important figure of myth for writers of the Romantic period. Lord Byron wrote an ode to Prometheus, and Percy Bysshe Shelley wrote a long poetic drama titled *Prometheus Unbound*. It would be simplistic to say that Prometheus in this poem is a figure of rebellion against tyranny, though that element is important. The poem includes the fall of Jupiter, and thus a new stage in the myth of succession, but Prometheus does not take his place as king of the gods; instead, the final vision of the poem is a utopian fantasy of love and harmony without rulers. This poem has been much admired, and it includes some beautiful passages, but it is not an easy read. Mary Shelley's *Frankenstein*, which is today more widely known than her husband's poetic drama, is subtitled *The Modern Prometheus*; just as Prometheus was the creator of human beings, the scientist Victor Frankenstein creates a new human life. Prometheus has also provided a subject for visual artists; a famous late Baroque sculpture (1762) by the French artist Nicolas-Sébastien Adam shows Prometheus attacked by the eagle in a whirl of dramatic movement and agony, whereas Gustav Moreau's painting of the same scene (1868) is almost contemplative.

Herakles when he became a god – there was an altar to her in Athens and a sanctuary in Philasia – but her name simply means Youth. We have seen that Prometheus has a role in several myths, and he often appears on vase illustrations. In Athens Prometheus had an altar, which was the starting point of a torch race (*Guide* 1.30.2). Aeschylus wrote a trilogy of plays about Prometheus; we have a tragedy titled *Prometheus Bound*, which may have been part of this trilogy (though some scholars believe that this play was written by another unknown playwright). But the name Prometheus simply means something like Foresight, and the name of his brother, Epimetheus, means something like Afterthought, so these gods also count as personifications. On the other hand, the names of some of the gods can be used more or less as synonyms for their powers, so a Greek could say that Zeus is raining, or that men are killed in Ares.

The Greek literary imagination found it easy to personify abstractions, and we cannot necessarily assume that a personification was more than a figure of rhetoric. But many personified abstractions had temples or received some kind of cult; these include Fear (Phobos); Youth (Hebe); Righteous Anger (Nemesis); Divine Law (Themis); Fair Fame (Eukleia); Health (Hygieia); Concord (Homonoia); Peace (Eirene); Democracy (Demokratia); Good Fortune (Agatha Tyche); and The People (Demos) (Stafford 2007: 74–82). There were some stories which were supposed to explain how one or another of these abstractions came to be worshiped at a particular place, though in some instances the worship may have come first and the story was invented later. In Corinth there was a shrine to Fortune, and there was a story that the hero Palamedes invented dice and dedicated them there (*Guide* 2.20.3).

After Apollo and Artemis had killed the monster Python, they came to Aigaleia, on the plain near Sikyon, to be purified. At a place called Fear, however they fell into a panic and fled. As a result, the citizens all became ill. The soothsayers said that Apollo and Artemis had to be placated. Seven boys and seven girls were sent to the river Sythas to pray, and the gods were persuaded to return and cure the disease. The sanctuary to Persuasion is built where they entered the acropolis (*Guide* 2.7.7).

For the ancient Greek mind the line between a rhetorical personification and a divine personification was easy to cross, and given the right circumstances almost any abstraction could have achieved divinity.

IV. BEYOND HESIOD

Hesiod's *Theogony* was not a sacred document, and no one was required to believe Hesiod's genealogy of the gods. Although the *Theogony* is extensive and comprehensive, it does not cover everything about the Greek gods or Greek religious thought. Some mythic stories add details which are not in Hesiod's account, but which do not conflict with it. A number of gods are missing from the *Theogony*: Pan, Priapos, Adonis, Asklepios, and the twins Kastor and Polydeukes, for instance. The *Theogony* has no account of the creation of the human race, although it does seem to explain the creation of woman. Hesiod's other poem, the *Works and Days*, includes the story of the Five Ages, but the process of creation of the human race and indeed the creator is left unclear. According to the travel writer Pausanias, in Phokis there are two large stones, more clay than stone, which smell like human flesh; these are what is left of the clay Prometheus used to make the human race (*Guide* 10.4.3). Certainly the great interest Prometheus shows in the human race would be explained if he were its maker.

Hesiod also leaves out the story of the flood (though it is possible that it appeared in the Hesiodic *Catalogue of Women*). This story is mentioned by many Greek writers, but no surviving Greek source gives us the whole story, and students usually read Ovid's Roman version. The two survivors of the flood were Deukalion and Pyrrha. Deukalion was the son of Prometheus (his mother was variously named or left without a name), while Pyrrha was the daughter of Epimetheus and Pandora. (Again there is a close connection between Prometheus and the origins of the human race.) In this story the human race was restored when Deukalion and Pyrrha threw stones over their shoulders, and these stones turned into human beings. In Athens there was a large split in the ground near the temple of Olympian Zeus, and according to the Athenians this was where the water drained away after the flood (*Guide* 1.18.7).

According the Hellenistic poet Callimachus, when Zeus was an infant Rhea hid him in Crete and set the Kuretes to guard him; they performed a war dance and beat their armor so that Kronos would not be able to hear him cry (*Hymn to Zeus*, 51–53; see also *Library* 1.4.) This story is not in the *Theogony*, but it does not contradict anything Hesiod says.

Other accounts, however, do conflict with Hesiod. Homer never presents any lengthy account of the origins of the gods, but in the *Iliad* Hera calls Okeanos "the genesis of the gods" and she links Okeanos to "mother Tethys" (14.201). Perhaps Homer knew a story in which Okeanos and Tethys are the first gods, rather than Chaos and Earth and Tartaros and Eros and Ouranos, as in Hesiod's *Theogony*. Homer also makes Aphrodite the daughter of Zeus and Dione, whereas in the *Theogony* she is born from the severed genitals of Ouranos.

A rather shadowy poet named Epimenides, of perhaps the late sixth century BCE, is supposed to have composed an account of the first gods in a poem titled *Oracles*, but only a few fragments quoted by later authors now survive. His cosmos evidently began with Air and Night, who produced two Titans, who in turn produced an egg, from which other gods were born (West 1983: 45–53).

The fullest divine genealogies other than Hesiod's *Theogony* were associated with the name of the mythical poet Orpheus and the religious groups called the Orphic cults.

According to Martin West, there were six of these Orphic genealogies, related to each other in complex ways.[5] The authors of these poems are not known, though scholars have made various conjectures. Some of the poems may date to the late sixth or early fifth century, but some are later. These poems probably played some role in Orphic cult, but here again there are more questions than answers. The following summary of some parts of what scholars call the Rhapsodies narrative is based on West's reconstruction.

The narrative, as West reconstructs it, begins with Time, in the form of a winged serpent, which coupled with Necessity. From this union were born Aither and Chaos, a great chasm covered with Night. Time then made an egg from Aither. This egg then hatched and brought forth Phanes (also called Metis), Erikepaios, Protogonos, Eros, Bromios, and Zeus. Phanes then brought forth other gods, including Ouranos and Ge. The narrative continues with the creation of other gods, and also the creation of a golden race of mortals under Phanes and a silver race under Kronos, but the details are not relevant here. Near the end of the narrative, Zeus proclaims that Dionysos (who is the child of Zeus and Persephone) will be the next divine king. The Titans decide to kill Dionysos; they whiten their faces with gypsum, they divert him with a mirror, apples, a pinecone, a bull-roarer, a ball, knucklebones, wool, and puppets. Then the Titans cut Dionysos into seven pieces, which they boil, roast, and taste. Athena saves the heart, which she takes to Zeus, who blasts the Titans with a thunderbolt. Apollo buries the limbs of Dionysos on Parnassus, but from the heart a new Dionysos is born. Zeus then creates a new race of mortals from the soot left by the blasted Titans. These mortals have immortal souls, which can pass through a series of transmigrations into human and animal bodies. When the soul in a human body dies it is judged; the good go to the meadow by the river Acheron, but the bad go to Tartaros and the plain of Kokytos. Souls spend 300 years in the other world and then they are reborn, but they desire release from rebirth. Zeus has appointed Dionysos and Kore (Persephone) to help mortals find release through sacrifices and rites (West 1983: 70–75).

The Rhapsodies narrative shares some features with more mainstream Greek thought, such as the idea of a succession of divine rulers and even many of the names of gods, such as Ouranos and Ge and Zeus and Dionysos. But there are clear differences as well. The story begins with divine forces not mentioned by Hesiod, such as Time and Necessity and Phanes. The egg produced by Phanes is not mentioned by Hesiod, though it is mentioned in the fragments of Epimenides. The roles played by Persephone and Dionysos are very different from anything in Hesiod or in more mainstream Greek myth. Some of the imagery is unlike the generally anthropomorphic imagery of Hesiod's gods: Phanes, for instance, has four eyes and four horns, gold wings, ram, bull and serpent heads, and both male and female genitals, whereas Persephone has two faces, four eyes, and horns. Hesiod's *Theogony* rather ignores mortals, though the myth of the Five Ages is found in the other Hesiodic poem, *The Works and Days*. The Rhapsodies narrative discusses both the creation of mortals, including three rather than five successive ages, and also their ultimate fate. One of the primary concerns of the Orphic cults was the fate of the soul after death.

It is not easy to tell how widely the Orphic poems were known. Most likely the Orphic cults were marginal to Greek society, but there are echoes and hints of Orphic theology in a number of Greek writers, including Herodotus, Euripides, Aristophanes, Plato, Aristotle, and others. West argues that the theogony at the beginning of Apollodorus' *Library of Greek*

Mythology has Orphic as well as Hesiodic elements (West 1983: 121–24). No doubt the divine genealogy presented in Hesiod's *Theogony* was the best known and most widely accepted, but it was not dogma, and other genealogies were in circulation.

V. MYTH AS RITUAL AETIOLOGY

Greek myth abounds in aetiologies, stories which explain the foundation of a ritual. [6] It seems, however, that an aetiological myth often was developed after the ritual practice, as an invention to explain what already existed. Aetiological myths may be associated with Panhellenic rituals, as the *Homeric Hymn to Demeter* is associated with the Panhellenic Eleusinian Mysteries, but they may also be local, as the story of the Bouphonia is associated with a local ritual in Athens, the Dipolieia. Hesiod's story of the sacrifice at Mekone justifies no particular ritual, but rather the general ritual division of the meat in a normal sacrifice. (The *Homeric Hymn to Hermes* includes another account of the beginning of sacrifice as instituted by Hermes.)

The evidence suggests that Greeks were very interested in aetiological myths, which are common throughout Greek literature. The travel writer Pausanias is a rich source of aetiologies. He tells, for example, an interesting and complex story about a ritual, called the Daidala, held in Plataia. (The word *daidalon* means a work of art, particularly a statue.) The Plataians make a statue from a specially chosen oak tree, dress it up, and put it on a wagon with a young woman beside it to act as bridesmaid. They drive the wagon to the river Asopos and then to the peak of Mount Kithairon, where they burn the statue along with cattle that have been sacrificed.

The Plataians explain this ritual with the following story. Once Hera was angry at Zeus and went away to Euboea. Zeus wanted to get her to come back, so he went to the king of Plataia, a wise man named Kithairon, who advised him to construct a wooden statue of a woman, dress it up in bridal clothing, and spread the word that he was marrying Plataia, the daughter of Asopos. (Asopos is the name of the river near Plataia, and Plataia is the name of the mythical heroine after whom the city is named.) Hera fell for the trick; she came and ripped the clothes off the statue, and when she saw it was a statue she was reconciled to Zeus (*Guide* 9.3.1–4).

There are many other examples of aetiological myths in Pausanias. For example, the Thebans held a sacrifice for Ashen Apollo in which a working ox was sacrificed, although ordinarily working animals were not sacrificed. According to Pausanias, one year when the sacrifice was about to take place, the bull chosen for the sacrifice did not arrive in time, and so the Thebans in this emergency sacrificed an ox from a wagon that happened to be there (*Guide* 9.12.1). Near Mount Kronion in Eleia there is a sanctuary for the goddess of childbirth, Eileithuia, where the people worship a spirit known as the City Savior. Once when the Arcadian army invaded the territory, a woman brought her baby to the Eleaian commanders and told them that she had been told in a dream to hand the baby over to the army so that he could fight in defense of the city. The commanders put the infant in the front line, and when the Arcadians charged, the little boy turned into a serpent. The Arcadians fell into a panic and fled. The serpent then disappeared into the ground, and on the spot the Eleaians built the sanctuary to the City Savior and to Eileithuia, who had brought the child to birth (*Guide* 6.20.2–6).

Greek literature is full of such aetiological stories, but aetiologies are also found in the monotheistic religions. The story of the Jews in Egypt is the aetiology for the Passover ritual, and the Last Supper is the aetiology for the Mass. People like to have a story to explain why they do what they do.[7] One effect of such aetiologies, both ancient and modern, is to connect the world of the past to the world of the present, to make historical time come alive. What is different about the aetiologies in ancient Greece is their profusion. We should not assume, however, that everyone in ancient Greece believed these stories. Pausanias himself often suggests that he is skeptical, and there were other skeptics, as we will see in Chapter Five. But these stories had a fascination and an effect even for a skeptic like Pausanias. We benefit from his fascination, for these aetiologies can illuminate what the ancient Greeks thought and what they did, and how their thoughts and actions came together in ritual.

VI. MYTH AND RITUAL IN GREEK SOCIETY

Greek ritual practice could occur in the household or in social and political groups, both small groups (such as the Attic demes) and in the city as a whole. Civic cults, both in smaller political units such as the deme and in the city as a whole, were fundamental to Greek life. To some extent ancient Greeks demonstrated their citizenship, their membership in a city, by participation in that city's rituals. Most civic festivals recurred on the same day in each year, and so we can speak of a calendar of festivals. In Athens, for example, in the month Hecatombaion there were three festivals, the Kronia, the Synoikia, and the Panathenaia, which was one of the great festivals of the year; in the month Metageitnion there were probably two festivals, the Metageitnia (about which almost nothing is known, beyond the fact that it was celebrated in other cities aw well), and a festival for Herakles at Kynosarges, in which non-citizens could participate; in the month Boedromion there were four festivals, the Genesia, a festival for Artemis Agotera, the Boedromia, and the celebration of the Eleusinian Mysteries, which stretched over several days in the middle of the month; and so on. A typical festival might have included a procession, a hymn sung to the god being honored, a prayer, a grain offering, a libation, or an animal sacrifice, and a communal banquet (Mikalson 2005: 27). Some festivals also included competitions, athletic, musical, or dramatic. Festivals varied in popularity; some were attended by only a small group, others attracted crowds of many thousands over several days.

Each city had its own calendar of festivals, but some festivals occurred in more than one city. (The names of the months varied from city to city, and because the Greek lunar calendar did not match the solar year, the months could fall at different seasons in different years.) Knowledge of the ritual calendars of cities other than Athens is incomplete, but there is at least some information about many hundreds of festivals performed around the Greek world.

VII. MYTH AND RITUAL IN THE *ORESTEIA*

Greek religion is the background for Greek myth, and in a circular fashion, Greek myth is the background for Greek religion. The great tragedies, for example, often pose theological problems and often put rituals on the stage, as can be seen in Aeschlyus' trilogy the *Oresteia*, made up of the *Agamemnon*, the *Libation-Bearers*, and the *Eumenides*. The basic plot of the trilogy is simple. In the first play, Agamemnon returns from the Trojan War and is killed by his wife Klytemnestra and her lover, Agamemnon's cousin Aigisthos (the only child surviving from the feast in which Thyestes unknowingly ate his children, served up by his father Atreus, the father of Agamemnon). In the second play, Agamemnon's son Orestes kills Klytemnestra and Aigisthos. In the third play, Orestes is driven mad and pursued by the Furies; he finally goes to Athens, where Athena presides over a trial in which he is declared innocent. All of these events occur within a context of theological speculation and ritual practice.

The *Agamemnon* takes place on the day of Agamemnon's return, but in the background of the play is a corrupted ritual. When the Greek fleet had gathered at Aulis to sail to Troy, the winds blew against them. The seer Kalkhas revealed that Artemis was angry and demanded the sacrifice of Agamemnon's daughter Iphigeneia.[8] By necessity or by choice – the critics disagree – Agamemnon agreed to the sacrifice. In some versions of the story, Artemis substituted a deer at the last moment and carried Iphigeneia away, but in the *Agamemnon* everyone believes that she has died. Klytemnestra kills her husband in large part because of the sacrifice of their daughter, and the language of sacrifice is used to describe his murder, as well.

There seems to be no strong evidence that human sacrifice was any regular part of Greek religion (although a ritual in Attica simulated human sacrifice when a man's throat was nicked to draw blood, and in Sparta young men were whipped at an altar (Burkert 1985: 59); see Chapter Four for stories of human sacrifice in Arcadia). In a number of myths, however, human sacrifice takes place or is threatened. The Athenian king Erechtheus sacrifices one (or more) of his daughters to save the city in war; the Trojan princess Polyxena is sacrificed on the tomb of Achilles; when the crops fail in Boiotia, Ino proposes that her stepson Phrixos be sacrificed, but he is saved by his mother, the goddess Nephele, and he flies away on the ram with the Golden Fleece. (Readers may also be reminded of the story of Abraham and Isaac in Genesis.)

Even as an idea rather than as an actual practice, human sacrifice raises a number of questions. For instance, in a society that accepts animal sacrifice, can human sacrifice be imagined as a kind of extreme case? Could the gods demand human sacrifice? If the gods were to make such a demand, would we have to obey? If we obey the gods' demand for human sacrifice, do we bear the guilt for the action? Is human sacrifice comparable to other human killings, such as war or executions? Can the sacrifice of one person be justified if it saves the lives of many others? All of these questions are posed in the *Agamemnon* or in other mythic stories.

Religion continues to be an important element throughout the trilogy. The second play, the *Libation-Bearers*, begins with a ritual, as Elektra, the daughter of Agamemnon, comes to make offerings at his tomb. This offering can be seen in the context of hero cult (see Chapter Six). The third play, The *Eumenides*, begins at Delphi, where Orestes has come, pursued by the Furies. The first character the audience sees is the Pythia, the priestess of the oracle of Apollo, and the second character is Apollo himself, Orestes' protector, and the patron of the oracle. Thus the beginning of the play firmly places the action in the context of religious practice.

The scene shifts to Athens, where Athena presides over a trial in which Orestes is acquitted. The Furies agree to take a place in Athenian religion as the Eumenides (Kindly Ones), also known as the Semnai Theai (Revered Goddesses). The transformation of the Furies into the Semnai Theai may be Aeschylus' invention, but there was a cult of the Semnai Theai in Athens, so his invention has a real basis in Athenian ritual.

This complex play raises a theological problem about the relationship of the "older" and the "younger" gods. At the very beginning of the play, the Pythia explains that the Oracle at Delphi originally belonged to Gaia, a goddess of the very earliest generation; then it belonged to Themis, then to Phoebe, and finally to Phoebus Apollo, an Olympian. Thus we see a transfer of ownership from the oldest generation of gods to the youngest. In some other versions of this story of the successive ownership of the Oracle, the transfer occurs violently (as the succession of generations in Hesiod's *Theogony* is also violent), but here each stage of the process seems to have occurred quite peacefully (Sourvinou-Inwood 1988: 215–41).

This myth of succession at the beginning of the play is then mirrored by a myth of succession at the end. In the trial, Athena rules that Orestes is innocent and that the Furies have no right to punish him. After Orestes and his protector Apollo have left the stage, the Furies complain bitterly to Athena that the younger gods have trampled on the laws of the older generation, and they threaten to bring plague and famine on Athens. But Athena manages to placate the Furies by promising an honored place for them in Athenian cult, so long as they use their powers to protect the city. Thus Aeschylus' myth of succession ends with the pacification of the Furies, as the older gods freely agree to take a new position in the cosmos.[9]

The *Oresteia* is a great work of literature, a magnificent poetic drama, with stirring action, vivid characterizations, and rich imagery. This trilogy is also the representation of a myth, and the myth itself is presented in the context of religious ritual and theological speculation. Any particular analysis may have to separate out one or another of these strands, but for the Greek audience, they were all woven together into a unified experience.

CONCLUSION

This chapter has explored various aspects of the relationship between Greek myth and Greek religion. The ancient Greeks' system of polytheism included a wide variety of divine figures, including Titans, gods, personifications of various kinds, nymphs, and various monsters. Many of these are listed in Hesiod's *Theogony*; this poem is an essential text for the understanding of Greek myth, but as extensive as it is, it needs to be supplemented by other myths and rituals as well. Hesiod does not cover all of the gods, nor does he show in detail how the various gods were honored in ritual.

Some myths explain the origin of particular rituals, but myth does not form a scripture for Greek religion. On the other hand, the rituals show that the gods were not simply characters in stories, but fundamental to Greek life through frequent social practice. Most rituals honored the Olympian gods, but there were ritual observances for such divine figures as Kronos and Prometheus, for gods who do not play any large role in the stories of myth, such as Hestia, as well as for some divine personifications. Rituals were performed at all levels of ancient Greek society, from the household to the polis to interstate institutions such as the Eleusinian Mysteries. Those performed at the level of the polis probably had a particular importance, since participation in civic rituals served to mark membership in a citizen body. The myths and rituals were a fundamental background for Greek social practice and thought, and their importance can be seen in the way they are woven into works of literature such as the *Oresteia*. Chapter Three will explore some of the ways the various myths are linked to each other in complex networks.

FURTHER READING

There are a number of good introductions to Greek religion; see, for example, Mikalson 2005, Price 1999, and Bruit Zaidman and Schmitt Pantel 1992. Burkert 1983 is a fuller and more extensive treatment of the topic. Ogden 2007 collects a number of worthwhile essays on various aspects of Greek religion, including Stafford 2007, which discusses personification in Greek religion. West 1966 is the standard commentary on Hesiod's *Theogony*. Hesiod's theological views are discussed in Clay 2003. Dougherty 2005 is a good introduction to Prometheus in ancient thought and in the Classical tradition. On Kronos, see Versnel 1988. West 1983 is a scholarly account of the Orphic poems. Parker 1996 is specifically concerned with religion in Athens. On the myth of succession in the *Eumenides*, see Sourvinou-Inwood 1988, and on religion in the *Oresteia* and in tragedy generally see Sourvinou-Inwood 2003.

Chapter Three

HOMER'S BEAUTY PAGEANT
The Traditions of Myth

What myths did the ancient Greeks know and tell? Which stories could an ancient author expect his audience to be familiar with? The tradition of Greek myth included an enormous treasure of narratives, some well known still today, others less known, and some now lost. But all of these were more or less part of the background of knowledge in the ancient Greek world. Many of these stories are linked to each other, often through genealogical relationships. Moreover, the literary representations of a myth will often include references to other myths, perhaps as parallels or contrasts to the principal story. This chapter begins with references to myth in the *Odyssey*, and continues with an extended reconstruction of one of these myths, the myth of the once famous hero Melampous, from various fragmentary sources. Section III explores references to myth in the *Iliad* and section IV discusses the most important ancient Greek catalogue of myth, the Hesiodic *Catalogue of Women*, which now survives only in fragments. The final section V turns to a visual rather than literary source, through a discussion of the various myths depicted on the famous François Vase.

I. FAMOUS WOMEN OF MYTH IN THE *ODYSSEY*

When Odysseus went to the Land of the Dead (as he tells the Phaiakians in Book Eleven of the *Odyssey*) he first met the soul of one of his crew who had recently died and had not yet been buried. Next he spoke with the soul of the blind seer Teiresias, and then with the soul of his mother. After that Persephone sent him a parade of women, women famous in myth before the Trojan War. Odysseus names 14 of these women – Tyro, Antiope, Alkmene, Megara, Epikaste, Chloris, Leda, Iphimedeia, Phaedra, Prokris, Ariadne, Maira, Klymene, and Eriphyle. Odysseus tells little stories about some of these women, but others he merely mentions by name. Most often the references to these women can be filled out with

Exploring Greek Myth. First Edition. Matthew Clark.
© 2012 Matthew Clark. Published 2012 by Blackwell Publishing Ltd.

information from later sources, but with some caution, since it is difficult to prove that Homer knew the details of a story unless he tells it himself.

The *Odyssey* was a Panhellenic epic, and the women in the catalogue became Panhellenic when Odysseus talked about them, unless they were already Panhellenic before the *Odyssey*. Perhaps they lend their own Panhellenic status to this upstart epic hero. Some of these women of myth remain famous today. Readers may know something about Alkmene, who was Herakles' mother; or Megara, Herakles' wife, the mother of the children he killed when he went mad; or Leda, the mother of Kastor, Polydeukes, Klytemnestra, and Helen of Troy; or Phaedra, who fell in love with her stepson Hippolytos; or Ariadne, who helped Theseus escape from the Labyrinth. Epikaste is a special case: her name may not be familiar, but as the wife of Oedipus she is famous no matter what she is called.

The others are not so well known today. Tyro was the daughter of Salmoneus, one of the great sinners in Greek myth. He attached bronze pots to his chariot and waved torches as he rode, in order to imitate the thunder and lightning of Zeus. Zeus naturally enough blasted him with lightning bolts, but Tyro was saved because she had opposed her father's irreverence. She married her uncle Kretheus and they had three children, Aison, Pheres, and Amythaon, but she and Poseidon also had two children, Pelias and Neleus. Aison, the father of Jason, was the king of Iolkos, but his throne was stolen by his brother Pelias, and then Pelias sent Jason off to fetch the Golden Fleece. Pheres is the father of Admetos, whose wife Alkestis died in his place. Amythaon is the father of Melampous and Bias (for more on Melampous see Section II below).

Neleus married Chloris, the sixth woman in the parade. She was the daughter of Amphion of Orchomenos, though Apollodorus in his *Library* says she was the daughter of the Amphion who was son of Antiope, number two in the parade. (This Amphion and his brother Zethus are mentioned briefly in Chapter One.) The children of Neleus and Chloris were Nestor, Chromios, Periklymenos, and Pero. Of these, Nestor is an important figure in both the *Iliad* and the *Odyssey*. Pero was courted by Bias, the brother of the seer Melampous.

Iphimedeia was the wife of Aloeus and mother (by Poseidon) of Otos and Ephialtes, the tallest men ever and the handsomest, after Orion. They threatened the gods and they planned to pile the mountain Ossa on top of Olympos, but Apollo killed them. Prokris was the wife of Kephalos; there are several stories about them; the best known (but not necessarily the most interesting) is that Kephalos killed her accidentally while he was hunting. Eriphyle was the wife of Amphiaros, who was one of the heroes who joined Polyneikes in the attack on Thebes when he and Eteokles were fighting over the throne. At first Amphiaros refused to join the expedition; he was a seer, and so he knew that the attack would fail and all the heroes except Adrastos would die. But Polyneikes bribed Eriphyle with a golden necklace and she persuaded Amphiaros to go.

Klymene is more difficult to identify. Odysseus gives us no information about her. There are several women in the mythic tradition named Klymene. One of these is a daughter of Okeanos, another is a Nereid, and a third is a nymph; none of these is likely to be in the Land of the Dead. Another is the daughter of Minyas and the mother of Iphiklos, who was Aison's brother-in-law and Jason's uncle (according to Apollonius of Rhodes), and one of the Argonauts; he also imprisoned Melampous. Most scholars believe that this Klymene, the mother of Iphiklos, is the woman Odysseus saw in the Land of the Dead.

There was, however, another Klymene, the mother of Palamedes, one of the Greeks who went to Troy. In one story, when Odysseus was trying to avoid joining the expedition against Troy by pretending to be insane, it was Palamedes who proved he was faking. Later on Odysseus plotted against him and managed to have him killed. None of this story, of course, is mentioned by Homer (though it is mentioned in the *Kypria*, an early epic poem which now survives only in fragments). Perhaps Homer did not know the story. If he did know the story, perhaps he left it out as unworthy of his hero. But this reference could also have been a sign to his audience that he knew the story, and knew that they knew it, and it was not by mistake that he left it out.

The intentions of poets are notoriously difficult to establish, even when something about the poet is known; since nothing at all is known about Homer, his intentions can only be deduced from reading his poems. Some scholars prefer to talk about the epic tradition rather than about Homer as an individual poet, but if it is difficult to talk about Homer's intentions, it is not much easier to talk about the intentions of the tradition. It may be better to say that whenever it was that Palamedes and his mother Klymene entered the tradition, this reference might bring them to the mind of the audience.

Odysseus tells us nothing about Maira, and there is little or no information about her from other surviving sources. According to an ancient marginal note on the *Odyssey*, and also the commentary on the *Odyssey* by the Byzantine bishop Eustathios, Maira was a follower of Artemis; she was the daughter of Proitos, the son of Thersandros, the son of Sisyphos. All of these except for Sisyphos are hardly known. She was seduced by Zeus, and Artemis found out and killed her (see Gantz 1993: 733–34). Perhaps this is the Maira Homer has in mind, but she does not seem to fit with the other women in the catalogue, who are all famous wives or mothers. Perhaps there was a Maira who figured in a story that has simply been lost.

But in any case Homer seems to assume that his original audience would have known about Maira without any reminders, just as he assumes that they knew about the others. A few of them he does describe, at least briefly, but probably not because of fear that his audience will not know who they are. It is not clear why some are selected for fuller treatment; the rhythm of oral storytelling may be part of the reason.

For a modern reader, it takes a few hours with a good encyclopedia to identify all of these women and trace their family histories. Homer's audience did not have any reference books, but they didn't need them. Their encyclopedia was simply in their minds, built up as memories from countless epic recitations. Homer's audience heard him tell the story of the anger of Achilles and the return of Odysseus, but as they listened to these epics they also heard many other stories. These other stories, in constant counterpoint to the main action, gave the epic experience a kind of depth modern readers should try to recapture, insofar as possible, in the effort to understand the mythic world of ancient Greece.

Why did Homer include this little catalogue of women from myth? Why did he put it into the mouth of Odysseus at this point in the story? These are questions about literature rather than about myth, but there is no point in drawing the boundaries of this discussion too strictly. The *Odyssey* overall does not refer to a large number of myths except when Odysseus is in the Land of the Dead. (The *Iliad* includes many more references to myth; see Section III below.) This, then, is a special passage in the *Odyssey*. At this point in the story Odysseus has just arrived in the land of the Phaiakians, with no companions, no property, in fact not even any clothing. He is entirely dependent on his hosts and their good will towards him. He has to make a good impression, and almost his only resource is his ability to tell stories. His tale of his trip to the Land of the Dead is surely impressive; only a few other heroes had ever made this trip before. His catalogue of heroines also suggests that he is a part of their world of myth. Of course if these are good stories for Odysseus to tell the Phaiakians, they are also good stories for Homer to tell his audience. They offer a kind of mythic resonance to the story, and they establish a place for Homer's story in the world of myth. Moreover, these famous women of myth provide a context for the women – Penelope, Helen, Klytemnestra – who figure so prominently in this epic.

II. THE MYTH OF MELAMPOUS

Many of the stories Homer tells or hints at in this catalogue of famous women can be expanded considerably from other sources. This section explores just one of these, the story of Melampous, as an example of the reconstruction of a myth Homer tells only in part. Melampous is not well known today, but from the time of Homer down to the Roman Imperial period he was a major figure of myth. Homer mentions Melampous twice, first, as we have seen, in Book Eleven of the *Odyssey*, and later in Book Fifteen. Among the works attributed to Hesiod was an epic poem about Melampous called the *Melampodia*; only a few fragments of this poem survive, but it is mentioned by the rhetorician Athenaeus in his *Scholars at Dinner* (*Deipnosophistae*) in the second century CE, by the Christian writer Clement of Alexandria in the late second or early third century CE, and by the Byzantine scholar Tzetzes in the twelfth century CE. An Athenian poet of the fifth century BCE named Pherekydes wrote about Melampous, but his version of the story survives only in a summary. Apollodorus tells the story at some length in his *Library of Greek Mythology*, Pausanias mentions Melampous several times, and other ancient authors mention him as well.

Homer seems to know two slightly different versions of the story of Melampous. In Book Eleven of the *Odyssey*, Odysseus tells the Phaiakians about Pero, the daughter of Neleus. She was courted by many men, but her father would give her only to someone who could obtain the cattle of Iphikles (the name is also sometimes spelled "Iphiklos"; this Iphikles should not be confused with the Iphikles who is the son of Amphitryon and brother of Herakles). An unnamed seer undertook the task. (Homer presumably expects his audience to know that he is referring to Melampous.) But this seer was captured and held prisoner by the herders. At the end of a year Iphikles released him, when he had told Iphikles all his prophetic knowledge (11.287–97). In Book Fifteen, Homer says that Melampous (and here he does name him) was a rich man in Pylos, but he fled from Neleus, and he was kept prisoner for a year in the house of Phylakos (according to Apollodorus, Phylakos was the father of Iphikles). Eventually Melampous was released; he drove the cattle back to Pylos and received Neleus' daughter Pero, whom he took to his brother. (Homer does not tell us the name of Melampous' brother, but later sources call him Bias.) Melampous then went to Argos and ruled there. In Argos Melampous married and had two sons (15.225–40). Thus in Book

Eleven, Melampous left home of his own free will to get the cattle of Iphikles, while in Book Fifteen it seems he was forced to go.

Apollodorus gives further details in the *Library* (1.9.11–12; 2.2.2). When Melampous was a child, he saw a servant kill some snakes. He burned the bodies of the snakes (as if on a funeral pyre?) and raised the baby snakes they had left. Later on these snakes came to Melampous while he was asleep and licked his ears with their tongues. When Melampous awoke he discovered that he could understand the language of the birds, and he used this knowledge to predict the future. He also learned to tell the future from observing sacrificial victims.

According to Apollodorus, when Melampous went to steal the cattle from Phylakos, he knew in advance that he would be imprisoned for a year. Towards the end of the year he heard some woodworms saying that they had nearly eaten through the beam in his room, so he asked the guards to move him to another room. The beam collapsed but Melampous was safe. His captor Phylakos heard what had happened and offered to free Melampous if he could cure Iphikles of his inability to have children.

Melampous found out from a vulture that Iphikles' impotence stemmed from what today might be called a childhood trauma, which occurred when he saw his father gelding sheep and became frightened. (According to Pherekydes, however, Phylakos saw his son Iphikles doing something improper – "atopon", "out of place" – and chased him with a knife.) Phylakos fixed the knife in a tree and the bark grew over it, but Iphikles' fear caused his impotence. Melampous, directed by the vulture, found the knife, scraped the rust from the knife and mixed it with wine. Iphikles drank this mixture and was cured.

According to Apollodorus, when Melampous was in Argos he cured the daughters of Proitos, who had been driven mad either for rejecting Dionysos or for mocking Hera. Melampous initially asked for a third of the kingdom if his cure should succeed, and Proitos turned him down. Now all the women of Argos became mad; they killed their children and ran off into the wilderness. Melampous raised his price for the cure and asked for an equal share in the kingdom for his brother. When Proitos agreed, Melampous gathered a posse of young men and they chased the women out of the wilderness. One of the daughters of Proitos died in the chase, but the others were cured, and Proitos married these daughters to Melampous and Bias.

The Myth of Melampous combines a number of traditional story elements. Some of these elements are perhaps more typical of folktale than of myth, though the line between these genres is hard to draw. There are many stories of animals that reward their benefactors, and many folktale heroes gain knowledge of the language of the animals.

Contests for the hand of a princess occur many times in folktales and also in Greek myths. One of the most famous is the foot-race set by Danaos to marry off his many daughters. This second set of marriages occurs after the daughters have killed their first husbands (Pindar, *Ninth Pythian*; *Library* 2.1.5). King Oinomaos of Pisa, the father of the beautiful Hippodameia, made each of her suitors try to outrun him in a chariot race; if Oinomaos could catch the suitor, he would kill him. After many suitors had died, Pelops won by trickery. There is also a story that Odysseus won Penelope in a foot-race set by her father Ikarios (*Guide* 3.12.1), and one might also include the test of the bow at the end of the Odyssey.

Cattle raids are also common in myth and folklore. In the Greek tradition we can note Nestor's stories about cattle raids in the *Iliad*, as well as Hermes' theft of Apollo's cattle and Herakles' theft of the cattle of Geryon. The most famous Celtic story of this kind is the medieval cycle called the *Cattle Raid of Cooley (Táin Bó Cúailnge)*.

The story of a prisoner with special knowledge can also be found in *Genesis*, Chapters 39–41: Joseph, in Egypt, was falsely accused by his master's wife and thrown into prison, where he interprets the dreams of two other prisoners. Pharaoh hears of his skill and asks him to interpret his two dreams, one of seven lean cows eating seven fat cows and another of seven withered ears of grain eating seven good ears of grain. Joseph tells him that God will bring seven years of plenty followed by seven years of famine. Pharaoh is so impressed that he releases Joseph from prison and makes him his overseer.

The story that Iphikles was cured by the rust of the knife that frightened him is similar to the story of the cure of Telephos, king of Mysia. When the Greeks were on their way to Troy, they attacked Mysia by mistake, and in the battle Achilles wounded Telephos with a spear. Once they realized their mistake, they sailed on, but they had no guide to show them the way to Troy. Meanwhile, Telephos' wound would not heal, and Apollo told him that it could be cured only by the man who had wounded him. Telephos found the Greeks, Achilles healed the wound with rust scraped from his spear, and Telephos showed them the way to Troy (*Library, Epit.* 3.17–20). Thus the story of Melampous seems to be constructed with a variety of traditional materials.

How much of the story of Melampous did Homer know? Certainly he knew that Bias courted Pero and that Melampous helped his brother by obtaining the cattle of Iphikles; he knew that Melampous was imprisoned and that he was released when he told Iphikles his prophetic knowledge. Since he knew that Melampous was a seer, he could have known the story about how he received his prophetic knowledge. He might have left it out because it was not really relevant to what he was talking about, or perhaps because he usually avoids the fantastic and magical. There is no trace of the story about the daughters of Proitos or the story about the cure of Iphikles. Quite possibly Homer did not know these stories, and perhaps they were not part of the tradition in Homer's day. Speculation is part of scholarship, but in the attempt to reconstruct a tradition, speculations must be controlled by what is actually known. The question of what Homer knew cannot always be decided.

III. MYTHIC TRADITIONS IN THE *ILIAD*

In Book Fourteen of the *Iliad* we find another little encyclopedia of myth. Hera wants to distract Zeus' attention from the battlefield, so she dresses up in her finest robe, and she borrows Aphrodite's sash (she tells a lie to get it), and she makes her way to the peak of Mount Ida where Zeus is watching the battle. As soon as he sees her, desire fills his heart as never before. As he tells her, he desires her more than he desired Ixion's wife, who was the mother of Perithoös (the companion of Theseus); or Danaë, the mother of Perseus; or Europa, the mother of Minos; or Semele, the mother of Dionysos; or Alkmene, the mother of Herakles; or Demeter, the mother of Persephone; or Leto, the mother of Apollo and Artemis (14.314–28). It is hard to imagine why Zeus would tell Hera about these other women, since she is typically jealous of his other loves, but he does, and from the way this list is presented it seems that Homer's audience probably knew all these stories beforehand.

Myths in the *Iliad* and *Odyssey*

Alkestis, who gave up her life for her husband Admetos (Il.2.715)

Bellerophon, who was falsely accused of attempted rape by Anteia, the wife of Proitos, and who killed the Khimaira (Il.6.155–202)

Daidalos, who built the Labyrinth (Il.18.592)

Ino, the daughter of Kadmos, who became the goddess Leukothea (Od.5.333–53)

Itys, who was killed by his mother Prokne to punish her husband Tereus (Od.19.523)

Jason, who went on a quest for the Golden Fleece (Il.7.468, Od.12.72)[1]

Lykourgos, who attacked Dionysos and his followers, and was struck blind and soon died (Il.6.130–40)

Marpessa, who loved the mortal Idas in preference to Apollo (Il.9.557–64)

Meleager, who killed the Calydonian boar (Il.9.529–99)

Niobe, who bragged about her children and saw them all killed by Artemis and Apollo (Il.24.602–17)

Minos, king of Crete, who now issues judgments in the Land of the Dead (Od.5.568)

Orion, the great hunter, who was loved by Eos, the goddess of the Dawn (Od.5.121, Od.11.572)

Perseus, who killed Medusa and rescued Andromeda (Il.14.320, Il.19.116)

Thamyris, who boasted that he could out-sing the Muses and was punished for his presumption (Il.2.594–600)

Tithonos, who was loved by the Dawn (Il.11.1, Od.5.1)

Sisyphos, who eternally rolled a rock up a hill in the Land of the Dead (Od.11.593)

Tantalos, who was tantalized in the Land of the Dead by food and drink he could not reach (Od.11.582)[2]

Tityos, who attacked the goddess Leto, and whose liver was eaten by vultures in the Land of the Dead (Od.11.576)

Homer alludes to myths here and there throughout the epics, and from these allusions it seems likely that Homer's audience probably knew a very large stock of mythic narratives. Some of Homer's references are just a name, and it cannot be known with any certainty that he knew of the story in the version familiar today. (And sometimes, as in the story of Oedipus, his version is different from later versions.) When he mentions Alkestis, for example, he only says that she was married to Admetos, that their son Eumelos was the leader of a contingent from Pherai in the Trojan War, and that she was the most beautiful of the daughters of Pelias. He does not include any reference to the story that she gave up her life for Admetos, as told by Euripides in his play *Alcestis*. Homer mentions Daidalos in Knossos, but he doesn't mention the Labyrinth or Ikaros. He does know that Theseus took Ariadne from Crete (*Odyssey* 11.322), so it is probably safe to assume that he knew about the Minotaur.

A few stories, however, Homer tells in some detail. Often fuller versions are put into the mouth of a character rather than told by the narrator. In Book Nine of the *Iliad*, for instance, Achilles' companion Phoinix tells the story of Meleager and the Calydonian boar in some 70 lines (529–99). This is no casual tale; Phoinix is using the story as an example as he tries to persuade Achilles to accept Agamemnon's gifts and return to battle. But Achilles refuses.

Meleager and the Calydonian boar

Artemis was angry at Oineus because he had not given her the proper offerings. As a punishment she sent a great boar to ravage the country. Meleager, the son of Oineus, gathered a great group of champions to hunt the boar. Once the boar had been killed, Artemis caused a dispute between the Kouretes and the Aitolians over the trophies of the hunt, the boar's head and hide. So long as Meleager fought for the Aitolians, they had the upper hand. But when his mother cursed him because of the death of her brother, he withdrew from the fighting, and the Aitolians began to lose. The elders begged him to relent and promised him great gifts in return, his father begged him, his sisters and his mother begged him, his friends begged him, but he would not relent. Finally his wife Kleopatra begged him. He returned to battle and saved the Aitolians, but they would no longer give him any gifts for his service, which came so late.

Later, in Book Twenty-four of the *Iliad*, Achilles uses the same technique of persuasion through myth. Priam has come to Achilles' hut to ask for the body of his son Hektor. Achilles takes pity on the old man and agrees to give up the body. He offers Priam a meal, and tells the story of Niobe, who lost six sons and six daughters; even in her grief Niobe remembered to eat, and so should Priam (602–17). Again, the story is told at length and in detail for its persuasive purpose. No other known version of the story says that Niobe remembered to eat; this seems to be an invention of the poet for this passage. Myth could be employed for a purpose, and it could be shaped to fit that purpose.[3]

IV. MYTHIC TRADITION IN THE *CATALOGUE OF WOMEN*

The most extensive early catalogue of heroic myth exists today only in fragments. This is the so-called *Catalogue of Women*,[4] which in the ancient world was attributed to Hesiod; the last two lines of the *Theogony* are the same as the first two lines of the *Catalogue*, and they could serve as a transition between the two poems. But most scholars today would say that the *Catalogue* was composed somewhat later by an anonymous author sometimes called the Catalogue Poet.[5]

The *Catalogue* in its current condition hardly makes for enthralling reading. Much of what survives comes from damaged scraps of papyrus recovered from the sands of Egypt, and other parts have been recovered from brief quotations in other ancient authors. Sometimes these fragments contradict one another. Sometimes a few lines can be read in sequence, but often all that remains of a story is only a few phrases or even a single word. But patient scholarship allows scholars to reconstruct the general sense of much of the poem, and for all of its difficulties it remains an important source for the understanding of the early stages of the mythic tradition in ancient Greece.

Further explorations

Many of the Greek tragedies include references to myths in addition to the primary myth which forms the plot of the play. Often these myths are used as either a parallel or contrast to the main story. Because many of these references are very brief, it seems that the audience must have been expected to know the myths without explanation. For example, the Chorus in Sophocles' *Antigone* refers to the myths of Danaë, Lykourgos, and Phineas in one ode (1002–41), and the Chorus in Aeschylus' *Libation-Bearers* refers to the myths of Meleager, Scylla, and the Lemnian Women in an ode (595–638). Pick one or the other of these passages; find the details (including possible variant forms) of these myths in Gantz 1993 or in some other good encyclopedia of myth, and write a short essay explaining the function and meaning of these myths in the play.

The poem begins with the first generations of mortals, Pandora, then Deukalion and Pyrrha, then Hellen, the ancestor of the Hellenes. This section is recovered from several ancient commentaries, and these commentaries give differing accounts of the genealogies of these first mortals in the *Catalogue*. In general, however, these early genealogical myths, in the *Catalogue* and elsewhere, understand the ethnic divisions of Greece as derived from family relationships among the early figures of Greek myth. Thus Hellen had three sons, Doros, Xuthus, and Aeolos (fragment 9), and later we learn that Xuthus had two sons named Achaeus and Ion (fragment 10); these figures are the ancestors of the Dorians, the Aeolians, the Achaeans, and the Ionians. Macedonia, however, was named after Macedon, who was the son of Zeus and Thyia, who in turn was a daughter of Deukalion (fragment 7).

The genealogies continue and very quickly present more names than can be easily remembered. Many of these figures seem to play no particular role in later myth, and the Catalogue Poet does not stop to tell stories about them. Others, however, do have little stories, some of which are familiar, some of which are now obscure. Fragments 16–17, for example, tell about Otos and Ephialtes, the sons of Iphimedeia, whom Odysseus saw in the Land of the Dead. Tyro's son Salmoneus, who tried to imitate Zeus, appears in fragments 26–27. Fragments 13–15 present the sons of Actor and Molione, who in some accounts were conjoined twins; there are several vase paintings of the Moliones, and in the *Iliad* Nestor says that in his youth he fought against them (11.709–10).

Thus there is considerable overlap between Homer's stock of stories and the stories in the *Catalogue*. But there are differences as well. Meleager appears in fragment 22 of the *Catalogue*, but according to the Catalogue Poet, he was killed fighting against the Kouretes, whereas Homer does not say how he died; and the surviving fragments do not tell the story of the curse of Althea, which is important in Homer's version of the story.

Sometimes the *Catalogue* gives some detail about a character who is only mentioned by Homer. When Odysseus sees Chloris in the Land of the Dead, he mentions that she is the mother of Nestor, Chromios, Periklymenos, and Pero. He tells us about Pero, and of course Nestor is a character in other parts of the *Odyssey*, but he doesn't tell any story about either Periklymenos or Chromios. Chromios is not mentioned in surviving myth, but according to the *Catalogue* (fragments 31–33), Poseidon gave Periklymenos the power to change into various animal forms, such as an eagle, a bee, an ant, or a snake. When Herakles brought an army against Pylos, Periklymenos killed many men in the attacking army. The fragment becomes hard to read at this point in the story, but evidently Periklymenos turned himself into one of his animal forms, perhaps a bee, but Herakles managed to kill him anyway. Homer doesn't mention this story, and it is not in the Homeric style to talk about people changing into bees.

There are also many figures in the Catalogue not mentioned by Homer at all, such as Atalanta (fragments 47–52), Asclepius (fragments 53–58), Erysichthon (fragment 69–71), Io (fragments 72–74), and Europa (fragments 88–91). All of these remained important in the later mythological tradition. Atalanta, for example, is mentioned by many later poets, including the Latin elegist Propertius; the story of Erysikhthon is told at length by the Hellenistic poet Callimachus in his *Hymn to Demeter*; Io is a character in Aeschylus' *Prometheus Bound*, and she also appears in Book One of Ovid's *Metamorphoses*. All of these later poets depend upon a long tradition of myth that we can trace back as far as the *Catalogue of Women*.

Later mythological catalogues

The tradition of writing catalogues of mythical stories continued for many hundreds of years. In his epic poem *Jason and the Golden Fleece*, the Hellenistic poet Apollonius of Rhodes includes an elaborate description of Jason's cloak, which has a number of figures from myth woven into it: the Cyclopes hammering out thunderbolts for Zeus; Amphion and Zethus and the walls of Thebes; Aphrodite looking at her reflection in Ares' shield; the Teleboans and the sons of Elektryon fighting over a herd of cattle; Pelops and Hippodameia in a chariot pursued by her father Oinomaos; Apollo shooting the giant Tityos, and Phrixus with the golden ram.

The literary tradition of mythological catalogues continued down into Roman Imperial times. A Latin poet named Marcus Aurelius Olympius Nemesianus wrote a hexameter poem titled *The Hunt (Cynegetica)*, which begins with a long list of mythic subjects: Niobe, Semele, Dirce (who kept the mother of Amphion and Zethus prisoner), Hippodameia, the daughters of Danaos (who all killed their husbands all on their wedding night, except for Hypermnestra, who spared her husband Lynkeus), Biblis (who fell in love with her brother), Myrrha (who fell in love with her father; Apollodorus and others call her Smyrna), Cadmus, Io, Hercules, Tereus and Philomela, Phaethon, the house of Tantalus, Medea, Nisus (whose daughter Scylla betrayed him for the love of Minos), Circe, and Antigone. All of these topics, the poet says, have been treated at length by other poets, so he will ignore them and write about hunting instead. Clearly this poet of the Imperial period expected his audience to know a large body of myth without any explanations.

V. MYTH ON THE FRANÇOIS VASE

Sometime around the year 570 BCE, an Attic potter named Ergotimos made a large bowl, about 66 centimeters tall, for mixing wine, and a painter named Kleitias decorated it; we know their names because they both signed the vase. Though it was made in Athens, it was exported to Italy, where it was found in 1844 in an Etruscan tomb in Chiusi by an Italian excavator named Alessandro François, and it is now known as the François Vase (see Figure 3.1).

The decorations include well over 100 figures whose names are inscribed beside them. These names identify several different mythological stories represented on the vase. In effect, the vase is a kind of visual catalogue of Greek myth, the visual equivalent to the literary catalogues we have been examining. The decorations are painted in six horizontal bands around the vase, and there are also illustrations on the handles.

The top band on one side of the vase shows the Calydonian boar hunt. The boar itself is very large and fierce. Two figures are standing side by side in front of the boar, attacking it with spears; the names Peleus and Meleager are clearly written beside them. Atalanta and Melanion are right behind them, and a number of other figures are attacking the boar from the rear. There are also several dogs in the illustration, and these also are named.

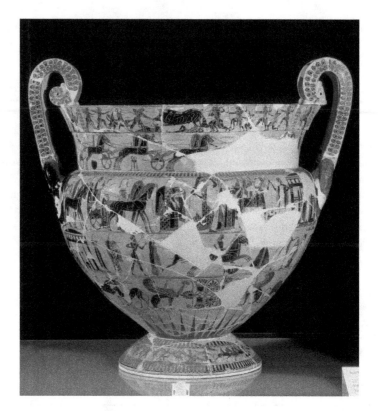

Figure 3.1   The François Vase. Kleitias and Ergotimos (ca. 570 BCE). Attic black-figure volute krater, from Chiusi. H. 66 cm. Restored 1902 and 1973. Museo Archeologico, Florence, Italy. Photo: Serge Domingie. Copyright © Alinari/Art Resource, NY

On the other side of the top band we see a ship coming to shore and a man jumping from it, and then a long line of men and women with their hands clasped. Facing them at the far end of the line is a woman holding a wreath and a ball of yarn. Her name has been damaged, but the man at the front of the line facing her and holding a lyre is clearly named Theseus. Thus the woman must be Ariadne, and the ball of yarn must be a reference to the trick which allowed Theseus to escape from the Labyrinth, while the line of young men and women are the Athenians who would have been food for the Minotaur if Theseus had not saved them.

According to one interpretation, this illustration shows Theseus landing on Crete, where he is welcomed by Ariadne with the yarn which will save him (see Walker 1995). Another interpretation places the scene on the island of Delos, after Theseus has escaped from Crete with Ariadne. When the Athenians reached Delos the young men and women from Athens performed a round dance, in celebration, and the line of men and women on the vase are performing this dance. This story explains a ritual during the summer month of Hecatombaion on the island of Delos, when young men and women performed a dance called the Crane Dance, which was supposed to mimic the winding path of Theseus out of the Labyrinth (Callimachus, *Hymn IV to Delos* 310–13; Plutarch, *Life of Theseus* 21).

The second band from the top probably shows the battle between the Lapiths and Centaurs on one side, and the funeral games for Patroklos on the other side. This part is damaged, but it is possible to read the names of Achilles, Diomedes, Automedon, and a few others.

The third band, the largest on the vase, shows the wedding of Peleus and Thetis. Thetis, the daughter of Nereus, was a minor goddess of the sea; according to a prophecy (either from Themis or from Prometheus), her son would be mightier than his father. Zeus had been attracted to her, but he was frightened off by the prophecy (perhaps remembering his own rise to power in the Myth of Succession). He therefore decided to marry her off to the mortal hero Peleus. Achilles was their son. Their wedding, which was attended by a multitude of the divinities, is said by some to have been the last time when the gods mingled freely with mortals. On the vase Peleus stands in front of his palace, and Thetis herself sits inside. Peleus is greeting the centaur Cheiron and Iris, the goddess of the rainbow and sometimes the messenger of the gods. (Underneath the clasped hands of Peleus and Cheiron the phrase "Kleitias painted me" appears.) Next in line Hestia, Chariklo, Dionysos, and the Horae. (Behind the Horae there is the phrase "Ergotimos made me".) Then come two of the Muses – Kalliope and Ourania – followed by Zeus and Hera in a chariot, four more muses – Thaleia, Euterpe, Kleio, and Melpomene – then Poseidon and Amphitrite. Among the other guests are Aphrodite, Ares, Apollo, Athena, Hermes, Maia, and Hephaistos, all identified by name.

The fourth band shows the story of the Ambush of Troilos. Homer merely mentions a son of Priam named Troilos who has been killed in the fighting (*Iliad* 24.257). The story of the death of Troilos was told in the lost epic called the *Kypria*, and Sophocles wrote a tragedy on the subject, though this also has been lost. According to Apollodorus, Achilles ambushed Troilos in the sanctuary of Thymbrian Apollo. On the vase Troilos on his horse races towards Troy, pursed by Achilles. Hektor and Polites are coming out of the city, while Priam is sitting in front with Antenor. The woman in front of Troilos is his sister Polyxena (who was sacrificed after the war on the tomb of Achilles). She has dropped a water jug, so perhaps she and Troilos were at the fountain, which is shown at the far right of the picture.

The other side of the fourth band shows an illustration of Dionysos leading Hephaistos, who is sitting on a mule, towards a group of gods, including Aphrodite, Zeus, and Hera. These figures illustrate the story that Hera threw Hephaistos off Olympos, and to get revenge he built her a throne with invisible bonds that would tie her down as soon as she sat in it. Eventually Dionysos convinced Hephaistos to return to Olympos and free her, and in return he was given Aphrodite as his wife. There are several other vase paintings of the story, as well as a wall painting in Athens, which no longer exists. Pausanias saw this painting and he tells the story (*Guide* I.20.2).

On the handles Ajax is shown carrying the dead body of Achilles, Artemis holding a lion and a stag, and Gorgons. The bottom band on the body of the vase does not show a narrative, but simply some animals, including sphinxes and other mythological beasts. And the foot of the vase shows the battle between the Pygmies and the Cranes, mentioned by Homer in the *Iliad* (3.3–7).

CONCLUSION

These four snapshots of the mythic tradition – in the *Iliad* and the *Odyssey*, in the *Catalogue of Women*, and on the François Vase – suggest the large number of myths widely known in ancient Greece. Many of these myths were linked together in complex genealogical relationships. These relationships were not hard and fast, however, but could vary from teller to teller in the tradition. Some of these stories became Panhellenic, and it is clear that epic poets and dramatists could refer to these stories and know that the audience would know them.

The tradition of myth, however, is not timeless. Some stories must have been formed very early, long before Homer, but the process of creating new stories did not stop. Before Sophocles' play *Antigone*, probably produced around 441 BCE, there is no known tradition that Antigone buried her brother Polyneikes; and before Euripides' *Medea*, produced in 431 BCE, no known tradition that Medea killed her children. Homer knew something about Theseus, but he says nothing about the deeds of Theseus as he made his way from Troezen to Athens, and many scholars believe that these stories were invented later.

Stories are created and told within a social and historical context, and they are taken up by tradition because they answer some need and provide some kind of meaning. Later chapters will explore the influence of history and politics on the creation and interpretation of various myths. But first it is necessary to have a better understanding of the sources for modern knowledge of ancient Greek myth, and this is the topic of the next chapter.

FURTHER READING

Much has been written about the gods in the Homeric epics, but rather less about Homer's use of previous heroic myth. Willcock 1999 discusses Homer's use of myth as paradigm in passages of advice, and the discussion of inset myths and other digressions is continued in Austin 1999 and Andersen 1999; all of these are conveniently collected in de Jong 1999. An English translation of the Hesiodic *Catalogue of Women* can be found in Hesiod 2007. On Melampous, see Dowden 1989: 71–115. For illustrations and discussion of the François Vase, see Boardman 1974: 33–34; Carpenter 1991: 13–17; Charbonneaux *et al.* 1971: 59–65; Lissarrague 2001: 10–21; Osborne 1998: 91–95; and also the photographs of the vase in the database of the Perseus Project.

Chapter Four

PELOPS' SHOULDER
Sources for the Study of Myth

In the days when schooling began with the classics of Latin literature, the most familiar source for Greek myth was the Latin poet Ovid. He was one of the first authors studied by every educated person in Western Europe, and his influence was enormous. Ovid was one of Chaucer's favorite authors, and one of Shakespeare's favorites as well. The Greek language and Greek literature were hardly known in Western Europe from the fifth century CE until the Renaissance, and even then Greek was a more specialized study than Latin, which was the basis of education. Chaucer did not know Greek, and Shakespeare's Greek was not nearly as good as his Latin. Greek myth, for most writers and readers, meant the stories that Ovid told, primarily in the *Metamorphoses*, but also in his other poems.

Ovid is no longer the primary source for Greek myth, but he has certainly not disappeared from the schools, and the introductory textbooks still include passages from his poems. He is always a compelling storyteller, and sometimes his version of a myth is the best told and the most complete that survives. But often something is lost in the translation from Greek myth to Latin poem. The qualities Ovid retains in these stories can be those which make the myths interesting to any audience, Greek, Roman or modern, but he leaves out the details which can show the place these stories had in Greek society and in the Greek mind.

An understanding of the place of myths in ancient Greece requires examination of all possible sources. These sources may include epic, drama, and lyric poetry, the works of mythographers, historians, and philosophers, and visual art. This chapter explores the sources for two related myths – the myth of Lykaon's feast and the myth of Pelops' shoulder – as case studies. Each section begins with the account Ovid gives in the *Metamorphoses* and continues with an examination of other sources, in order to get a better idea of the various ways each story was told and the different purposes that might lie behind these various versions.

Exploring Greek Myth. First Edition. Matthew Clark.
© 2012 Matthew Clark. Published 2012 by Blackwell Publishing Ltd.

I. LYKAON IN LATIN POETRY AND GREEK MYTH

Ovid tells the story of Lykaon's feast almost at the beginning of the *Metamorphoses*, and it should be seen in its context.[1] Ovid starts with the creation of the world out of the chaotic jumble of fundamental elements (*Met.* 1.5–68). He continues with the creation of living things, including human beings (*Met.* 1.69–88) and then the myth of the four ages, leaving out Hesiod's age of heroes (*Met.* 1.89–150). Next comes the battle of the gods and giants, which Ovid conflates with the story of Otos and Ephialtes, who piled Mount Pelion on Mount Ossa on Mount Olympus. Jupiter blasts the giants with his thunderbolt, and the earth is soaked with their blood. The warm gore takes on human form, "but this generation was also scornful of the gods and greedy for savage slaughter and violent. You would know they were born from blood" (*Met.* 1.151–62).

As father Jupiter looked down upon this scene, he groaned and remembered the feast of Lykaon, a recent occurrence and not yet widely known. He calls a council of the gods and tells them the story. He had decided to see for himself if the stories about the evils of the age were true. He came down from Olympus, put on human form, and traveled the lands. It would take a long time to tell the tale of the crimes he saw; the rumors were less than the truth. He reached Arcadia, the mountainous region in the center of the Peloponnese, where King Lykaon had his palace. He gave a sign that a god had come, and the people began to pray to him.

Lykaon laughed and decided to test this new arrival to see if he was in fact mortal. He prepared to kill Jupiter, and he prepared another test as well. He cut the throat of a hostage sent from the Molossians, chopped the body into pieces, boiled some pieces and roasted the rest. But as soon as he placed this meal on the table, Jupiter blasted the palace with his flames. Lykaon fled in terror, and when he reached the silence of the countryside, he howled and tried in vain to speak. The foam of his mad fury dripped from his mouth, he turned his desire for slaughter against the herds, and still he delighted in blood. His clothing turned into a shaggy coat of fur, his arms into legs, but he had the same grey hair, the same ferocious face, the same gleaming eyes, the same wild image. He was a wolf (and the Greek word for wolf is "lykos"). "One house has fallen," Jupiter told the other gods, "but not just one is worthy to perish. As far as the earth extends, the Furies rule. You would think they had sworn an oath to crime. Let them all pay the penalty they deserve." All the gods agreed, and Jupiter sent the great flood, which only Deukalion and Pyrrha survived (see Chapter Eight).

Ovid's story is dramatic and engaging, as Ovid's stories always are. It announces a number of themes which he will explore throughout the *Metamorphoses*, including human depravity, divine punishment, the persistence of character despite a change in outward form, and also, in the divine council, a certain satirical view of the gods. But it doesn't tell us much about the Greeks.

Ovid's version is the longest ancient account of Lykaon's story that survives, but there are a few important references in surviving Greek literature, and these show something about how the story fits into the network of Greek myth and into Greek culture in general.

According to Apollodorus (*Library* 3.8.1–2), Lykaon was the son of Pelasgos, who was born from the earth, or else he was the son of Zeus and Niobe (this Niobe is the daughter of

Phoroneus, not the Niobe who was the daughter of Tantalos and the mother of the children killed by Apollo and Artemis). Lykaon had 50 sons, and Apollodorus names 49 of them. These sons were the most impious of all men; Zeus visited them disguised as a laborer; they offered him hospitality, but they killed a child and mixed his entrails into the sacrificial meat and served the dish up to their guest. Zeus overturned the table (Greek "trapeza") at a place now called "Trapezous", and he blasted Lykaon and his sons with his thunderbolts, though the youngest son, Nyktimos, was saved. Nyktimos became king, and Deukalion's flood took place during his reign; some people say it was caused by the impiety of Lykaon's sons. Apollodorus then tells the story of Kallisto, who according to some sources was Lykaon's daughter. (Ovid tells the story of Kallisto in Book Two of the *Metamorphoses*; see Chapter Five.)

The story as Apollodorus tells it places Lykaon within a family tree, and in fact it makes his sons responsible for the sacrilegious meal; but Lykaon also pays the penalty for the crime, so there is perhaps a suggestion that he was in some way involved. According to Apollodorus, Nyktimos, the youngest son of Lykaon, was spared, but he does not say why; perhaps he refused to take part in the crime. But Apollodorus makes no mention of Lykaon's transformation.

Pausanias, in his *Guide to Greece*, gives more details. He says that Pelasgos was the first king of Arcadia (which at that time was called Pelasgia), and he quotes the genealogical poet Asios, who says that Pelasgos was born from the earth. Pelasgos invented huts and sheepskin tunics, and he discovered that the acorns of the Dodona oak trees were edible; before then the people had eaten leaves and grass and roots (*Guide* 8.1.1–5).

Lykaon, the son of Pelasgos, founded the city Lykosura, gave Zeus the epithet Lykaeus, and founded the Lykaean games. He was a contemporary of Kekrops, the first king of Athens, but Kekrops was wiser about religion. Kekrops was the first to call Zeus the Supreme, and he established the custom of sacrificing honey cakes rather than living animals. (The Bouphonia was the first meat offering in Athens; see Chapter One.) But Lykaon sacrificed a human baby on the altar of Zeus, and he was immediately changed into a wolf (*Guide* 8.2.1–3). Pausanias now links this story to events still occurring in his own time: "ever since the time of Lykaon a man has changed into a wolf at the sacrifice to Lykaean Zeus, but that change is not for life; if, when he is a wolf, he abstains from human flesh, after nine years he becomes a man again, but if he tastes human flesh he remains a beast for ever" (*Guide* 8.2.6).

Somewhat later in his discussion of Arcadia, Pausanias describes Mount Lykaeus. He mentions the precinct of Lykaean Zeus, which no one may enter; if anyone does enter, he will die within a year; moreover, there is a story that people and animals who do enter the precinct do not cast shadows (*Guide* 8.38.6; cf. Plutarch, *Greek Questions* 39). Then on the highest point of the mountain there is an altar with two pillars. "On this altar they sacrifice in secret to Lykaean Zeus. I was reluctant to pry into the details of the sacrifice; let them be as they are and were from the beginning" (*Guide* 8.38.7). Pausanias probably believed that the sacrifice to Lykaean Zeus included a meal of human flesh. In another section of the *Guide*, Pausanias mentions an Olympic victor named Damarchus, an Arcadian, who is supposed to have been a wolf for nine years after he participated in the sacrifice of Lykaean Zeus, though Pausanias does not believe the story (*Guide* 6.8.2).

All of these accounts are rather late: Ovid wrote during the time of Augustus Caesar, Pausanias wrote in the second half of the second century CE, and the *Library* of Apollodorus probably dates from around the same time. There are, however, earlier references to the story. One of these comes from Plato's *Republic* (565d–e). Here Socrates is talking with Adimantus about the tendency of champions of the people turn into dictators:

> "So what makes a champion change into a dictator? Isn't it obviously when a champion starts to behave in the same way as what the stories tell us happens to people in the sanctuary of Zeus Lykaeus in Arcadia?"
>   "What's that," he asked.
>   "That anyone who tastes even a single morsel of human entrails mixed in among those of other sacrificial offerings is bound to become a wolf. Haven't you heard this story?"
>   "Yes, I have."

The transformation of Lykaon is also mentioned in a pseudo-Platonic dialogue titled the *Minos* (315c), and there is a reference in Porphyry's *On Abstinence* (2.27), probably derived from Theophrastus, who was Aristotle's successor as head of the Lyceum. The Athenian playwrights Xenokles and Astydamas each wrote a play titled *Lykaon*, but these are now lost. There are three brief references to Lykaon in the *Catalogue of Women* (fragments 111, 112, 114), but they show only that the author knew of Lykaon and knew that he had committed some transgression against Zeus. There are a few other references as well.[2] These various references suggest that the story of Lykaon was known perhaps from very early times down to the Imperial period. Outside of Arcadia the story was perhaps more a rumor than a myth. But inside Arcadia, it played a part in a larger cultural context.

For Ovid, Lykaon was simply a villain, but in Pausanias' account he is a complicated figure. He is the son of the first king of Arcadia, who was a culture hero, and he was a kind of culture hero himself, as the founder of a city and the founder of the Lykaean games. Moreover, he seems to have a special relationship to Zeus, to whom he gave the epithet Lykaios. Pausanias agrees with Ovid that Lykaon performed human sacrifice and was turned into a wolf, but this sacrifice still continued down to the time of Pausanias, so even in this regard he was a founder. The Arcadians evidently did not feel the kind of revulsion against this sacrifice that was felt by people outside.

The story of Lykaon is a myth with (at least) two meanings: a local meaning, as a myth of initiation, and a Panhellenic meaning, as a myth of Arcadian savagery. As a local myth, it may have been related to a ritual of initiation, of which the sacrifice was one part (see Burkert 1983: 84–93). It is impossible to know for certain exactly what happened at this Arcadian sacrifice. It is not necessary to assume that there really was human sacrifice and cannibalism, though the possibility can't be ruled out. Perhaps the boys who were being initiated were told that the stew they were served included bits of human flesh, and if anyone happened to taste a piece, he would become a wolf. Perhaps some boys believed that they had become wolves, in a sense, and ran off into the bush for some time, perhaps even nine years (though the number nine in Greek can just mean "a long time"). These are speculations, but they are consistent with initiation rituals found elsewhere.

As a Panhellenic myth, the story is part of a larger complex of Greek ideas about Arcadia: the Arcadians were born from the earth, they inhabited Arcadia even before the moon was created, they ate acorns, they wore animal skins, and Pan was their god (see Borgeaud 1988: 3–44); no wonder they performed human sacrifice and turned into wolves. Thus the same mythic elements can be interpreted in different ways in different contexts. This story has a place in Greek thought and Greek culture we could never guess from Ovid's dramatic fable.

II. PELOPS' SHOULDER

Whereas Ovid's version of the feast of Lykaon is a full-scale dramatic treatment of the story, his version of the story of Pelops' shoulder is just a brief reference at the end of another story, the myth of Niobe, Pelops' sister (*Met.* 6.150–312).[3] Once Ovid has killed off Niobe and her children and husband, he turns to her brother (*Met.* 6.402–11):

> The people mourned the death of Amphion and his offspring,
> the mother was blamed. Just one is said to have wept
> for her, Pelops – he tore the clothing from his chest
> and left shoulder and revealed the ivory.
> This shoulder, when he was born, had been flesh
> and the same color as the right; then, they say,
> the limbs cut by paternal hands were joined by the gods.
> The other parts were found, but the part between the throat
> and the upper arm was gone. Ivory was fitted in to serve
> for the missing part, and when this was done, Pelops was whole.

If we fill in some of the details left out by Ovid, here is the story in brief: Tantalos was favored by the gods, who even feasted with him. One day he killed his son Pelops, cut him up, and made a stew which he served to the gods. Demeter, who was upset because of the disappearance of her daughter Persephone, ate the shoulder. The other gods realized what Tantalos had done, and they brought Pelops back to life, and the missing shoulder was replaced with ivory.

Ovid's minimal narrative probably assumes that the readers will know the whole story. The story was indeed well known and popular. Brief summaries of the story can be found in Euripides (*Iphigeneia in Tauris* 386–88 and *Helen* 388–89), Hyginus (*Fab.* 83), Apollodorus (*Library*, *Epit.* 2.3), and elsewhere.

The crime and punishment of Tantalos

According to Homer, Tantalos is one of the sinners punished in the Land of the Dead, but Homer does not explain why he is being punished. The story of Pelops' shoulder could provide the explanation, but there are other possibilities. In one story, Zeus prom-ised Tantalos whatever his heart should desire, and Tantalos asked to be able to indulge all his appetites and live always as the gods live. Zeus had to grant the wish, and so he surrounded Tantalos with all good things, but he also suspended a rock above his head, which evidently would fall and crush him if he should reach for any of the delights (Athenaeus, *Deip.* 7.14).

Plato also says that Tantalos had a rock suspended over his head in the Underworld (*Cratylus* 395d). According to Pindar (see text below) Tantalos stole ambrosia and nectar from the gods, while Elektra in Euripides' *Orestes* said that he could not control his tongue, though what he said she does not specify; he is punished by hanging in the air with a rock over his head (*Orestes* 4–10). The ancient commentaries say that he is suspended between heaven and earth to keep him from hearing the gods or from talking to mortals. Iphigeneia in Euripides' *Iphigeneia in Tauris*, however, says that Tantalos served a child's flesh to the gods, so evidently Euripides knew more than one version of the crime. The ancient commentaries to the *Odyssey* say that Zeus buried Tantalos under Mount Sipylos because he had stolen a living golden dog which belong to Zeus' shrine on Crete.

The oldest surviving account of the feast of Tantalos occurs in Pindar's first *Olympian Ode*, written in honor of Hieron, ruler of Syracuse, who won the race for single horse at the Olympic Games in 476 BCE. As is usual in these victory odes, the praise of the victor is placed in the context of a myth: here the myth of Pelops. But Pindar announces that he will tell a story different from the traditional tale. Tantalos, he says, invited the gods to a banquet. At this banquet Poseidon saw the young Pelops and snatched him away, just as Zeus had snatched away Ganymede. When people looked for him and were unable to find him, a jealous neighbor spread the rumor that the gods had cut him up and then cooked him and ate him. But Pindar cannot call any of the gods a savage or a glutton. Tantalos, however, was unable to deal with the great favor the gods had shown him, and he stole ambrosia and nectar, which had made him deathless; Zeus punished him by suspending a rock over his head, and they sent his son Pelops back to earth and a mortal life.

Pindar now turns to the other major myth of Pelops. When Pelops began to grow a beard, he wanted to win Hippodameia in marriage, though her father Oinomaos had already killed 13 suitors who failed to win the chariot race he had set as a contest for her hand. Pelops went to the seashore where he called to Poseidon for help. Poseidon sent him a golden chariot and a team of tireless horses, with which he defeated Oinomaos. And now, Pindar says, Pelops receives sacrifices at his tomb where the Olympic Games are held.

Pindar's account is complex. He rejects what he considers the traditional story, that the gods cooked Pelops and ate him, and instead he asserts that Pelops disappeared only because he was taken away by Poseidon. So our earliest source for the story tells it only to reject it. We can conclude, however, that the version Pindar rejects must have been the version most widely known, and some scholars believe that Pindar made up the new version. It is interesting, however, that the version he rejects seems to say that the gods rather than Tantalos cooked Pelops. Pindar also tells the story of Pelops and Hippodameia, but whereas most versions of this story say that Pelops won the race against Oinomaos by trickery (for instance, Hyginus *Fab.* 84; *Library*, *Epit.* 2.6–8; Diodorus 4.73.3), Pindar says that he won it with a chariot he received from Poseidon.

The race between Pelops and Oinomaos was represented on an Attic black-figure lekythos from around 500–490 BCE, which shows the horses of Pelops with wings, as Pindar said, and on an Attic red-figure amphora from about 410.[4] It was also represented on the great chest of Kypselos, which is now lost, but which is described in detail by Pausanias

(*Guide* 5.17.5–5.19.10).[5] The race was also represented in sculptures on the pediment of the temple of Zeus at Olympia; Pausanias describes this also (*Guide* 5.10.6–7), and pieces of it have been found (see Shapiro 1994: 82; Woodford 2003: 37). This group of sculptures, according to Pausanias, includes the charioteer Myrtilos, who was Pelops' accomplice, so this representation probably assumed the story that Pelops won by cheating.

As Pindar notes, Pelops was closely associated with the Olympic Games, and in a sense he was their founding hero.[6] As Pausanias says, "the Eleans honor Pelops as much above all the heroes of Olympia as they honor Zeus above the rest of the gods" (*Guide* 5.13.1). The geography of Olympia was littered with reminders of Pelops and his myths. In addition to the sculptures on the temple of Zeus, there was a monument with the bones of Hippodameia, where women offered annual sacrifices (*Guide* 6.20.7); in the racecourse itself there was a mound which some said was built by Pelops as a cenotaph for Myrtilos (*Guide* 6.20.17); a few miles away there was a temple to Athena where Pelops offered sacrifice before the race (*Guide* 6.21.6); not far away was a mound where Hippodameia's unsuccessful suitors were buried (*Guide* 6.21.9); nearby there was a temple to Artemis Kordax, so called because Pelops' followers performed a dance there called the "kordax" after his victory, and also a building with a chest containing Pelops' bones (*Guide* 6.22.1); Pelops' gold-handled dagger was kept in a building in an area called Altis (*Guide* 6.19.6); also in Altis, near a temple to Zeus, there was an enclosure dedicated to Pelops, where there was an annual sacrifice of a black ram (*Guide* 5.13.1); at one time a huge bone said to be Pelops' shoulder blade was kept there, but it had disappeared by the time Pausanias visited (*Guide* 5.13.4–6).

In Pindar's time, the most prestigious event at the Olympics was the chariot race, and it is easy to see Pelops' race with Oinomaos as its aetiological myth. But the chariot race was added to the festival perhaps only in 680 BCE (*Guide* 5.8.7). Before that time, the most important event was the foot-race, and in the lists of Olympic victors only the victors in the foot-race are recorded from the supposed beginning of the contests in 776 BCE. Gregory Nagy (following Walter Burkert) argues that the foot-race was associated with the myth of the feast in which Pelops' shoulder was eaten (Nagy 1990a: 116–35; see Burkert 1983: 93–103). According to Nagy, Pindar's rejection of the story of Pelops' shoulder – in favor of a story about Pelops' relationship with Poseidon, who then gives him the chariot with which he defeats Oinomaos – reflects the historical development of the Olympic festival, as the chariot race came to supplant the foot-race as the most prestigious event. Pindar's poem is thus understood in the context of Panhellenic myth and ritual.

III. LYKAON AND PELOPS

The Panhellenic myth of the feast of Tantalos is in some ways like the local myth of Lykaon. In each story, a mortal is favored by the gods, who even share meals with him. For some reason the mortal kills a baby and offers it to the god or gods at a feast. The meal is rejected by the god or gods and the perpetrator is punished (see Burkert 1983: 94 and 100; Nagy 1990a: 125-26). Moreover, each myth is closely connected to a festival in which there were sacrifices and athletic contests.

The myths are not identical, however. The principal character of the myth of Lykaon is the perpetrator of the crime, and the victim is less important. In some versions, he is unnamed; either a hostage, as in Ovid, or just a local child, as in Pausanias. In the story of Tantalos' feast, the victim is always Pelops, and in a sense the story is as much about Pelops as it is about Tantalos. It was the sacrificer Lykaon who founded the Lykaean games, but the sacrificial victim Pelops who founded the Olympics.

According to Lycophron, however, the victim of Lykaon's feast was Nyktimos (*Alexandra* 481), who elsewhere is named as one of his sons (*Guide* 8.2.1). According to Hyginus the victim was Arkas, the son of Lykaon's daughter Kallisto; Zeus put Arkas back together, just as the gods put Pelops back together (*Astronomica* 2.4). The Arcadians are named after him (*Guide* 8.4.1). These versions bring the story of Lykaon's feast closer to the story of Tantalos' feast. If Lykaon's victim was Arkas, then the story continues with a further myth, in which Arkas hunts his mother, who had been changed into a bear, with various results in various versions (see Ovid, *Met.* 2.409–530; Hyginus, *Astronomica* 2.1.2 and 2.4.1). This continuation is very unlike the later story of Pelops, the race against Oinomaos.

The crime of Lykaon is his feast, and his punishment is his metamorphosis, but the crime and the punishment of Tantalos vary from story to story. Moreover, the crime and punishment of Lykaon are re-enacted in a ritual which may have continued at least to the time of Pausanias. The sacrifice at the Olympic Games, even if it was intended to recall the feast of Tantalos, was not a re-enactment, and the participants did not think that they had eaten human flesh there, nor did they run off into the bush to become wolves. The myth of Lykaon's feast was perhaps associated with a local rite of initiation, while the myth of Tantalos' feast was associated with a Panhellenic athletic contest. Nagy (1990a: 118–19), however, argues that athletic contests were in a sense initiatory. Though the myths are similar, each should be understood within its own context.

Another way of looking at the stories would place them within Greek ideas of food and sacrifice, and they can be compared with other stories such as the feast of Thyestes or the myth of Prokne and Tereus. In general, ancient Greek thought distinguished mortals from gods above and animals below. The gods eat only ambrosia and nectar, and they enjoy the smoky odor of the roasted sacrificial meat; Hesiod explains that this diet was established by Prometheus' sacrifice at Mekone. Animals, on the other hand, eat uncooked food, and they even eat each other. Mortals eat cooked meat and they do not eat each other; cannibalism is a reduction to the level of the beasts (see Detienne 1979: 56–57; Detienne and Vernant 1989.) The feasts of Lykaon and Tantalos, however, take place in the period when the gods shared meat with mortals; after these feasts, perhaps because of them, the gods withdrew from human association and no longer ate meat. When Lykaon and Tantalos offer human flesh to the gods, they are throwing the system into confusion. Because Lykaon served human flesh to Zeus, he is no better than an animal, and so he becomes a wolf. Tantalos is presented with all the delights of food and drink, but he cannot eat them. In another version, his crime is the theft of nectar and ambrosia, the food of the gods; also a violation of the culinary code, but from the other direction (see Nagy 1990a: 133). Thus these stories function not only within Greek ritual practice but also within Greek thought.

IV. THE SOURCES OF GREEK MYTH

This exploration of the myth of Lykaon and the myth of Pelops has used a wide variety of sources. One important source was Ovid's *Metamorphoses*, a long mock epic poem which includes hundreds of myths – some told at length, some merely summarized. This poem is one of the major works of Western literature; it was never intended to be an encyclopedia or textbook of myth, but it served that purpose for hundreds of years and is still an engaging introduction to many important stories. Sometimes Ovid is the best source for a story, but he was writing for a Roman audience, and he was not particularly interested in or knowledgeable about the details of Greek culture and society. Ovid's purposes are primarily literary, and he uses the myths as vehicles to express his own very complex and sophisticated view of the world. (Ovid's unfinished poem the *Fasti* concerns Roman traditions, but it also includes some Greek myths, such as the story of the abduction of Persephone; see Chapter One.)

Other literary works are also important sources for myth. Homer narrates the events of the Trojan War and its aftermath, but he also refers to a host of other stories, as shown in the previous chapter. Homer is the earliest source to describe the punishment of Tantalos. Hesiod and the Hesiodic *Catalogue of Women* are other important early sources for myth, as are the *Homeric Hymns*, such as the *Hymn to Demeter* which was discussed in Chapter One.

All but one of the surviving Athenian tragedies are based on myth, and most of them include abundant references to other myths: thus there were references to Tantalos in Euripides' *Helen* and *Iphigeneia in Tauris*. In addition to the 33 surviving tragedies, there are surviving fragments or titles of many more, and these can give worthwhile information. The Athenian playwrights Xenokles and Astydamas wrote plays about Lykaon, and thus, although the plays are lost, it is clear that this story was of some interest to people outside Arcadia.

The lyric poet Pindar wrote a series of odes for victors in the various important athletic contests, and almost all of these include a reference to some mythic story; the story of Pelops in the first *Olympian Ode*, the voyage of the Argonauts in the fourth *Pythian Ode*, the infancy of Herakles in the first *Nemean Ode*, the marriage of Thetis in the eighth *Isthmian Ode*, to give just a few examples. Pindar hardly ever tells a complete story; he assumes that his audience knows what he is talking about, and he selects just those details which contribute to the point he is making. Pindar's contemporary Bacchylides also wrote odes and dithyrambs which include references to myth.

The Hellenistic Greek poets were also interested in myth – for example, Apollonius of Rhodes (*The Voyage of the Argo*), Callimachus (*Hymns* and the fragmentary poems *Hecale* and the *Aetia*), and

Further explorations

The Athenian tragedies by Aeschylus, Sophocles, and Euripides are an essential source for our knowledge of myth, and because these plays are so famous, they have in part determined what modern students regard as belonging to the tradition of Greek myth. But out of the thousand or so tragedies produced in Athens during the fifth century BCE, only 33 survive, and these are only a small sample of the stories presented to Athenian audiences. The titles of many lost plays are known, however, and some fragments exist. Using Aeschylus 2009, Sophocles 1996, and Euripides 2008 and 2009, write a short essay exploring the range of myths in Athenian tragedy.

Lycophron (*Alexandra* – a very difficult poem that purports to be the prophecies of the Trojan princess Cassandra). It was Lycophron who said that Lykaon's victim was his son Nyktimos and thus brought the story closer to the story of Pelops. Roman poets such as Propertius and Horace also used Greek myths.

Encyclopedias of myth began to appear in the Hellenistic period. The best of the ancient encyclopedias is *The Library of Greek Mythology*, attributed to Apollodorus; this is a basic text which every student of myth should consult regularly. In the early Imperial period, the Latin writer Hyginus composed about 300 brief summaries of various myths, titled *Fabulae*, and also a work titled *De Astronomia*, which tells the stories of the constellations.

The Greek historians were sometimes skeptical about the mythic tradition, but myth was such an important part of ancient Greek culture that they were not able to ignore it completely. Some historians treated myths about the genealogies of the supposed founders of cities. Often they reinterpreted myths in order to rationalize them as historical accounts.

The philosophers were at times hostile to myth, but like the historians they were unable to ignore it. Plato mentions many myths, such as the myth of Kronos and Zeus in the *Euthyphro* and the myth of Lykaon in the *Republic*. (Plato's use of myth is the topic of Chapter Twelve.) Theophrastus, who was a student of Aristotle, was an important source for the later philosopher Porphyry, whose book *On Abstinence* was mentioned in the earlier discussions of the Bouphonia and the story of Lykaon.

The Greek travel writer Pausanias, who wrote in the second half of the second century CE, is an important source for knowledge of rituals and other customs in Greece. He rarely tells a complete story, but he often includes odd details of local versions of myth. Serious students of myth will find Pausanias indispensable and endlessly fascinating.

Many other Greek and Latin writers can provide information about myth. This chapter, for instance, drew on information about Lykaon and Pelops in Plutarch's *Greek Questions*, Pliny's *Natural History*, and Athenaeus' *Deipnosophistae* (or *Scholars at Dinner*). Some early Christian writers also include references to Greek myth. St Augustine, for example, told a version of the story of Lykaon.

Ancient commentaries to texts were often written in the margins of manuscripts. The technical term for a marginal note is "scholion" (plural "scholia"). The scholia include many interesting if brief comments on myth. Various collections of scholia have been published, but few of these have been translated into English.

A last but very important source of information about myth is visual art. Several thousand painted vases from ancient Greece survive, also many sculptures, both freestanding figures and reliefs, and many of these paintings and sculptures represent moments from mythic stories. Almost all large paintings from ancient Greece – paintings on boards or on walls – have disappeared, but ancient writers, including Pausanias, have left descriptions of some lost paintings and other lost art works. The visual representation of a story, or of some variant of a story, can show that the story or the variant was known at a particular time or place, though the absence of a representation does not mean that no one knew the story. Sometimes the visual representation shows a detail or a variant that is not found in any surviving literary source. For example, an Attic red-figure cup made by Douris about 470 BCE shows Jason being disgorged by a dragon; the golden fleece hangs behind them, and Athena, holding an owl and dressed in her helmet and aegis with the Gorgon's face, stands in front of them (see Carpenter 1991: 277). No known story says that Jason was eaten and disgorged by the dragon; possibly it was simply made up by the artist, but it could represent a traditional part of the story now lost to us.

CONCLUSION

The serious study of a myth should include as many versions from as many sources as possible, rather than relying on any single version, no matter how famous or well told. The various tellers of a tale have their own reasons and perspectives, and these can influence how the tale is told. Ovid was primarily a literary artist; he selects his tales for their aesthetic impact, and he crafts them to express his sophisticated and ironic view of the world. In so doing, he often leaves out details which would be important for a Greek audience but not interesting for Romans – such as the information that Io was a priestess of Hera or that Lykaon was a culture hero associated with Zeus in Arcadia. Apollodorus and Hyginus are interested in providing brief summaries of a large number of myths, with little interest in artistry, but also with little interest in local details. Plato chooses myths which will contribute to the philosophic argument he is constructing, while Pausanias gathers information about local variants as part of his project as a guide to the Greek past. Each source will have its own purpose, and each of these purposes is legitimate in its context, but the student of myth needs to keep them all in mind in reconstructing the place of these myths in ancient Greek culture. Chapter Five explores some of the different meanings that different versions of myths can convey.

FURTHER READING

The primary sources of myth include all of the works mentioned above. In addition, Gantz 1993 lists extensive references to various versions of the myths. Fowler 2000 is an important scholarly source for early Greek mythography, but the text is only in Greek; the second volume, yet to appear, will include commentary. Trzaskoma *et al.* 2004 has selections from a wide variety of ancient sources. For visual art, the fundamental source is the multi-volume collection *Lexicon Iconographicum Mythologiae Classicae* (LIMC); good selections of visual art can be found in Carpenter 1991, Shapiro 1994, and Woodford 2003. The standard scholarly edition of the fragments of Aeschylus, Sophocles, and Euripides is the five-volume collection edited by Bruno Snell *et al.* 1977–2004, but this edition leaves the passages in Greek and so is of limited usefulness for students. There are, however, good selections of the fragments published in Loeb editions, with Greek text and English translation on facing pages; see Aeschylus 2009, Sophocles 1996, and Euripides 2008 and 2009.

Chapter Five

IKAROS' WINGS, AKTAION'S DOGS
Myth and Meaning

Sometimes myths are told in works of literature, such as Ovid's *Metamorphoses* or the Athenian tragic drama, and these literary works can be interpreted through the methods developed over the years by literary scholars. But myth is not just the same as literature, and literary interpretation does not exhaust the meaning of a myth. Unlike most literary narratives, myths typically have variant versions, and each variant must be interpreted in its own terms. Some of these variants may take literary form, and these can be interpreted with the methods of literary criticism, but other variants may be found as summaries in encyclopedias, as references or allusions in works of history or philosophy, or as stories told along the way in a traveler's guidebook. Myths can also have a function within a society, perhaps as the explanation of a ritual or some feature of the landscape, or as the justification of some social practice. In a sense, a myth does not have one meaning, but rather a potential to take on various meanings, depending on the purposes of the teller and the telling. The interpretation of a myth, then, is not the search for the correct meaning of the story, but rather the investigation of the range of meanings it has been given. Much of the rest of this book will concern various ways of interpreting myths; this chapter demonstrates some methods of interpretation through the examination of versions of two myths, the myth of Aktaion and the myth of Ikaros.

I. OVID AND AKTAION'S ERROR

The myth of Aktaion is one of the most famous of the Greek myths, but the earliest complete version of the story is found in a Latin source, Ovid's *Metamorphoses* (3.138–252).[1] Aktaion, Ovid tells us, went hunting with his companions. In the heat of the day, he called a halt, and

---

Exploring Greek Myth. First Edition. Matthew Clark.
© 2012 Matthew Clark. Published 2012 by Blackwell Publishing Ltd.

he and his dogs wandered off to find a place to rest. They came to a wooded valley, where Diana (Artemis in Greek) was bathing. Her attendants tried to shield her from his view, and Diana, in her anger, sprinkled Aktaion with water, which changed him into a deer. When he ran off his dogs chased him and tore him apart, urged on by his companions in the hunt.

Ovid seems to have two primary points in mind in his telling of the story. First, he is interested in the pathos of the situation. Aktaion retains his human intelligence but he has lost his power to speak, so he cannot appeal to his own dogs as they tear him apart. This pathos, however, is combined with wit, in a confusion of feeling typical of Ovid's manner (*Met.* 3.242–48):

> His unknowing companions urge on the rabid pack
> with their usual cries; they look for Aktaion
> and they keep calling "Aktaion" as if he were absent
> (he lifts his head at his name) and they complain he isn't there,
> lazy fellow, and won't see the show of the prey they have found.
> Indeed he wishes he were absent, but he's there,
> he wishes he could watch and not feel the dreadful deeds of his own dogs.

Ovid's second point has to do with the cruelty of the gods. At the very beginning of the story he clearly says that Aktaion was not guilty of any crime (3.141–42):

> But if you look carefully for the blame in this bad luck,
> you will not find a crime; for what crime is there in an error?

Aktaion did not intend to spy on Diana, in Ovid's version of the myth; he just happened to be in the wrong place at the wrong time. But his innocence makes no difference to Diana, who punishes him just as much as if he had acted deliberately. At the very end of the story, Ovid emphasizes Diana's rage (3.249–52):

> The dogs stand all around and sink their teeth in his body
> and rip apart their master in the false image of a deer
> and not until his life has ended in endless wounds
> is the anger of quiver-bearing Diana satisfied.
> On all sides the dogs stand around him and sink their teeth
> into his body and tear their master apart in the false form of the deer,
> and not until his life has ended in a host of wounds
> (so they say) is the anger of quiver-bearing Diana satisfied.

Diana's revenge then becomes a topic for discussion within the world of the epic (3.253–55):

> Opinion is divided: to some the goddess seems
> more violent than fair; others praise and say she befits
> her strict virginity; each side finds its reasons.

This passage invites the reader to judge the goddess; she, not Aktaion, seems to be the guilty party.

The story of Aktaion can be compared to some other stories Ovid tells about gods and mortals. In Book One, for example, Apollo spots Daphne, who is hunting in the woods. He chases her, but she appeals to her father, the river god Inakhos, and to Earth, and she is changed into a laurel tree (452–567). A little later in Book One, Jupiter spots Io at midday, a dangerous time for mortals; he pursues her and takes her virginity; then he changes her into a cow to keep Juno from knowing what he has done (588–624). In Book Two (409–531), Jupiter rapes Kallisto, and Juno takes her revenge by turning her into a bear.

The myth of Kallisto in Ovid's *Metamorphoses* (2.417–507)

Kallisto, the daughter of Lykaon, was a hunter and one of the companions of Diana. One day she is resting from the midday heat, when Jupiter spots her. He changes himself into the image of Diana and greets her as she rests from her hunting. Kallisto replies, "Greetings, goddess, in my opinion greater than Jupiter, and he himself may hear it." Jupiter was delighted that she preferred him to himself and he gave her kisses neither moderate nor of a sort to be given by a maiden. He has his will of her, despite her resistance, and she becomes pregnant. She hides her shame from Diana, though the other nymphs seem to guess her secret. Nine months later Diana and the nymphs are weary from the hunt, and they seek shelter from the heat of the sun. Diana suggests that they all go swimming. Kallisto tries to delay disrobing, but the other nymphs tear her clothing away, and reveal Kallisto's crime (as Ovid calls it). Diana exiles her from the company of nymphs; a little later Kallisto's son Arkas is born.

Juno, meanwhile, has figured out what has gone on, and as soon as Arkas is born, she turns Kallisto into a bear. Fifteen years later, as Arkas is hunting, he comes across his mother. Somehow she knows that this hunter is her son, but of course he does not realize that this bear is his mother. She approaches him and he is about to attack her, when Jupiter finally intervenes and turns them both into constellations.

In each of these stories a mortal suffers because of the actions of the gods. Apollo lusts after Daphne, Jupiter lusts after Io, and he also lusts after Kallisto. Daphne escapes her pursuer by praying for a change in form; Io and Kallisto are raped and transformed. But Diana does not lust after Aktaion, nor (in Ovid's version of the story) does he lust after her. He has, however, violated a sexual taboo when he has seen her bathing, and even though his transgression was involuntary, Diana punishes him. The gods Jupiter and Apollo can get away with rape, but the mortal Aktaion is punished for an innocent error.

These various stories in the *Metamorphoses* show a complex interaction of two binary oppositions: male versus female, and mortal versus immortal. A god can lust after a mortal woman, but (at least in these stories) no goddess lusts after a mortal man, nor does a mortal man lust after a goddess.[2] The mortal women who receive the sexual attentions of a god all suffer from the experience, and this mortal man who happens to catch sight of a goddess also suffers. Aktaion is in a way Ovid's victim as well as Diana's, as his suffering becomes an opportunity for the display of Ovid's wit.

This brief discussion does not exhaust the meaning of the myth of Aktaion in the *Metamorphoses* (see, for example, the discussion of Aktaion's voicelessness in Heath 1992), but it shows at least some of what Ovid was able to make of the story. Other versions of the story, however, present other meanings.

II. AKTAION'S CRIME

The Hellenistic poet Callimachus tells the story of Aktaion briefly in the context of another myth. His fifth *Hymn*, "The Bath of Pallas", tells the story of the blinding of Teiresias. A nymph named Chariklo, the mother of Teiresias, was one of Athena's companions. One day Athena and Chariklo went bathing at noon, and Teiresias accidentally stumbled upon them. He was immediately blinded, and when Chariklo angrily complained, Athena told her that the blinding was not Athena's will, but a result of a law established by Kronos. Moreover, Teiresias was better off than Aktaion will be, for when Aktaion accidentally sees Artemis bathing he will be killed by his own dogs. Moreover, Athena granted Teiresias prophetic powers as compensation for his blinding. (But according to Ovid (*Met.* 3.316–38), it was Juno who blinded Teiresias and Jupiter who gave him the gift of prophecy.)

The story of Aktaion as Callimachus tells it is similar to Ovid's version, but its context is quite different. Ovid's version comes after a series of stories in which mortal women are raped by gods, and its interpretation is colored by this context. Ovid invites the reader to condemn Diana's action, and he emphasizes the pathos of Aktaion's punishment. In Callimachus' hymn, the story of Aktaion is clearly subordinate to the story of Teiresias and Athena, and it seems to be designed to show Athena's benevolence. Athena was not responsible for the blinding of Teiresias, the punishment of Teiresias was far less serious than the punishment of Aktaion, and Teiresias receives a compensating gift. The meaning of the myth depends in part on the context in which it is used. (A Freudian interpretation might also suggest that Athena in Callimachus' *Hymn* is a substitute for Teiresias' mother Chariklo; in this interpretation the story is really about the boy child's guilty desire to see his mother naked.)

The story of Aktaion is also found in the Latin novel *The Golden Ass* (or *Metamorphosis*), written by the Latin writer Apuleius in the second century CE. In Book Two of the novel, the hero, Lucius, has arrived in Hypata and finds himself at the home of a woman who turns out to be a distant relative. There he sees a remarkable statuary group; Diana in the center, striding forward, clothes blown back by the breeze as she walks. The goddess is surrounded by dogs, sculpted so well that if you should hear a bark, you would think that the sound came from these stone dogs. At the feet of the goddess there is a pool, and above her Aktaion is hidden among some branches, looking eagerly down at the goddess (*The Golden Ass* 2.4).

Apuleius and his narrator Lucius trust the reader to know the story from the description of the statuary group. In a sense the story is not told, but shown. Two details in the description, however, suggest that Apuleius has crafted the statuary group for the purposes of the novel as a whole. According to Lucius, Aktaion is hiding in the branches and looking eagerly down at Diana, waiting for her to disrobe. This is not the pose of an innocent person who has accidentally stumbled upon the goddess. As John Heath (1992: 104–06) points out, the theme of curiosity dominates the story of Lucius; his transformation into an ass comes about because he wanted to look at something forbidden, and throughout the story there are many instances of curiosity. The representation of a curious Aktaion thus fits the thematic design of the story.

Another detail in the statuary group may also be related to the novel's thematic design. As Lucius describes the group, the dogs seem to belong to Diana rather than to Aktaion. Heath (1992: 109) notes that ancient paintings of the story often give the dogs to Diana, or at least show Diana urging the dogs to attack Aktaion (see, for example, illustrations 130 and 133 in Carpenter 1991). The organization of the visual representation of the story forces Diana and the dogs to be grouped together against Aktaion; moreover, as Heath points out, a curious Aktaion would only be encumbered by a pack of dogs. In Ovid's version of the story, however, pathos is created when Aktaion is killed by his own dogs, as he tries to tell them who he is but fails because he has lost his human voice.

Aktaion in art

The story of Aktaion has been a popular subject of art since ancient times. Many ancient representations show Aktaion attacked by his dogs; sometimes Artemis is represented as well. Sometimes Aktaion is shown as a human being with horns or with the head of a deer to suggest his transformation. In addition to the two illustrations in Carpenter 1991, there are two illustrations in Caskey and Beazley 1931–63 of vases at the Museum of Fine Arts in Boston (plates LXII and XLVII, Boston 00.346 and Boston 10.185; see Figure 5). A krater painted by the Painter of the Woolly Satyrs, perhaps based on the lost play *Toxitides*, is now in the Louvre; a vase by the Dolon Painter, painted around 390 BCE, is now in the British Museum; a lekythos dating to 470 BCE is in the National Archeological Museum in Athens.

Roman artists continued to be interested in the story. Woodford 2003 shows a Roman statue of the second century CE (plate 129). There are several paintings of Aktaion in the ruins of Pompeii, one in the House of D. Octavius Quartio; another in the House of the Orchid, which shows two scenes from the story, the moment when Diana is surprised by Aktaion and also the moment when he is torn apart by his dogs (Ling 1991, figure 17); another in the Casa del Marinaio (Franklin 1990: 27); and another in the House of Menander. The story is also depicted on a marble sarcophagus dating to about 125 CE, now in the Louvre. The story has also been popular with painters and sculptors since the Renaissance.[3]

Euripides refers to Aktaion several times in his play *The Bacchae*, which concerns Pentheus and Dionysos, who are both cousins of Aktaion: Aktaion is the son of Autonoë, Pentheus is the son of Agave, and Dionysos is the son of Semele, and these three mothers are sisters, daughters of Kadmos, the brother of Europa. The theme of curiosity is also prominent in this play, especially when Pentheus goes to spy on his mother and the other women of Thebes as they revel on the mountain Cithaeron. But Aktaion's crime in the play is arrogance rather than curiosity. Early in the play, Kadmos reminds his grandson Pentheus about the fate of Aktaion, torn apart by his own dogs, because he boasted that he was a better hunter than Artemis. He warns Pentheus not to make the same mistake, not to put himself above this new god Dionysos (*Bacchae* 337–42). Pentheus does not heed this warning and suffers a worse fate: he is torn apart not by his dogs but by his mother. (There are further references to Aktaion at lines 1227–28, 1290–92, and 1371.) It is true that Pentheus wanted to see what he should not have seen, but his fundamental crime is that he put himself above a god. Thus the crime of Aktaion, in Euripides' version, fits the overall theme of the play. Euripides' version belongs to a group of stories in which a mortal boasts superiority to a god or goddess and is punished (for example Niobe and Leto; Arachne and

Figure 5.1 Aktaion attacked by his own dogs as Artemis prepares to shoot an arrow at him. The Pan Painter (ca. 470 BCE). Attic red-figure bell krater. H. 37 cm; D. 42.5 cm. Museum of Fine Arts, Boston, MA, USA. Julia Bradford Huntington James Fund. 10.185. Copyright © Museum of Fine Arts, Boston

Athena; Thamyris and the Muses; Marsyas and Apollo). Evidently the Greeks found it important to remind themselves often that mortals were weaker than the gods and that it was dangerous to think otherwise.

Other versions of the story accuse Aktaion of other crimes. The earliest reference to the story of Aktaion is found in fragment 161 of the Hesiodic *Catalogue of Women*. According to this fragment, Aktaion was punished because he wanted to marry his aunt Semele; the word "marriage" here ("gamon" in Greek) is perhaps a euphemism for rape. Semele was one of Zeus' lovers – their son was Dionysos – so perhaps Aktaion's crime was daring to be Zeus' rival. According to Apollodorus (*Library* 3.4.4), the archaic poet Acusilaos (who wrote in the sixth century BCE) gives the same reason for Aktaion's punishment, but Apollodoros then adds that most versions say Aktaion saw Artemis bathing.

The mythographer Hyginus says that Aktaion saw Diana bathing and wanted to rape her (180–81), and the late epic poet Nonnus says that Aktaion spied on Artemis because he desired her (*Dionysiaca* 5.287–551). The historian Diodorus Siculus (in his *Bibliotheca Historica*) says that Aktaion was punished either because he tried to consummate a marriage with Artemis or else he boasted that he was the better hunter, or perhaps for both reasons (4.81.4–5). Although gods and goddesses were certainly allowed to lust after mortals, a mortal was not allowed to lust after a deity. Ixion, for example, lusted after Hera; he is punished variously in various sources; sometimes he was tied to a whirling winged wheel, perhaps on fire, perhaps in the Underworld (cf. Pindar's second *Pythian Ode*, Apollodorus' *Library*, and so on; for illustrations, see Carpenter 1991, figure 132 and Shapiro 1994, figures 57 and 58). In some sources, the great hunter Orion tries to rape Artemis (Hyginus, *Fab.* 195, for example).

Thus different versions of the story have different meanings. As Ovid tells the story, Aktaion is innocent, and his punishment shows the arbitrary cruelty of Artemis; the story is placed in the context of other stories that show the gods abusing mortals. Callimachus places the story in the context of the myth of Teiresias, in order to make Athena look better than Artemis. Apuleius suggests that Aktaion's curiosity was less than innocent, like the curiosity of his hero Lucius.[4] In other sources, such as the *Catalogue of Women*, Hyginus' *Fabulae*, Nonnus' *Dionysiaca*, Euripides' *Bacchae*, etc., Aktaion either lusted after Semele, Artemis, or Hera; in these versions he fully deserved his punishment. Thus there is no single meaning to the myth; it can take various meanings depending on its context and the way it is shaped by a particular author.

III. LOCALIZATION AND RATIONALIZATION

When Pausanias was traveling from Eleutherai to Plataia he saw a rock called Aktaion's Bed, because Aktaion supposedly rested there after hunting. He also tells us about a spring nearby, where Aktaion saw Artemis bathing. He then refers to a poem by the archaic poet Stesichoros, in which Artemis changed Aktaion into a deer by throwing a deerskin over him and then made his dogs kill him to keep him from marrying Semele. Pausanias thus refers to the story that Aktaion saw Artemis bathing and also to the story that Aktaion wanted to marry his aunt Semele. But then Pausanias says the gods had nothing to do with the death of Aktaion; his dogs must have been rabid (*Guide* 9.2.3). Later Pausanias tells another quite different story about Aktaion: the Orchomenians consulted the Oracle at Delphi because an apparition was devastating their countryside, and the Oracle advised them to find whatever was left of Aktaion and bury it, then to make a statue of him; according to Pausanias, the people there burn offerings to Aktaion annually (*Guide* 9.37.4).

Pausanias thus places the story of Aktaion within the Greek landscape. For Pausanias, and no doubt for most Greeks, the stories of myth were not foreign abstractions, but a part of daily life. If you lived near Thebes, then you lived where Aktaion was killed by his dogs, where Amphiaraos was swallowed by the earth in the battle of the Seven Against Thebes (*Guide* 9.8.1), where Kadmos sowed the serpent's teeth (*Guide* 9.10.1); if you lived in Athens, you lived where the waters from Deukalion's flood were absorbed by the earth (*Guide* 1.18.7), where Talos, murdered by his uncle Daidalos, was buried (*Guide* 1.21.6); if you lived in Eleusis, you could see the well where Demeter was resting when the daughters of Keleus first spoke to her (*Guide* 1.39.1), and so on. Moreover, the myths and the figures from myth are often associated with local rituals, such as the annual offerings to Aktaion reported by Pausanias. These local identifications and rituals were part of the meanings of the myths for the ancient Greeks, though it is difficult to put meanings of this sort into words. When a

Greek myth appears outside of its home, when it appears, for example, in a Latin writer such as Ovid, it has likely lost this local meaning and lost its connection to the landscape and to ritual. On the other hand, when a myth loses its local connections, it becomes available for new meanings, as can be seen in literary representations such as Ovid's *Metamorphoses*.

Pausanias was fascinated by the mythical stories and their place in Greek thought and Greek society, but he does not simply believe them, as he explains to the reader quite directly (*Guide* 2.17.4). Since Pausanias does not believe that Aktaion was turned into a deer, he has to find some way to explain what happened, some way to rationalize the unbelievable aspects of the story: if Aktaion was killed by his own dogs, they must have been rabid. Rationalizations occur throughout his account. He says, for example, that the Trojan Horse was a device built by military engineers to break down the walls of Troy (*Guide* 1.23.10); he refuses to believe that Kyknos, the king of the Ligurians, was changed into a bird (*Guide* 1.30.3); he doubts the story that men grew from serpents' teeth sowed by Kadmos (*Guide* 9.10.1).

On the other hand, Pausanias believes stories that would seem incredible to most people today. He is willing to believe in the Minotaur, because even in his own time women gave birth to more remarkable monsters (*Guide* 1.24.2). When Seleukos, one of Alexander's generals, was sacrificing to Zeus at Pella, the firewood spontaneously moved to the altar and started to burn (*Guide* 1.16.1). When the inhabitants of Pioniai are about to sacrifice to Pionis, the founder of their city, smoke rises from the grave spontaneously, as Pausanias himself saw (*Guide* 9.18.3). These examples show that Pausanias tries to understand the myths within his standards of what is rational, but his idea of what is rational does not necessarily match ours.

A different rationalization of the story of Aktaion is told by a somewhat obscure Greek author named Palaephatus, who was perhaps associated with Aristotle's school in Athens in the late fourth century BCE. His book, *On Unbelievable Tales*, which survives only in part, consists of 45 short rationalizing explanations of famous myths, with another seven mythical tales added from another source. His treatment of the story of Aktaion is typical of his manner of retelling the myths in a way which he feels makes them believable. He begins by rejecting the idea that Aktaion was eaten by his own dogs, because dogs, he says, love their masters. He also rejects the story that Artemis changed Aktaion into a deer, though he grants that Artemis could do whatever she wanted. The real story, he says, is that Aktaion squandered all his money on his hunting dogs, and so people said that he had he was eaten up by his dogs. Rationalizations can be found in other authors, including Herodotus and even Euripides. The skeptical spirit is another important aspect of the meaning of Greek myth. (For more on rationalizations of Greek myth, see Chapter Twelve.)

IV. THE FALL OF IKAROS

The stories of Daidalos – the inventor and architect who built the Labyrinth – and his son Ikaros – the boy who flew too near the sun – are well known today. Oddly enough, however, they have left little trace in surviving Greek sources. Homer says that Daidalos built a dancing floor for Ariadne in Knosos (*Iliad* 18.592), but he doesn't mention Ikaros. There is no reference to either Daidalos or Ikaros in Hesiod's *Theogony* or *Works and Days*, nor in what survives of the *Catalogue of Women*. Bacchylides mentions Daidalos and Pasiphaë and the bull in his fragmentary Ode 26, but there is not enough of the poem left to tell us much. There may have been references to Daidalos in two lost plays by Sophocles (the titles of these plays are not certain) and the lost play the *Cretans* by Euripides. Plato mentions Daidalos several times as a great craftsman and sculptor, though his work would be obsolete in Plato's own time (*Ion* 533a; *Laws* 677d; *Republic* 529e; *Greater Hippias* 282a; *Meno* 97d, 15b; *Euthyphro* 11b), but he never mentions Ikaros.

Daidalos

Daidalos was related to the mythical royal family of Athens, though he had different ancestry in different sources. He was variously described as an inventor, an architect, and a sculptor. His statues were said to be so lifelike that they could walk, but others say only that he was the first person to sculpt figures in a striding position. He fled Athens for Crete because he had killed his nephew, who was his apprentice but who threatened to outshine his uncle's inventive ability. In Crete Daidalos built a dancing floor for Ariadne (*Iliad* 18.592); he also built a hollow wooden cow which Queen Pasiphaë could use to indulge her lust for the bull that King Minos had refused to sacrifice to Poseidon. The offspring of this union was the Minotaur, who was hidden away in the Labyrinth built by Daidalos. According to some sources, it was Daidalos who showed Theseus how to escape from the Labyrinth though in other sources Ariadne figured out the trick with the thread by herself.

Minos now imprisoned Daidalos and his son Ikaros in the Labyrinth. Daidalos constructed wings from wax and feathers, but when he and Ikaros flew away Ikaros flew too close to the sun; the wax in the wings melted and Ikaros fell into the sea, which is now called the Icarian Sea. Herakles found the body of Ikaros and buried him on the island now called Icaria. Daidalos landed in Sicily, where he took refuge with King Kokalos. Minos then searched for Daidalos. Wherever he went, he would produce a spiral conch shell, and he would offer a reward to anyone who could pass a thread through its windings. King Kokalos gave the shell to Daidalos, whom he had hidden. Daidalos tied a thread to an ant and waited until the ant made its way from end to end through the spiral. King Kokalos tried to pass the solution off as his own, but Minos concluded that he must be hiding Daidalos. Before Minos could take action, either the king's daughters or Daidalos himself killed him, either with boiling oil or boiling water. (See Diodorus, *Library* 4.76.2–77.9; Hyginus, *Fab.* 39, 40, 42; *Library* 2.6.3, 3.1.3–4, 3.15.9, *Epit.* 1.8–15; *Met.* 8.236–59; Herodotus, *Histories* 7.169–79.)

The first literary reference to the story of Ikaros, from the late fourth century BCE, is found in Palaephatus' book *On Unbelievable Tales*. According to his rationalizing version of the story, when Daidalos and Ikaros were imprisoned by King Minos of Crete, they let themselves down through a window and sailed off in a small boat. Because the winds were strong, they seemed to be flying. When Minos pursued them, their boat capsized and Ikaros drowned.

It is only an accident that the earliest surviving version of this story is a rationalization. A rationalization of the story was necessary only because the mythic version was already popular, so Palaephatus' rationalized account can be taken as evidence that the traditional story that Ikaros flew too close to the sun was well known by his time. There is also artistic evidence that the story of Ikaros was known as early as the middle of the sixth century – a small fragment of a vase shows two winged feet with the name "Ikaros" written clearly beside them (Athens Akr 601 frr; see LIMC sub Daidalos et Ikaros, no. 14). Two vases of the late fifth or early fourth century show Daidalos fitting wings to Ikaros (LIMC sub Daidalos et Ikaros, nos. 19–20).

Summaries of the story can be found in the historian Diodorus Siculus (first century BCE) and in the mythographers Hyginus (first century CE) and Apollodorus (second century CE). But these summaries present just the bare events, with no interpretation.

Pausanias offers a rationalizing version of the myth not unlike the version in Palaephatus' *On Unbelievable Tales*, but with some different details. According to Pausanias, Daidalos made two boats in which he and Ikaros escaped from Crete, but he adds that Daidalos was the first to use sails, and thus he maintains Daidalos' reputation as an inventor. But Ikaros didn't know how to use the sails, and so he upset his boat. Herakles came across the body and buried it, and even now, Pausanias says, there is a small tumulus; the island and the sea around it are named after Ikaros (*Guide* 9.11.3). Pausanias does not tell us about any rituals performed at this tumulus; perhaps there were none. Nonetheless, Ikaros was represented in a visible feature of the ancient Greek landscape.

V. IKAROS IN ROME

Although the story of Ikaros is not widely told in surviving Greek literature, it became popular in Rome. Vergil tells the story oddly by not telling it. At the beginning of Book Six of the *Aeneid*, Aeneas and his followers have just landed in Italy, at Cumae, near Naples. There Aeneas finds a temple to Apollo, with huge doors decorated by Daidalos, who had landed at Cumae after his flight from Crete. On these doors Daidalos has represented the death of Androgeos, Minos' son, whose death in Athens was compensated by the tribute of Athenian youth, as also shown on the doors. Pasiphaë and the bull were there, and also the Minotaur and the Labyrinth. Now the narrator addresses Ikaros himself: "You also should have a great role in such a work, if grief allowed. Twice Daidalos attempted to represent your fall in gold, twice the father's hands fell" (*Aeneid* 6.30–33). The absence of the story is evidence of the father's sorrow. This version fits in well with the theme, so prominent in the *Aeneid*, of the love between fathers and sons.

Ovid told the story of Ikaros twice, once in the *Art of Love* (2.19–98) and once in the *Metamorphoses* (8.152–235). At the beginning of Book Two of the *Art of Love*, Ovid says that it is not enough to catch a girl, now you must keep her; but Cupid is fickle and his wings make it difficult to keep him in one place (2.19–20). Likewise, Ovid says, Minos tried to prevent the escape of Daidalos, but Daidalos found a way out with wings. Ovid then proceeds to tell the story in some detail, particularly the fashioning of the wings and the flight itself, with much emphasis on the cleverness of Daidalos, and also on his prudence, as he gives Ikaros careful directions about the flight. He explains that if they fly too close to the sun, the wax in the wings will melt, but if they fly too close to the sea, the wings will become waterlogged, so they should fly between the two (2.59–62). As they put on their wings and prepare to fly, Daidalos kisses his son with tears in his eyes (2.69–70). As Ikaros boldly flies away, an angler sees him and drops his fishing rod (2.77–78).

Now Ikaros rashly soars too high and the wax in the wings melts; he flails his bare arms but the thin air will not support him. He falls and calls out "Father, Father!" as the sea closes over his mouth. His father calls out "Ikaros, Ikaros! Where are you?" and then he sees the wings in the water. Now the bones of Ikaros are covered by the earth, and the sea is called by his name (2.83–96). Ovid ends the story by returning to the comparison he made at the beginning: "Minos was not able to restrain the man with wings, but I am ready to hold on to the flying god" (2.97–98).

If we take Ovid at his word – never a safe procedure – the point of the story is simply the comparison between Minos and the poet, Daidalos and Cupid. But if that is really the point, then the story is developed beyond necessity, and in any case the fate of Ikaros doesn't really fit. Perhaps Ovid is simply taking pleasure in the story and his own narrative skill. Important elements of this version are the inventive power of Daidalos, the youthful rashness of Ikaros, the virtue of the middle path, the surprise of the fisherman, and the pathos of the death of Ikaros.

Ovid tells the story again in the *Metamorphoses* (*Met.* 8.152–235), with some differences of emphasis. In general the poet fits each version to the points in the larger context of each poem. The version in the *Metamorphoses*, for example, drops the comparison of Cupid and Daidalos, but it develops the story of Pasiphaë and the Minotaur, which is appropriate to the theme of transformation. Some parts of the story are expanded – for example, when Daidalos and Ikaros fly away, they are seen by a fisherman, a shepherd, and a plowman, who think the pair must be gods – and some are abbreviated; in some spots Ovid even borrows the wording of the *Art of Love* for reuse in the *Metamorphoses*. Both versions were often read and imitated.

Roman painters were also interested in the story of Ikaros (LIMC sub Daidalos et Ikaros, nos. 36–43). Some ten paintings of the story have been found at Pompeii. A wall painting in the Villa Imperiale in Pompeii (LIMC sub Daidalos et Ikaros, no. 36) shows in the upper left a figure wearing wings and flying, while at the bottom there is a figure lying on the surface of the sea; in the middle right a woman's figure looks down at the fallen body. A wall painting in the House of the Priest Amandus (LIMC sub Daidalos et Ikaros, no. 38; Ling 1991, figure 116) shows a walled city in the background, two oared boats in the lower middle, two female figures in the bottom left. The women and the men in the boats are looking up at Ikaros, who is falling; the center is unfortunately damaged, but it is possible to see the tips of another pair of wings. In the lower left of the painting, the corpse of Ikaros is lying on the beach, and a male figure is looking at it. Thus the painting shows two moments in the story, the fall itself, and then the body of Ikaros after he has fallen.

VI. IKAROS IN THE WESTERN TRADITION

There are innumerable references to the story of Daidalos and Ikaros in the later Western tradition, some long, some just brief allusions. In Canto 17 of the *Inferno*, Dante is perched on the back of the flying monster Geryon; his fear, he says, was as great as the fear of Phaethon, when he dropped the reins and burned the sky, or as great as the fear of Ikaros, when he felt the wax melt in the heat of the sun (100–05). For Dante, Ikaros is an example of fear of flying. Geoffrey Chaucer, in his dream poem the *House of Fame*, says that he was seized by a giant eagle, which carried him aloft. When they were high in the air, Chaucer looked down and saw that the world had become just a point. The eagle tells him that no person had ever been so high, and he gives examples of those who in the past had supposedly flown high in the air: Alexander the Great, Scipio (in Cicero's *Dream of Scipio*), and Daidalos and Ikaros. For Chaucer, Ikaros is an example of a high flier.

Shakespeare's *Henry VI, Part Three* deals with the continuing civil conflict between the ineffective King Henry VI, who represents the Lancastrian faction, and the Yorkist faction, led first by Richard, Duke of York, and after his death, by his three sons, Edward (later King Edward IV), George, and Richard (later King Richard III). In Act Five, the Yorkists have defeated the Lancastrians, and King Henry's son, Prince Edward, has been brutally murdered. Richard now goes to the tower of London, where Henry is imprisoned. Henry guesses that his son has been killed, and Richard tells him, "Why what a peevish fool was that of Crete/ That taught his son the office of a fowl/ And yet for all his wings the fool was drowned" (5.618–20); that is, Henry had taught Prince Edward to fly too high, and thus his death was his father's fault. Henry replies, "I Daedalus, my poor boy Icarus,/ Thy father Minos that denied our course,/ The sun that seared the wings of my sweet boy/ Thy brother Edward, and thyself the sea/ Whose envious gulf did swallow up his life" (5.6.21–25). Thus Henry turns Richard's insulting reference into a complete allegory of his own situation. If he was Daidalos, he says, and his son was Ikaros, then the villains of the story are Richard, Duke of York, who played the role of Minos, and then his sons Edward and Richard, who combined to kill the boy. The Yorkists are the villains of the allegory; Prince Edward was perhaps rash, but he was innocent, and Henry himself is the grieving father.[5]

According to Sir Francis Bacon, the story of Ikaros is a parable of moderation:

> The path of virtue goes directly midway between excess on the one hand and defect on the other. Icarus, being in the pride of youthful alacrity, naturally fell a victim to excess. For it is on the side of excess that the young commonly sin, as the old on the side of defect. (Bacon 1864: chapter 27)

Pieter Breugel's *Landscape with the Fall of Icarus* is perhaps the most famous of the many artistic representations of the story. The painting is dominated by a farmer plowing in the center foreground; behind him is a shepherd, and in the lower right corner there is a fisherman. Behind these figures is a seascape, with several ships, and in the lower right, just above the fisherman, two legs are visible, all that can be seen of the fallen Ikaros. Breugel has evidently modeled his painting on the version of the story in Ovid's *Metamorphoses* – thus the farmer, the shepherd, and the fisherman – but he has turned the story to his own purposes. The landscape and seascape now dominate, along with the prosaic activities of ordinary working men, and the mythic hero is not noticed by the people within the picture and hardly to be seen by the viewer. Breugel's painting has inspired poems by William Carlos Williams, Charles F. Madden, and W. H. Auden.[6]

The Italian writer Lauro de Bosis used the myth of Ikaros to present an anti-fascist message in his play *Icaro*, published in 1930. De Bosis sets the story in Cnossos on Crete, where the dictator Minosse is holding the inventor Daedalo and his son Icaro prisoners.

Further explorations

Greek myth has remained alive in popular culture. Some myths and mythic characters are used as brief references or allusions, for example in songs or in television commercials, but others are the subjects of extended representations, in popular novels, movies, and graphic novels. Pick a character from Greek myth and write an essay on how this character is used in popular culture. Pay particular attention to new or different elements in the modern version and explain what these changes may mean for modern audiences. You may find useful the final chapter in Doherty 2001, with bibliography noted there.

When Minosse decides to wage war against Asia, Daedalo provides him with a new material, iron, for his weapons. Icaro, however, opposes the war. He plans to spread a message of peace by flying away from the island, using the wings his father has invented. Minosse orders that the wings be burned, but his daughter Fedra, who is in love with Icaro, convinces her father to allow Icaro to leave. When Icaro flies away, he meets the Athenian Teseo sailing towards Crete, and before he dies he tells Teseo to fight, to resist the tyranny of Minosse. De Bosis saw Icaro as a symbol of resistance, and he turned this symbol into personal action. In October 1931 he flew an airplane over Rome and dropped hundreds of thousands of anti-fascist leaflets; he then flew away and was not seen again.

CONCLUSION

These two examples – the myth of Aktaion and the myth of Ikaros – suggest that any myth can have a variety of meanings, depending on how the story is told on any particular occasion. Perhaps Aktaion was just in the wrong place at the wrong time, perhaps he was too curious to see what no mortal should see, perhaps he boasted that he was better than a divinity, perhaps he desired his aunt, the consort of Zeus, perhaps he even tried to rape a goddess. Ikaros can stand for youthful exuberance, he can teach the value of the middle way, he can be the cause of a father's grief, he can show that even remarkable events can pass unnoticed, or he can be the symbol of resistance to tyranny. No myth can mean just anything – the basic framework of the characters and events limit the range of meanings possible – but the basic structure of a myth may offer itself for varying interpretation depending on the purposes of the teller. This flexibility is one of the reasons Greek myth has remained important throughout the history of Western culture.

Myths are often interpreted in terms of one or another theory of myth, and several of these theories will be explored in later chapters. Comparative and Jungian interpretation will be highlighted in Chapter Eight, gender theory in Chapter Nine, historical interpretation in Chapter Ten, and structuralist interpretation in Chapter Eleven. The connection between myth and ritual is a continuing interest throughout this study, as is the related interest in how Greek myth was part of ancient Greek society. These theories, and others, have provided important insights into the study of myth, but an exclusive reliance on any one theory, while it may illuminate certain aspects of myth, would leave other aspects in the dark. Myths typically exist in different versions, and these versions may express a variety of meanings. An eclectic approach is required to do justice to the adaptability of the myths themselves.

FURTHER READING

Heath 1992 presents a detailed literary analysis of the story of Aktaion in four major sources: Callimachus' fifth *Hymn*, Ovid's *Metamorphoses*, Apuleius' *The Golden Ass*, and Nonnus' *Dionysiaca*. The statue of Aktaion in *The Golden Ass* is discussed in Elsner 2007: 180 and 289–302. Palaephatus' *On Unbelievable Tales* has been translated by Jacob Stern (1996). Fontenrose 1981 places the myth of Aktaion in the context of a general Myth of the Hunter and the Huntress, including the stories of Orion, Kallisto, Kephalos, and Prokris, etc. For discussion of De Bosis (and other modern uses of myth in drama), see Belli 1969. For discussion of theories of myth and methods of analysis, see Csapo 2005 and Edmunds 1990.

Chapter Six

THE BONES OF ORESTES
Heroes in Myth and Society

In many cultures, myths are primarily stories about divinities. Ancient Greek myth, however, prominently features heroic myth, stories about mortal heroes (though gods may play a secondary role in these heroic myths). The word hero in Greek, however, does not mean what it means in English. A hero in Greek myth may be descended from a god and a mortal, like Achilles, or from two mortal parents, like Odysseus. Some heroes did remarkable deeds, but others had committed crimes, and some were infants whose only important action was to die. Mostly the heroes were felt to have power even after death. The heroes were also closely connected to rituals and social practices. They often became the recipients of local cult, and it is often possible to link heroic myths with local rituals. The myths were not just stories to be told for entertainment; an important part of the meaning of the heroic myths came from their association with ritual practice or features of the landscape.

Hero cult, defined most narrowly, involved regular ritual observance, usually at the tomb of the hero or heroine. In some instances the rituals for heroes and heroines were clearly different from divine rituals, but sometimes the distinction was not so definite. In the eighth century BCE, hero cult was often performed at Mycenaean graves; it was no longer known who had been buried in these graves, and so they were free to be associated with the heroes of the mythic tradition. Later on cult could be paid to historical people, such as Olympic athletes, and there were also many heroes without names. In addition to hero cult proper, heroes and heroines could be associated with other ritual practices. This chapter examines the ritual associations of four heroes: Orestes, Orestes' sister Iphigeneia, the Athenian hero Theseus, and a lesser-known heroine, Hyrnetho, who was given honors in both Argos and Epidaurus.

I. THE BONES OF ORESTES

Orestes, the son of Agamemnon, who killed his mother Klytemnestra and her lover Aigisthos, was a prominent figure in Greek myth: in the *Odyssey*, as an example for Telemachos; in Pindar's *Eleventh Pythian Ode*; and in six Greek tragedies (Aeschylus' *Libation-Bearers* and *Eumenides*, Sophocles' *Elektra*, and Euripides' *Elektra*, *Iphigeneia in Tauris*, and *Orestes*). But he is not simply a character in these works of literature; he also played a role in the life of ancient Greece.

Sometime in the mid-sixth century BCE, the Spartans were engaged in a war with the Tegeans, who lived some 50 miles or so to the north, in Arcadia. According to the historian Herodotus, the Spartans asked the Oracle at Delphi how they could win the war, and the Oracle told them to find the bones of Orestes. They asked where they could find these bones, and the Oracle gave a riddling response: they should look for a place where two winds were blowing, and where there was striking and counter-striking.

At first the Spartans were unable to understand this riddle. But then a Spartan elder named Lichas took advantage of a temporary truce and traveled to Tegea. There he came across a smithy, where he saw iron being worked. The smith had two pairs of bellows – two winds – and he was forging iron with a hammer and anvil – striking and counter-striking. When Lichas expressed his amazement at the process, the smith told him about something even more amazing: not long before, he had been digging in his yard and he dug up a huge coffin containing enormous bones, then he buried it again. Lichas realized that the Oracle had been fulfilled, and that the bones the smith had dug up were the bones of Orestes. He managed to take out a lease on the smith's yard, dug up the bones, and took them back to Sparta. Ever since that time, the Spartans had the advantage over the Tegeans (Herodotus, *Histories* 1.67–68). When Pausanias visited Sparta, he saw the grave where the bones of Orestes were buried (*Guide* 3.11.10; 3.3.5–6), and in Tegea he saw a monument marking the spot where the bones were dug up (*Guide* 8.54.4).

The bones of Orestes clearly had a kind of power, even though Orestes himself was dead. As a matter of history, Sparta did not conquer Tegea after the bones were found and moved, but they did establish a kind of control over Tegean foreign policy. It is impossible to establish causation in such a case, but Herodotus, at least, thought that the story was worth telling in his account of the growth of Spartan power in the region; ever since the Spartans found the bones, he says, they had the better of the Tegeans.

The meaning of the transfer of the bones at the time – assuming that this incident, or something like it, really did happen – has been debated. Some scholars believe that the Spartans, as Dorians, were seen as relative newcomers, and that they were trying to connect themselves to the pre-Dorian heroic age through Orestes; moreover, they claimed to have the sanction of the Oracle at Delphi for their actions. Other scholars have argued that the transfer of the bones showed their respect for the non-Dorian ancestors of the Tegeans; in effect, the transfer was intended to replace warfare with diplomacy. A third position is that the effect of the transfer was internal to Spartan society, as it created a symbol of general Spartan identity beyond the claims of particular families (McCauley 1999: 89). And it is possible that all of these meanings played some role in the effectiveness of this incident.

Orestes was a Spartan hero, so it is no surprise to see that he had power there. But the Athenians also had an interest in Orestes. According to Athenian myth, after Orestes killed his mother he came to Athens where he was put on trial. The story of Orestes in Athens provides an aetiology for one odd feature of a complex Athenian ritual, though, as is often the case, it is hard to say which came first, the ritual or the myth. The festival of the Anthesteria, a festival for Dionysos, was held over three days, the eleventh to the thirteenth of the month of Anthesterion. On the second day of this festival, called Choes, or "Wine Jugs", people gathered for an odd drinking party. Usually wine for a party was mixed in a large bowl called a krater and then served out to each drinker. On this day, however, each person at the party brought his own individual jug and even his own supply of wine. Moreover, the party was held in silence.

According to the aetiological myth, it happened that Orestes arrived in Athens, pursued by the Furies, during the festival of the Anthesteria. He was polluted, because he had committed a murder. The king, however, managed to find a way to welcome Orestes while avoiding the pollution. Since Orestes could not drink with anyone or talk with anyone, everyone would drink by himself and keep silent. And the festival has been observed in this way ever since. This story is told by Euripides (*Iphigeneia in Tauris* 947–60), and also by a Greek historian named Phanodemus (quoted in Parker 2005: 293).

Pausanias tells a similar story about Troezen, where he saw a building called the Booth of Orestes. When Orestes arrived there, he was lodged in this shed until he had been purified. And still the descendants of those who purified him have a dinner there on designated days. The material used to purify Orestes was buried near the booth, and a laurel tree grew up which was still there when Pausanias visited. Pausanias also saw the stone Orestes sat on when he was purified (*Guide* 2.31.8; 2.31.4).

In Arcadia Pausanias saw a sanctuary to goddesses called the Madnesses, who he thought were the same as the Eumenides; the local inhabitants said that Orestes went crazy there after he murdered Klytemnestra, and not far away Pausanias saw a mound with a finger made of stone on it, because Orestes supposedly bit off one of his fingers there, and also a place called Remedy where Orestes recovered from his madness, and another place where he cut his hair (*Guide* 8.34.1–3). But in Lakonia, near a town called Gythion, there was a stone where the local people say that Orestes recovered from his madness (*Guide* 3.22.1). Such differences of opinion about the location of events and graves were common. Because the bones of a hero were felt to have power, it was common for more than one location to claim a hero's grave, or, as in the story of Orestes, to try to get possession of the bones. These disputes became particularly important when two states were antagonists. But even when the physical relics were not in question, a place one of the heroes had visited was felt to retain some power.

II. BEARS FOR IPHIGENEIA

According to a popular version of the myth, at the very moment when Iphigeneia was about to be sacrificed at Aulis, so that the Greek fleet could sail to Troy, she was snatched away by Artemis, who had demanded the sacrifice in the first place. A deer was substituted in her place, though no one at the sacrifice noticed the switch. (In other sources, however, such as

Pindar's *Eleventh Pythian Ode*, it seems that Iphigeneia was not rescued by Artemis, but died at Aulis.) Artemis carried Iphigeneia away to be a priestess among the savage Taurians, who had the barbaric custom of performing human sacrifice for Artemis. Many years later her brother Orestes found her among the Taurians and brought her back to Greece. There are references to this story in many sources, especially in Euripides' *Iphigeneia in Tauris*. Herodotus, writing some years before Euripides' play was produced, has a somewhat different version; he says that that Taurians had a custom of sacrificing shipwrecked sailors to Artemis, and they claim, he says, that the goddess to whom they sacrifice is Iphigeneia. This version agrees with Euripides' play that Iphigeneia was not killed at Aulis, but it differs in turning Iphigeneia into a goddess (Herodotus, *Histories* 4.103).

Orestes, Iphigeneia, and Elektra in the classical tradition

These three children of Agamemnon were popular characters in ancient drama and they have continued to be popular in the later Western dramatic tradition. In 1674 the French playwright Jean Racine produced *Iphigénie*, based on Euripides' *Iphigeneia at Aulis*, but with the addition of an extra character, Eriphile, whose real name turns out to be Iphigeneia, and who is sacrificed instead of Agamemnon's daughter. Christoph Willibald Gluck's opera *Iphigénie en Aulide* was first produced in 1774, and his *Iphigénie en Tauride* in 1779. These are based on the plays by Euripides, but with some changes. Mozart's opera *Idomeneo* includes Elektra as a character, but the plot of the opera is only distantly related to anything in Greek myth.

Richard Strauss's opera *Elektra*, with libretto by Hugo van Hofmannsthal, was first produced in 1909. Eugene O'Neill's trilogy of plays, *Mourning Becomes Electra*, first performed in 1931, is set around the time of the American Civil War; the Agamemnon character, for example, is a general in the Union army, returned from the war, while his son Oren corresponds to Orestes and his daughter Lavinia corresponds to Electra. T. S. Eliot's play *The Family Reunion*, first presented in 1939, places the action in modern times; the plot is a symbolic imitation of the original myth rather than a close adaptation. Jean-Paul Sartre's *The Flies*, produced in 1943 during World War II, is set in ancient Greece, but it has clear reference to the events of its own time. It follows the basic outline of the myth, but with changes in order to expresses Sartre's own philosophic views. Of these various versions, the plays by Racine and Sartre are particularly effective.

When Orestes and Iphigeneia left the Taurians, according to Euripides, they took with them a statue of the goddess Artemis, supposedly by the design of Athena, who wanted the statue taken to Attica; she tells Orestes to build a temple for the statue at the region called Halai, on the [eastern] edge of Attica, where people will worship Artemis Tauropolos ("Bull-hunter"). In the ritual to be held there, the celebrants will touch a man's throat with a sword just enough to draw blood; this ritual will make up for the sacrifice of Orestes which did not occur in Tauris. Iphigeneia will become the priestess of Artemis at Brauron, near Halai; she will be buried there, and offerings will be made to her for women who die in childbirth (*Iphigeneia in Tauris*, 1435–74). An important festival for young Athenian girls was centered at the sanctuary for Artemis at Brauron (see Chapter Nine for more on the rites at Brauron).

Pausanias saw an ancient wooden idol of Artemis at Brauron, and he knew the story that Iphigeneia landed there after she fled from the Taurians (*Guide* 1.33.1), but he says that he does not believe that the statue there is the statue stolen by Iphigeneia. The Spartans also claimed to have the statue, and Pausanias says that their claim is more likely. The Cappodocians and the Lydians also claimed to have the statue (*Guide* 3.16.7–8).

Pausanias describes a Spartan ritual reminiscent of the ritual Euripides places at Halai. Once when the Spartans were sacrificing at the statue, so the story goes, they began to argue and fight. Many people were killed at the altar, and then more died afterwards of disease. An oracle told them to stain the altar with human blood. At first a human victim was chosen by lot and sacrificed at the altar, but later the Spartan lawgiver Lycurgus changed the ritual, and instead young men were whipped at the altar (*Guide* 3.16.7–10). This again is a story of human sacrifice changed to a milder form of bloodshed.

In Euripides' version of the story, Iphigeneia eventually died and was buried at Brauron, but Pausanias reports a story that Iphigeneia's tomb is at Megara (*Guide* 1.43.1). There was a statue of Iphigeneia at a shrine for Artemis in Aigeira in Arcadia, and a statue of Artemis as well; the priestess of Artemis at this shrine was a virgin who served until she married (*Guide* 7.26.3). The association of Iphigeneia with Artemis was very close, and at Hermion, near Corinth, Artemis had the epithet Iphigeneia, which can be understood as Artemis Strongbirth (*Guide* 2.35.1), while a fragment of the *Catalogue of Women* says that Artemis made Iphigeneia immortal and that Iphigeneia is now called Artemis of the Road (frag. 19). Emily Kearns suggests that when Artemis was worshiped in connection with childbirth, she was originally called Artemis Iphigeneia, and that this aspect of the goddess eventually became separated off and thought of as a mortal heroine closely connected to the goddess (Kearns 1989: 32–33).

III. THE BONES OF THESEUS

Theseus was the most important of all the Athenian heroes. In a sense he was the Athenian counterpart to Herakles, particularly in his role as a hero who kills monsters. He was also a founding figure for the Athenians, as the leader who brought the various villages of Attica together into one political unit, and as the oddly royal symbol of the democratic city. He did not die in Athens, however, and he was not buried there, at least at first. Towards the end of his life, political disputes drove him away from the city and he went to the island of Skyros, where he was treacherously killed by King Lycomedes (Plutarch, *Theseus* 35.3–5; *Cimon* 8.5–6). Many years later, in 476/5 BCE, the Delphic Oracle told the Athenians that they should recover his bones. The Athenian general Cimon, son of the general Miltiades, attacked and took the island, which at that time had been held by Dolopian pirates. When he went looking for Theseus' grave, he saw an eagle pecking at the ground and tearing it with its talons. He dug there and found a coffin containing an enormous skeleton, a bronze spear, and a sword. When he took these back to Athens, the Athenians welcomed them with a parade and sacrifices, as if Theseus himself had returned to the city. His grave, near the gymnasium, is a sanctuary for runaway slaves and others of low position (Plutarch, *Theseus* 36.1–2). It is easy to see that Cimon's own political interests were served when he was able to associate himself with the great hero (McCauley 1999: 91).

Myths of Theseus

The story of Theseus is a complex myth with many parts: his birth in Troezen, perhaps with two fathers, one mortal (King Aigeus of Athens) and one divine (Poseidon); the tokens left under the rock by King Aigeus; Theseus' journey from Troezen to Athens and his glorious feats along the way; his recognition by Aigeus, despite the plotting of Medea; his trip to Crete and the killing of the Minotaur; the abandoning of Ariadne and the death of Aigeus; the battle of the Lapiths and the centaurs; the kidnapping of Helen and the attempted kidnapping of Persephone; the expedition against the Amazons; the marriage with Phaidra and the death of Hippolytos; his protection of Oedipus and his assisting of Adrastos; his exile from Athens and his death at Skyros. There are many sources for these various stories, both literary and visual, but no single source tells the whole myth, which has to be pieced together from here and there.

Theseus was associated with several Athenian festivals. Three of these took place in the month Pyanepsion. The feast of the Pyanepsia, which gave its name to the month, was held on the seventh day of the month. The word "pyanepsia" means something like "boiled beans", and the festival included a meal of boiled beans, though other vegetables were included in a kind of vegetable stew. According to myth, Theseus and his companions had returned to Athens from Crete on this day, and when they arrived, they made a stew out of whatever provisions they had left (Plutarch, *Theseus* 22.4). Also on this day boys went around to houses singing begging songs and carrying an olive bough, called the "eiresione", festooned with wool and various fruits, and pastry formed into the shapes of cups and harps; Plutarch also relates this custom to the story of Theseus (*Theseus* 22.5), but his reasoning seems rather weak, and perhaps he is just trying to relate as much of this festival to Theseus as he can. Most likely the festival was originally an agricultural festival to which the name of Theseus was attached when he became an important Athenian hero.

Another festival, the Oschophoria, was also held on the seventh day of Pyanepsion. During this festival, there was a procession in which two young men dressed as women carried vine branches with grapes still attached to them. This custom was supposed to derive from another part of the myth of Theseus. According to the myth, when the group of young Athenian men and women went to Crete to be fed to the Minotaur, Theseus passed off two young men as women, presumably to increase the number of fighters in the group. According to Plutarch, he changed their appearance by having them take warm baths and by keeping them out of the sun, by doing their hair, and by smoothing their skin with oils and cosmetics. He also taught them to imitate girls in their speech and their posture (*Theseus* 23.2).

The procession included a number of women called Deipnophoroi, or "dinner carriers", who carried food used in the ceremonies and told stories at the banquet. According to the myth, when Theseus and his companions were getting ready to sail for Crete, their mothers brought them food and told them stories to keep their spirits up (Plutarch, *Theseus* 23.3).

The participants in a festival ordinarily wore garlands on their heads, but the herald in this procession carried his garland on his staff. According to the myth, when Theseus came back from Crete, he sent a herald ahead to announce his arrival. The herald discovered, however, that King Aigeus, Theseus' father, had thrown himself into the sea because Theseus had forgotten to change his sails from black to white as a signal that he was safe. When the people of Athens offered a garland to the herald as a mark of their joy that Theseus had returned safely, he refused to wear it and put it on his staff instead of on his head (Plutarch, *Theseus* 22.2).

When Theseus returned from Crete, his feelings and those of the Athenians were mixed; happy because he had returned safely, sad because Aigeus had died. In a similar way, after the procession of the Oscophoria, the participants cried out "Eleleu!", which is a cry of triumph, and "Iou! Iou!", which is a cry of consternation (Plutarch, *Theseus* 22.3).

On the eighth of Pyanepsion, the day after the Pyanepsia and the Oscophoria, the Athenians held a feast called the Theseia, specifically devoted to Theseus. This feast supposedly marked the anniversary of the day Theseus returned from Crete (Plutarch, *Theseus* 36.3), though other accounts say that he returned on the seventh (*Theseus* 22.4). The Theseia was a major festival, including a procession, a large feast provided to the general population of Athens, and an extensive array of athletic contests. According to Parke, this festival was established only in 475 BCE, when Cimon brought the bones of Theseus back from Skyros (Parke 1977: 81).

On the sixteenth of the month of Hekatombaion, in midsummer, there was a festival called the Synoikia, which celebrated the formation of the unified Attic state. This process of bringing the various Attic villages together into one political unit was called "synoikism", from "syn" meaning "together" and "oikos", meaning "household", and according to myth it was Theseus who brought it about. Thucydides mentions the festival and says that it was founded by Theseus (*History* 2.15.2), and Plutarch says that the festival was still held in his time (*Theseus* 24.4).

In addition to these major festivals, there was a festival, the Kybernesia, honoring the pilot and the lookout on the voyage to Crete, according to the historian Philochorus. This festival may have been held on the eighth of the month Boedromion at Phaleron, where there were hero-shrines to these two minor heroes associated with Theseus (Philochorus, in Jacoby's *Fragmente der griechischen Historiker* 328 F; Plutarch, *Theseus* 17.6). And according to Plutarch, it was Theseus who established the great festival of the Panatheneia, which was held on the twenty-eighth of the month Hekatombaion (*Theseus* 24.3).

On his way home to Athens from Crete, Theseus stopped at Delos, so the story goes, and there he performed a dance which, according to Plutarch, was still performed in his own day. The dance, called the Crane Dance, imitated the windings of the Labyrinth (*Theseus* 22.1–2). Some scholars argue that this Crane Dance is represented on the François Vase (see Chapter Three for discussion of the François Vase).

Theseus is connected with another interesting Athenian ritual, as discussed in Plato's dialogue, the *Phaedo*. As the dialogue begins, Echecrates, who lives in Phlius, is asking Phaedo about the circumstances of Socrates' death. Echecrates has heard that there was quite a long time between the trial of Socrates and his execution, and he wants to know why. Phaedo explains that the day before the trial the Athenians had just finished putting garlands on the stern of the ship which every year they send to Delos. According to the Athenians, Phaedo says, this is the ship which took Theseus and his companions to Crete and back. The Athenians made a vow that the ship would be sent to Delos every year on a mission of thanksgiving if the young people returned home safely. But there is a law that while the ship is on its trip, there can be no executions. This time the winds were bad, and so there was a long time before the execution could occur (Plato, *Phaedo* 57a–58c). Almost certainly what Plato says here is historically accurate, both about the specific circumstances of the death of Socrates and also about the mission to Delos.[1]

A complex story like the myth of Theseus does not come into being all at once. Henry Walker suggests that it may be possible to date the various episodes, but some caution is required in this kind of argument, since the evidence, both literary and archeological, is full of gaps. Walker notes that five main episodes were probably known in the eighth century (if this is the proper date of the Homeric epics) and certainly in the seventh; these are "the abductions of Helen, Ariadne, and Persephone, and the fights against the Minotaur and the centaurs" (Walker 1995: 20). The fight against the Minotaur was the most popular story, and it may have been the earliest (Walker 1995: 16). The François Vase, which dates from around 570 BCE, shows Theseus and the Lapiths; the first representation of the killing of the Bull of Marathon can be dated to 550–540 BCE (Walker 1995: 41). The stories of Theseus' early deeds (the killing of Sinis, the sow, Skiron, Kerkyon, and Procrustes) was organized into a cycle only around 510 BCE (Walker 1995: 38). Individual stories in this group may be earlier, however. A vase made by a potter named Skythes around 515 BCE shows Theseus and the sow and perhaps Theseus and Skiron (Walker 1995: 42). Walker correlates the appearance of some of these deeds to political events: the killing of the sow and of Skiron is connected to Athenian conflict with Megara during the time of the tyrant Hippias, while the cycle as a whole came together at the time Athens gained control over the island of Salamis, perhaps around 509 BCE (Walker 1995: 50–51). The connection between Theseus and Troezen appears only after the Persian invasion, when the Athenians took refuge there (Walker 1995: 55). The killing of Periphetes, which eventually became the first in the series of early deeds, is first known after 450 BCE, and only after 430 BCE is Theseus linked to Herakles' expedition to get the girdle of Hippolyta (Walker 1995: 66).

The large number of festivals and rituals associated with Theseus shows his importance in Athenian society. Moreover, although the myth of Theseus probably began in Aphidna, which is outside of Athens in northern Attica, the cult of Theseus was restricted to Athens itself. Walker argues that the myth "goes back to a time when Aphidna and its lord had some kind of independent existence", while the cult of Theseus "is a product of the newly united state of Athens" (1995: 21). According to Emily Kearns, "the most important factor lying behind the creation of the Theseus saga was the desire for a heroic figure who would express in himself the developed forms and ideals of Athenian political life" (1989: 120).

Although references to Theseus go back to the very earliest mythic records, the evidence suggests that he became much more prominent in Athenian thought in the sixth and then in the fifth century BCE. Some scholars (including Kearns and Walker) have argued that the popularity of Theseus in Athens was linked to the democracy, which was established by Cleisthenes after the overthrow of the Pisistratid tyranny in the late sixth century. Jonathan Hall, however, argues against the view that the myth of Theseus became prominent in Athens only when it was used as democratic propaganda after the fall of the Pisistratid tyranny. He notes that the stories about the early deeds of Theseus could have been in oral circulation before they appear in the written or artistic record; he casts doubt on the accuracy of dating archeological finds; he lists a number of artistic representations of the story from the time of the Pisistratids; and he catalogues a number of reasons that Pisistratus and his sons might have favored the story of Theseus (Hall 2007: 338–46). The meaning of a myth is often quite open and available to be adapted to the interests of whoever is telling it at any particular moment. There is little doubt that the Athenian democracy found the myth of Theseus useful, but it could also have served the purposes of the tyrants.

IV. HYRNETHO'S OLIVE GROVE

Orestes, Iphigeneia, and Theseus are all major figures of Panhellenic myth, and they all remain well known today. There were many other heroes, however, who were local rather than Panhellenic and who are now known only to specialists. Even though they are not well known, their stories and the rituals associated with them can be very informative about aspects of Greek history and Greek thought.

Pausanias mentions quite a few of these local heroes; one of the most interesting is a heroine named Hyrnetho who was honored in Argos and in Epidaurus. Hyrnetho's story is part of a larger story, which claims to explain how the Dorians became the rulers of Argos and other territories in the Peloponnese. Since this is a mythical story, it is not surprising to find that these versions do not all agree.

Part of the story we can get from Diodorus Siculus, and part from Apollodorus. After Herakles died, his children initially fled from Eurystheus, but then they returned, fought against Eurystheus, and killed him. Then they attempted to seize the cities in the Peloponnese, but they were forced to leave, and went to live in northern Greece with King Aigimos, the son of Dorus, the founder of the Dorians. One of the three tribes of the Dorians, the Hylleis, is named after Hyllus, the son of Herakles (the other two tribes, the Pamphyloi and the Dymaneis, are named after sons of Aigimos). An oracle promised the descendants of Herakles that one day they would return and become rulers of the Peloponnese. According to this story, then, the Peloponnese really belonged to the descendants of Herakles, who had become closely related to the Dorians (Diodorus 4.57–58; *Library* 2.167–80).

Pausanias tells a slightly different story. He says that Tyndareus (the father of Helen and Klytemnestra) was ruling in Argos, but he was driven out by his brother, Hippocoon. Herakles then killed Hippocoon, and so he presumably had the rights to the throne. He then gave Argos back to Tyndareus, but only in trust. Orestes, Tyndareus' grandson and therefore a descendant of Pelops, eventually ruled in Argos and Sparta, and he was followed by his son, Tisamenos. But according to Pausanias, the descendants of Pelops held the land, but the descendants of Herakles (who was in turn the descendant of Perseus) had the superior claim. The inference is that eventually the descendants of Herakles would return and Argos should then be returned to them (*Guide* 2.18.5–7; see also Thucydides, *History* 1.9 and 1.13).

During the time that Orestes' son Tisamenos was ruler in Argos, the descendants of Herakles returned to the Peloponnese, bringing the Dorians with them. This story, then, is designed to explain where the Dorians came from, and how it is that they became rulers of parts of mainland Greece even though they were absent from the earlier stages of Greek mythology, such as the stories about Thebes, the Trojan War, and the House of Atreus.

One of the returning descendants of Herakles was named Temenos. He drove Tisamenos out of Argos and became ruler. He had a number of sons – according to Pausanias they are Ceisos, Cerynes, Phalces, and Agraeus, but other sources give different names – and also a daughter, whose name was Hyrnetho. Hyrnetho was married to Deiphontes, who was also a descendant of Herakles. Temenos openly favored his son-in-law Deiphontes over his sons. The sons became jealous and formed a plot; one of them, Ceisos, took over the throne of Argos, presumably having killed his father, and Hyrnetho and Deiphontes were driven away (*Guide* 2.18.7 and 2.19.1).

With this background, it is now time to look at what Pausanias says about Hyrnetho herself. In Argos he came across the grave of Hyrnetho: at least the people of Argos say it is the grave of Hyrnetho, but Pausanias disagrees. It might be an empty grave erected to her memory, he says, but he does not believe that the body of Hyrnetho is there, and he says that only those who don't know the history of Epidaurus could believe that this is the grave of Hyrnetho (*Guide* 2.23.3). At this point he does not tell us about the history of Epidaurus. But Epidaurus is the next city he visits. He explains that the last king of Epidaurus before the arrival of the Dorians was Pityreus, who was a descendant of Ion. (Ion, who was king of Athens, was the founder of the Ionians.) According to Pausanias, Pityreus voluntarily handed the kingship of Epidaurus over to Deiphontes, the husband of Hyrnetho (*Guide* 2.26.1). Thus, according to this story, an Ionian king of Epidaurus handed the city over to a Dorian.

Pausanias begins his story of Hyrnetho, as he often does, with a landmark: a grove which the Epidaurians call the Hyrnethium, where wild olives grow.[2] Hyrnetho's brothers, he says, wanted to cause trouble for Deiphontes, and so they decided to take Hyrnetho away from him. Two of the brothers, Cerynes and Phalces, drove their chariots to Epidaurus and parked under the city wall. They sent a herald to the sister, asking for a meeting.

When she came to see them, they made accusations against Deiphontes, and begged her to return to Argos. They promised her a new and better and more powerful husband. Hyrnetho defended Deiphontes and told them that they should be called the murderers of their father Temenos rather than his sons. Her brothers then grabbed her and put her in their chariot and drove off with her. When Deiphontes heard what had happened, he rushed out to the rescue, followed by the citizens of Epidaurus.

When Deiphontes caught up with his brothers-in-law, he shot at Cernyes and killed him. He was afraid to shoot at Phalces, who was holding Hyrnetho, so he came up to them and tried to grab her away. But Phalces held on to her violently and in the struggle he killed her; she was pregnant at the time. Phalces drove madly off, while Deiphontes and his children took the dead body of Hyrnetho to the grove of wild olives, which is now called the Hyrnethium. They built her a hero-shrine, and they established the custom that no one could carry away any of the branches of the trees from the grove; they are left on the spot, sacred to Hyrnetho (2.28.3–7).

Pausanias is the only substantial source for the story of Hyrnetho, though other evidence suggests that her story was at least moderately well known.[3] Clearly she was regarded as a heroine, and she was given heroic honors in two cities. The Epidaurians told a dramatic story about her; no Argive story is known, though Pausanias makes it clear that the Argives claimed to have her body. Moreover, in addition to the three tribes of the Dorians – the

Hylleis, the Pamphyloi, and the Dymaneis – the Argives had a fourth tribe called the Hyrnethoi; evidently this tribe was made up of non-Dorian inhabitants of the cities (Larson 1995: 141; Kearns 1998: 106–07). Perhaps there was a tribe of Hyrnethoi in Epidaurus as well. Too much has been lost to allow any detailed reconstruction of the situation, but clearly the myth of Hyrnetho was connected to political disputes between Argos and Epidaurus and also to the social structure within these cities.

Further explorations

(1) In general the ancient Greeks made a clear distinction between the immortal gods and mortal human beings, but this distinction was challenged by some of the heroes, including Herakles, Asclepius, Ino (also known as Leukothea), Kastor and Polydeukes, and Helen, who were sometimes and in some places thought of as mortal and at other times and other places thought of as immortal. Write a short essay explaining how these heroes complicate the Greek view of the difference between gods and mortals. (2) Many of the heroes of myth were given heroic honors; some of these include Aias, one of the great heroes in the *Iliad* and also the eponymous hero of a play of Sophocles; Machaon, mentioned as a healer in the *Iliad*; Amphiaraos, one of the Seven Against Thebes; and Hippolytos, the eponymous hero of a play by Euripides. Write a brief essay on the relationship between these characters in myth and in ritual. Primary sources for these two topics could include Pausanias, Homer, Pindar, Herodotus, Aeschylus, Sophocles, and Euripides; secondary sources could include Farnell 1921, Clader 1976, Burkert 1979, Austin 1994, and Larson 2007, with further bibliography noted in these texts.

CONCLUSION

This chapter has explored the stories of four heroes, Orestes, Iphigeneia, Theseus, and Hyrnetho. Three of these heroes were figures in Panhellenic myth, as represented, for example, in Athenian tragedy, but they also have a place in local myth and local ritual. The bones of Orestes become the center of cult, and they play a role in the political conflicts between Sparta and Tegea; he also figures in aetiological myth in Athens and Troezen; he is associated with a sanctuary and features of the landscape in Arcadia and Gythion. Iphigeneia is closely associated with an important Athenian ritual practice for young girls at Brauron and also with sacrificial rituals at Halai in Attica and in Sparta. Theseus had his own festival in Athens and was associated with features of several other festivals. He was credited with bringing the towns of Attica together into a single political unit, and he became a representative figure, useful perhaps for more than one political group. Hyrnetho was a local heroine with cult in two cities, and also the subject of a local myth. Moreover, she was the eponym of one of the tribes in Argos. Like Orestes and Theseus, she became a tool of political propaganda, even if it is now impossible to recover exactly how her story was used.

There were literally hundreds of heroes in ancient Greece. Emily Kearns lists more than 250 heroes attested just in Attica. Most of these are little known today, and some were nameless even when they were the objects of cult. Today the heroes are remembered mostly as the great characters of epic and tragedy, but it is important to see them in their relation to Greek religion, society, and politics as well.

FURTHER READING

Farnell 1921 offers some useful background on hero cult but is now somewhat out of date and must be used with care. Burkert 1985: 190–215 is a good short introduction; likewise Felton 2007 and Ekroth 2007 (both in Ogden 2007). For general discussion of the concept of the hero in Greek myth, see Nagy 1979. For more specialized studies, see Kearns 1989 on Attic heroes, Larson 1995 and Lyons 1997 on heroines, and Pache 2004 on baby and child heroes. On the bones of Orestes, see Malkin 1994: 26–29 and Boedeker 1993. The complex details of many Athenian festivals are described in Parke 1977 and Parker 2005. On the festival at Brauron, see Dowden 1989: 9–47, Kearns 1989: 27–35, and Parker 2005: 232–48. On Theseus see Walker 1995.

Chapter Seven

BORN FROM THE EARTH
Founders of Cities and Families

Greek thought was often concerned with beginnings. An interesting set of myths describes the beginnings of various cities and the founders of important families in myth. These myths can give citizens the sense of a common ancestry and explain their place and the place of their city or social group in the broader Greek world. In some of these myths, such as the story of the early kings of Athens, the founders or first inhabitants sprang from the earth itself, and on this mythic basis the citizens of Athens claimed to be the most Greek of the Greeks. Other famous founders – such as Pelops, Kadmos, and Danaos – were immigrants from non-Greek territories. Pelops came from Lydia to Greece, married Hippodameia, gave his name to the Peloponnese, and founded one of the most important families in Greek myth, the House of Atreus; Kadmos, a descendant of Io, came from Phoenicia; he founded the Greek city of Thebes and the early kings of this city were his descendants. (His sister Europa gave her name to Europe.) Danaos, another descendant of Io, came to Greece from Egypt. He did not found a city, but his famous descendants included Perseus and Herakles. These immigrant heroes connected the world of the Greeks to the larger world of the Mediterranean. The foundations of the Greek colonies also placed Greeks in the larger world. Colonies often were given mythical backgrounds, and their founders, such as Battos, the founder of Kyrene in North Africa, were often regarded as heroes.

All of these founders – founders of cities within Greece, founders of important families, founders of colonies outside Greece – could be culture heroes, inventors of important social customs and rituals, and foundation myths also can be linked to features of the landscape, which often share their names with members of the founding families. These stories of foundation form part of the background of the Greek mythic tradition.

Exploring Greek Myth. First Edition. Matthew Clark.
© 2012 Matthew Clark. Published 2012 by Blackwell Publishing Ltd.

I. THE EARLY KINGS OF ATHENS

Kekrops, the first king of Athens, was born from the earth, rather than from the biological union of male and female, and he had the tail of a snake instead of legs. During his reign Poseidon and Athena held a contest for possession of the city. There are various versions of this dispute, but according to Apollodorus, Poseidon arrived in Athens first, and with a blow of his trident he created a saltwater sea on the Acropolis. Athena made her claim by planting an olive tree. The gods awarded the city to Athena; Poseidon became angry and flooded the Thriasian plain to the north-west of Athens (*Library* 3.14.1). According to another version, the people of Athens voted to determine the victor; the women all voted for Athena, and the men all voted for Poseidon. As it happened, the women had a majority of one, so the decision was made to name the city after Athena. In order to placate Poseidon the women were deprived of any future right to participate in political decisions (Augustine, *City of God* 18.9, quoting Varro).

Kekrops was something of a culture hero; he established the twelve townships of Attica; he established the bloodless sacrifices to the gods; and he originated the custom of marriage. But these stories about Kekrops may date only from the fourth century BCE (Parker 1988: 197–98).

Kekrops had a son, Erysichthon, and three daughters, Aglauros, Herse, and Pandrosos, but Erysichthon died, and Kekrops was succeeded by another earthborn king, Kranaos. According to Apollodorus, Deukalion's flood occurred during the reign of Kranaos; this version of the story seems to assume that the flood was local rather than universal (*Library* 3.14.5). According to Pausanias, the Athenians claimed that Deukalion lived in Athens; they said that he had built the ancient sanctuary to Olympian Zeus, and they also pointed out a crack in the earth where they said the water from the flood had run into the ground (*Guide* 1.18.7). Kranaos had a daughter named Atthis, and after she died Kranaos gave her name to Attica. Kranaos was succeeded by Amphictyon. Some sources say that Amphictyon was earthborn, but others say that he was the son of Deukalion. Amphictyon was driven out by Erichthonios, who was also born from the earth (*Library* 3.14.2, 3.14.5–7). Kranaos and Amphictyon have almost no function in this series, and many versions leave them out entirely, so that Kekrops, the first king, is immediately succeeded by Erichthonios.

Exactly how Kekrops was born is not explained in any surviving myth, but the story of the birth of Erichthonios is well known. Hephaistos, overwhelmed by passion, chased Athena and managed to catch her, but she resisted, and he ejaculated on her leg. She wiped the semen off with a piece of wool and threw it on the ground. The earth (the goddess Ge) then produced the child Erichthonios. Thus Erichthonios represents two forms of generation: spontaneous generation from the earth, and generation from male and female. Something like this version of the birth of Erichthonios was known very early, as is shown by a reference in the *Iliad* (though Homer calls him Erechtheus); among the Achaeans who went to Troy were

> those who held the well-built city of Athens,
> the people of great-hearted Erechtheus, whom Athena once
> nurtured, the daughter of Zeus, and the grain-giving field bore him,
> and she established him in Athens in her rich temple.
> There the young men of Athens propitiate him
> with bulls and sheep as the years turn in their course. (2.546–51)

This passage suggests that the Athenians had established hero cult for their earthborn king as early as the time of Homer.

When Ericthonios was born, Athena put him in a chest and gave him to the daughters of Kekrops with orders not to open the chest. They were unable to resist, of course, and when they opened the chest they saw a snake inside with the baby. Some say that the snake killed the girls, but others say that they were frightened and jumped off the Acropolis to their deaths (*Library* 3.14.6). Some say that only Herse and Aglauros looked in the chest and died, while the third daughter, Pandrosos, did not look in the chest and was saved.

The birth of Erichthonios is often depicted on Athenian vases of the fifth century BCE. For instance, a red-figure cup by the Kodros Painter (ca. 440 BCE) shows the goddess Ge rising from the earth holding a child, who is reaching out to Athena, while Hephaistos and Kekrops, with the tail of a snake, look on (see Figure 7.1). The daughters of Kekrops are also depicted in the painting, as well as Erechtheus and Aegeus, both later Athenian kings. As Nicole Loraux notes, the painting brings together four generations of myth in a timeless gathering.[1]

Figure 7.1   Gaia hands the baby Erichthonios to Athena as Kekrops, Hephaistos, and Herse watch. The other side of the vase shows Aglauros, Erechtheus, Pandrosos, Aegeus, and Pallas. Kodros Painter (5th century BCE). Attic red-figure kylix. Antikensammlung, Staatliche Museen, Berlin, Germany. Inv. F2537. Photo: Ingrid Geske-Heiden. Copyright © bpk, Berlin/Staatliche Museen/Ingrid Geske-Heiden/Art Resource, NY

Erichthonios does not figure in any myths after his birth and infancy. According to Apollodorus he was succeeded by his son, Pandion, the first king not born from the earth, and Pandion was succeeded by his son, Erechtheus (*Library* 3.14.7; 3.15.1). Erechtheus and Erichthonios are often confused with each other. The passage above quoted from the *Iliad*, for instance, gives the name Erectheus to the king who was born from the earth and nurtured by Athena. At some point they may have been the same figure. Sometimes they may form a sort of double, with Erichthonios as the infant part and Erechtheus as the adult part of the double, and sometimes they are clearly different (see Loraux 1993: 46–47; Parker 1988: 201).

During the reign of Erechtheus there was a war between the Athenians and the Eleusinians, who were led by Eumolpos, the son of Poseidon.[2] When Erechtheus consulted the oracle, he was told that the Athenians would be victorious if he sacrificed one of his daughters. He performed the sacrifice and his other daughters then killed themselves, perhaps because they had made a pact; but Kreousa, who was just an infant, did not die. In the following battle Erechtheus killed Eumolpos, and Poseidon in turn killed Erechtheus by driving him into the ground (*Library* 3.15.4; Euripides, *Ion* 267–82). So this king, descendant of the earthborn kings, in his death returned to the earth.

II. ATHENIAN AUTOCHTHONY

Because Erichthonios was born from the earth, the citizens of Athens had a special connection to their land, a connection to the land closer than that of the other Greeks, who had come to their cities from elsewhere, or so the Athenians believed. Because their first ancestor was earthborn, all Athenians were autochthonous ("born from the earth itself", from "autos", meaning "same" or "self", and "chthon", meaning "the earth"). The autochthony of the founder establishes the autochthony of the succeeding generations.

Autochthony was evidently an important element in Athenian thought. Not only was the birth of Erichthonios from the earth frequently depicted on vases, the idea of autochthony comes up in various literary works. Thucydides notes that early Greek history was generally characterized by a series of migrations, as a stronger tribe would push a weaker tribe to move. The only exceptions he makes are the Arcadians and the Athenians, and he specifically says that Attica was always inhabited by the same race. His explanation does not depend on myth, however; he argues that those who live in fertile areas are most likely to be displaced, while Attica was left alone because of its poor soil. Pericles, in the funeral speech Thucydides reports and perhaps partly invented, says that the Athenians have always lived in the same land (*History* 1.1; 2.36).

Lysias, in his funeral speech, makes the point very directly: "it was very fitting for our ancestors to be of one mind about the fight for justice, since the beginning of their way of life was just; for they did not, like the rest, gather together from hither and thither and expel other people and live in a land belonging to others, but being autochthonous they have possessed the same mother and fatherland" (Lysias, *Epit.* 17).

Plato, in the strange parody of a funeral speech he puts in the mouth of Socrates, also notes the importance of Athenian autochthony. He begins his praise of the noble dead by praising their forefathers. "Their ancestors were of noble birth, nor were they interlopers, nor were their fathers immigrants who came to this land from elsewhere, but they were autochthonous, actually living and dwelling in their fatherland. They were not nourished by stepmothers, as others were, but by the mother land in which they live, and now in their death they lie in their own land that gave them birth and nourished them and received them." And it is no surprise that the Athenians stood up for the Ionians against the Persian king, since the Athenians have no mixture of barbarian blood, as do the descendants of Pelops, Kadmos, Aigyptos, and Danaos (Plato, *Menexenus* 237b, 245c–d; cf. Plato, *Timaeus* 23d).

These speeches assume that autochthony gives the Athenians a kind of special status in the Greek world, though the precise implications of autochthony are never clearly stated. Perhaps it was a matter of self-understanding rather than any actual consequences in the real world. In somewhat the same way, the story of the Pilgrims has been used to give young citizens of the United States an understanding of themselves as citizens, even those whose ancestry has no close connection to these early British settlers.

The Athenian funeral speeches make no direct reference to the myths of the early kings of Athens, but the myths are the background to the speeches and without the myths these speeches would not have taken the form they have. The myths themselves, however, are prominent in Euripides' play *Ion*, which dates from between 420 and 410 BCE, after the funeral speech of Pericles but before the speeches written by Lysias and Plato.

The principal characters of this play are Kreousa, the only surviving daughter of Erechtheus; Ion, her child by Apollo; and Xouthos, her husband. When Kreousa was still unmarried she was raped by Apollo. She managed to hide her pregnancy, and when she gave birth, she hid the baby (with a few birth tokens) in the cave where Apollo had raped her. Apollo then sent Hermes to take the baby to Delphi, where he was brought up as the temple servant. Kreousa then married Xouthos, who was Aeolian rather than Athenian, but who had helped Athens in their war against the Euboeans. They have no children, and as the play begins they have come to Delphi to ask the Oracle for help.

The first dialogue of the play occurs between Ion and his mother Kreousa, though of course neither knows the truth about their relationship. When she approaches the temple he asks her a series of questions that amount to a little summary of the myths of early Athens, almost a catechism. Who are you, he asks, what is your family, and where do you come from? She says that she is from Athens, her name is Kreousa, and her father is Erechtheus. He congratulates her on her good fortune, and she tells him the good fortune goes only so far. Is it true, he asks, that your father's ancestor grew from the earth? Yes, she answers, Erichthonios, but this lineage was no advantage to her. And did Athena receive him from the earth? Yes, she took him in her hands, though she had not given him birth. And then, as we see in the pictures, she gave him . . .? To the daughters of Kekrops, Kreousa says, finishing his sentence, though they were to keep him safe, and not to look at him.

But I have heard, Ion says, that they opened the basket of the goddess. And so they jumped from the crag, she says, and died. And is it true, he asks, that your father sacrificed your sisters? Indeed, he had to kill the maidens as sacrificial victims. But you alone of the daughters lived? Yes, I was a newborn baby in my mother's arms. And did a chasm of the earth hide your father? Yes, blows from the sea god's trident killed him (Euripides, *Ion* 265ff.).

The conflict of this play is precisely the threat to the continuation of Athenian autochthony from Erechtheus down to later Athenian society. At the beginning of the play, both Kreousa and Xouthos believe that they are childless. When Xouthos asks the oracle for a child, he is told that the first person he meets as he leaves the temple would be his son, and that person turns out to be Ion. He remembers that in his youth he had dallied with a girl in Delphi, and Ion would be just the right age to be the child of that union. He accepts Ion as his son and promises him wealth and power in Athens.

When Kreousa learns that Xouthos has accepted Ion as his bastard son, she believes that she has lost any hope of producing an heir to the throne of Athens and she fears that the lineage of Erechtheus will end. She decides to poison Ion in order to eliminate this threat to herself and the house of Erechtheus.

There is a further complication, unstated, but certainly in the background to the play. According to the Athenian law at the time the play was written, even the child of Xouthos and Kreousa would not be an Athenian citizen. (Of course mythic heroes were not bound by later law, but Euripides often creates a clash between myth and contemporary reality.) The play itself offers a solution. When Ion, saved from the poisoning, confronts Kreousa, the truth about his birth comes out through the tokens she had left when she exposed him. She realizes that Ion is really her child, and Apollo's: presumably the child of a god can be an Athenian and can continue the autochthonous lineage of Erechtheus. Athena herself appears at the end of the play to explain the situation and confirm the solution. She tells Ion and Kreousa to keep the secret to themselves, however, so that Xouthos will think that Ion is his own son. She adds that Kreousa and Xouthos will have two sons, Doros and Achaios. Thus the four major divisions of the Greek people are established: Aeolians, Ionians, Dorians, and Achaeans. The Aeolians seem to have precedence, since Xouthos is an Aeolian before Ion is born and adopts Ion as his son, but the Ionians have precedence over the Dorians and Achaeans, and the various Ionian cities all descend from an Athenian king.

Most Greeks, however, would not have accepted the genealogy presented by Euripides in this play. According to the Hesiodic *Catalogue of Women*, the ancestor of all the Greeks was Hellen, and his sons were Doros, Xouthos, and Aeolos (*Catalogue* frag. 9). Apollodorus, many centuries later, presents a complicated and at times confusing genealogy. He begins with Deukalion and Pyrrha, who had two sons, Hellen and Amphictyon (who became king of Athens after Kranaos), and a daughter, Protogeneia. Hellen then had three sons, Doros, Xouthos, and Aeolos. Xouthos and Kreousa had two sons, Achaios and Ion. Hellen then gave various territories to his sons: Xouthos received the Peloponnese, Doros received the area northwest of Mount Parnassos, and Aeolos received Thessaly (*Library* 1.7.3). This genealogy does not explain how Ion fits into the lineage of the Athenian kings. Later on Apollodorus lists the Athenian kings: Kekrops, Kranaos, Amphictyon, Erichthonios, Pandion, Erechtheus, another Kekrops, and another Pandion. Ion is not mentioned in this list, although Kreousa is mentioned as one of the children of Erechtheus and as the wife of Xouthos (*Library* 3.14.1–7, 3.15.1). Apollodorus does grant that Kekrops and Erichthonios were born from the earth, but he doesn't seem to care about Athenian autochthony and the unbroken lineage of Erechtheus.

According to Pausanias, Xouthos, the son of Hellen, was driven away from Thessaly by his brothers; he went to Athens, married Kreousa, the daughter of Erechtheus, and their children were Achaios and Ion. When Erechtheus died, Xouthos was asked to choose the next king, and he gave the throne to Erechtheus' eldest son, Kekrops. The other sons drove Xouthos away, but Achaios went to Thessaly and became king there, while Ion became king of the Aigialians in the Peloponnese. But when the Athenians fought against the Eleusinians, they asked Ion to be their general. Ion was buried in Attica, but his descendants stayed in the Peloponnese until they were driven out by the Achaeans, who in turn had been driven out by the Dorians (*Guide* 7.1.2–5).

Each of these genealogies implies a particular version of the relationships among the various ethnic divisions of the Greeks. Only Euripides makes Ion a child of Apollo and a king of Athens, and only Euripides is greatly concerned with the Athenian claim to autochthony.

The myths of Athenian autochthony can be seen as part of Athenian thought about their relation to their land, their position as leaders of the Ionian Greeks, and even their claim to be the most Greek of the Greeks. As Robert Parker says, "The ideal of autochthony was a form of collective snobbery. Athenians *en masse* were invited to despise other states (Dorians above all). . . . Athenians were, so to speak, the only authentic citizens of Greece, all other groups being mere immigrants" (Parker 1988: 195). These myths – in particular, the representation in Euripides' *Ion* – can also be interpreted in their relation to Athenian thought about gender and the position of women in society, as Nicole Loraux argues in her study of Athenian ideas about autochthony (Loraux 1993).

Women held a curious position in Euripides' Athens. On the one hand they were not themselves citizens, but on the other hand they were necessary for the creation of new citizens. Athena, the patron goddess of Athens, was famously born from Zeus, and although in a sense she had a mother – Metis, whom Zeus swallowed – in another sense she was born from the male rather than from the female. Kekrops was not born from any sexual union. Erichthonios was born because Hephaistos desired Athena, but there was no sexual union; he was born simply from Hephaistos' semen thrown onto the ground; again from the male without the female. (Hephaistos, as the story was usually told, also was born from only one parent, but in this instance from the female, Hera.)

The early kings of Athens had some difficulty producing heirs. According to one genealogy, Kekrops was not followed by his son Erysichthon, but rather by the earthborn Kranaos, who in turn was followed by the earthborn Amphictyon, who was driven out by the earthborn Erichthonios. Autochthony and the continuity of the lineage of Erechtheus are important in Athenian thought, but autochthony is evidently not a secure form of reproduction.

Ion himself, as Euripides tells his story, also calls ordinary reproduction into question. At the beginning of the play, Ion has neither mother or father; in the first – false – recognition scene, he gains a father without a mother; and in the second – true – recognition scene, he gains a mother without a father.

These Athenian myths left their traces both in Athenian thought and also in the Athenian landscape and in Athenian ritual. Kekrops and Erechtheus were among the ten eponymous heroes of the Athenian tribes, and statues of both were among the statues to the eponymous heroes in the Agora.[3] On the classical Acropolis there was a large temple to Erechtheus, the Erechtheion, north of the Parthenon, beside the site of the temple to Athena Polias, which had been destroyed in the Persian invasion of 480 BCE. The surviving foundation of the temple to Athena Polias passed underneath the Porch of the Maidens, attached to the south side of the Erechtheion, as it still does today. The tomb of Kekrops, the Kekropeion, was attached to the west side, and the west cella of the temple contained the very spot where Poseidon had struck with his trident to create the salt sea on the Acropolis, and the sacred olive tree created by Athena in the contest was just outside the building (Rhodes 1995: 131; Parker 1988: 198). According to Pausanias, there was sea-water in a cistern inside the temple, and when the south wind blew there was a sound of waves; furthermore, when the olive tree was burned by the Persians, it produced a new shoot four feet long the same day (*Guide* 1.26.6; 1.27.2).

Just to the north of the Kekropeion was the Pandroseion, devoted to the one daughter of Kekrops who did not disobey Athena's order not to look inside the basket where she had placed the baby Erichthonios, and the precinct of Aglauros, who jumped from the Acropolis, is placed below the slope; and as Parker notes, "the most famous inhabitant of the Acropolis was the sacred snake that lived, very suitably, in the precinct of Erichthonios/Erechtheus, and was believed to guard the wonder child" (Parker 1988: 195–96).

According to Pausanias, there was a shrine to Hephaistos above the Kerameikos, with a statue of Athena beside it; he did not find the grouping of the two surprising, he says, since he knew the story of Erichthonios. He also mentions Ion's tomb in Attica (*Guide* 1.15.6, 1.31.2).

The Athenian ritual called the Arrephoria was most likely connected to the story of the daughters of Kekrops and the baby Erichthonios, though the very meager surviving evidence does not allow certainty. Evidently, a small group of young girls was selected every year (though some scholars say every four years) to serve as Arrephoroi (the meaning of the word is not now known; see Aristophanes, *Lysistrata* 638–47). The office was a matter of some pride, and a number of dedicatory statues have been found celebrating girls lucky enough to have been selected. These girls then lived "with the goddess" for a while (presumably on the Acropolis). They dressed in white and they were not allowed to wear gold ornaments (Parker 2005: 219, 223). They helped in the weaving of the garment for Athena (the *peplos*) which was carried in the procession of the Panatheneia. In addition to this task, the girls also took part in a ceremony which is described only by Pausanias. On the night of the ceremony, the priestess of Athena gave the girls objects in some sort of covered container. According to Pausanias, "neither she who gives it knows what it is nor do the ones carrying it understand"; whoever put the objects in the container must have known, but that operation must have been secret. The girls put the containers on their heads and then carried them down a natural underground passage near an enclosure called "Aphrodite in the Gardens". When they got to the bottom, they left the containers there and brought back other covered containers which they found there. Pausanias does not explain who had left these other containers at the bottom. This was the end of their task (*Guide* 1.27.3). According to an obscure note to the text of the satirist Lucian, the objects were models of snakes and male genitals made from dough (Parker 2005: 221).

As Parker notes, the ritual is in some ways like the story of the daughters of Kekrops and in some ways different: "the ritual moves to an ending – the bringing back to the acropolis of new sacred objects – quite absent from the story." In the ritual, then, "the real *arrephoroi* pass a test which their mythical prototypes have failed" (Parker 2005: 222). Evidently the myth and the ritual were connected in a way which made sense to the Athenians, but given the state of the evidence, it is impossible to say much more.

III. OTHER CITIES AND THEIR FOUNDERS

Although Athenian myth claimed that the Athenians alone were autochthonous and that the citizens of all other Greek states were immigrants, not everyone in Greece thought that the situation was quite so simple. Some founders, certainly, were immigrants, and myths of immigration were an important part of the Greek mythic repertoire. The most famous immigrants were Pelops, Kadmos, and Danaos; one can perhaps also add the Heraklids, whose return to the Peloponnese was discussed briefly in Chapter Six. But there were autochthonous founders outside Athens, and some foundation stories combine autochthony and immigration.[4]

Some people thought that Pelasgos, the ancestor of the Arcadians, was born from the earth. Pausanias quotes part of a poem by Asios of Samos to that effect (*Guide* 8.1.4), and Apollodorus says that Hesiod made the same claim (*Library* 3.8.1). Nothing of this is found in Hesiod's surviving works; probably Apollodorus found it in some part of the *Catalogue of Women* that is now lost. But Apollodorus seems to favor a story by Acusilaos which said that Pelasgos was the son of Zeus and the nymph Niobe. In either case, his son was the Arcadian king Lykaon, so the Arcadians were not immigrants to their land. The Greeks generally agreed that the Arcadians had lived in Arcadia from the beginning (see Chapter Four). Autochthony thus can have more than one implication: Arcadian autochthony meant that the Arcadians were primitive and almost savage, while Athenian autochthony meant that Athenians were the most Greek of all the Greeks.

Pelasgos occurs in some other stories. Pausanias says he lived in Argos and welcomed Demeter, and he locates in Argos a shrine to Pelasgian Demeter and the grave of Pelasgos himself (*Guide* 1.14.2, 2.22.1). Apollodorus says he was the ancestor of all the Peloponnesians (*Library* 2.1.1).[5]

Another early man was Phoroneus, the first inhabitant of Argos. In one of Plato's dialogues Phoroneus is called the first man (Plato, *Timaeus* 22a). He was the son of the river Inakhos, who in turn was the son of Okeanos and Tethys, although Apollodorus says that Inakhos was a man, and that the river Inakhos was named after him. He was the father of Apis and Niobe, and Niobe was the mother (with Zeus) of Pelasgos and Argos, from whom the city of Argos received its name (*Library* 2.1.1). When Hera and Poseidon were competing for Argos, Phoroneus was the judge, and he gave the city to Hera. Poseidon was angry and held back water from the region, and this is why the rivers there, including the Inakhos, dry up unless it rains. This contest is clearly very much like the contest between Athena and Poseidon for Athens. Phoroneus' tomb was in Argos (*Guide* 2.15.2, 2.20.2).

The Lakonians said that the first king in their region was the autochthonous king Lelex (*Guide* 3.1.1).[6] Lelex was followed by his son Myles, whose name means "mill" and who is supposed to have invented the millstone for grinding grain. Myles was followed by his son Eurotas, who drained the swamps to create land for cultivation; the river Eurotas is named after him. Eurotas had no male children, but he had a daughter named Sparte, who married Lakedaimon, who was the son of Zeus and the nymph Taygete, after whom the mountain Taygetus was named. Lakedaimon was followed by his son Amyklas, who was followed by his son Argalos, who was followed by his brother Kynortas. Kynortas had two sons, Oibalos and Perieres; according to Apollodorus, Perieres married Gorgophone, the daughter of Perseus, but Pausanias says that it was Oibalos who married her. In another version, Oibolos was the son of Kynortas, while Perieres was the son of Aeolos, and Gorgophone married both of them, first Perieres and then Oibalos; she was the first woman to have two husbands (*Guide* 2.21.8).

Oibalos and Gorgophone had three sons, Hippocoon, Ikarios (the father of Penelope, Odysseus' wife), and Tyndareus. After some troubles among the brothers Tyndareus became king. He had several daughters, among them Helen and Klytemnestra, who married Menelaos and Agamemnon respectively (*Guide* 3.1.1; 3.20.2; 2.21.7; *Library* 3.10.3).[7] Thus there is a direct succession (though not in the male line) from the autochthonous founder Lelex down to the point when this family merges with the immigrant family of Pelops.

Pelops (see Chapter Four), was the son of Tantalos, who was the son of Zeus and a woman named Plouto; though one source says that Tantalos' father was Tmolos (see Gantz 1993: 536) and another says that Pelops' father was Lydos (*Guide* 5.1.6). Pelops came from Sipylos, in Lydia, on the Aegean coast of Asia Minor, and he went to Pisa, near Olympia, in the northwest part of the Peloponnese, to marry Hippodameia, the daughter of Oinomaos. His sons were Atreus and Thyestes (and in some sources Pittheus, the father of Aithra, who was the mother of Theseus), and the sons of Atreus were Agamemnon and Menelaos. So these Peloponnesian royal families were a mixture of the autochthonous and the immigrant.

The line continues with the marriage of Orestes, the son of Agamemnon and Klytemnestra, and Hermione, the daughter of Menelaos and Helen. Their son was Tisamenos, who was driven away by the descendants of the Heraklid Aristomachus, including Temenos, the father of Hyrnetho, when the descendants of Herakles returned to claim their rights as rulers in the Peloponnese (see Chapter Four). Although Herakles himself was never king of any city in the Peloponnese, he served to justify the rule of his descendants and their Dorian followers. The return of the Heraklids and the establishment of Dorian rule were seen as crucial events, more important than the genealogical links with the autochthonous Lelex. As Irad Malkin notes, "not only were the Dorian Spartans new to their country but so was the ancestor of their 'returning' Herakleidai leaders. This is a far cry from the intimate, primordial, and autochthonous links with the soil which were the pride of Athenian rhetoric. Instead of hoary continuity, the Spartan alternative thrived on the break with a primordial past" (1994: 17).

Many of the figures in this early mythic history of Lakonia and the Peloponnese have left their names on the landscape or in the names of cities – the river Eurotas, the mountain Taygetus, the city Sparta, the city Amyklai, the whole region Lakedaimonia, and so on. Clearly the return of the Heraklids did mark a break in Lakonian history, but this break did not obliterate the mythic past.

Thebes, according to many sources, was founded by Kadmos, a descendant of Io, who was the daughter of the river Inakhos, which flows in the west of the Argolid. She was seduced by Zeus, who then turned her into a cow to prevent Hera from figuring out what had happened.

Further explorations

Women were not ordinarily founders of cities (but see *Guide* 5.5.5 and 8.8.4), though some – such as Io or Danaë – could be considered the mortal founders of important mythic families. In addition, many cities, regions, or aspects of the landscape were named after women. According to Pausanias, Sparta, for example, was named after Sparte, the wife of Lakedaimon, one of the early kings in Lakonia, and the mountain Taygetus near Sparta was named after Taygete, the mother of Lakedaimon (*Guide* 3.1.2; *Library* 3.1.2). Write a short essay on the use of heroines' names in ancient Greece. A good first resource for your research is the list of heroines in the Appendix to Lyons 1997; you should then consult the works referred to there for full information about the heroines in question.

But Hera, of course, did figure it out, and she sent a gadfly to torment Io.[8] Io ran over a huge portion of the known world and eventually settled in Egypt, where she became human again and where her son Epaphos was born. Epaphos married Memphis, the daughter of the Nile, and their child was Libya, who in turn was the mother of Agenor and Belos. Belos, who was the father of Aigyptos and Danaos, stayed in Egypt, but Agenor moved to Phoenicia. Thus large parts of North Africa and the Near East became linked to the traditions of Greek myth.

Agenor had two children, Kadmos and Europa, and when Europa was kidnapped by Zeus, Agenor sent Kadmos to find her.[9] Eventually he came to Delphi, where the Oracle told him to forget about Europa, but to find a cow which would guide him to a place where he should found a city. He did so, and the cow led him to a location in Boiotia. (The name "Boiotia" is related to the Greek word for "cow".) When he went to get water from a nearby spring, he found that it was guarded by a dragon, which he killed (see Figure 7.2). Athena then told him to sow the teeth of the dragon, and from these teeth grew a company of armed men, who fought with each other until only five were left alive. In most sources those five were named Echion, Oudaios, Chthonios, Peloros, and Hyperenor, and they were the first inhabitants of the new city. The names of the first four certainly suggest a connection to the earth: "Snakeman", "Earthman", "Groundman", and "Monster"; "Hyperenor" means "overweaning".[10]

Kadmos himself married Harmonia, daughter of Aphrodite and Ares, and they had four daughters, Autonoë, Ino, Semele, and Agave, all of whom are famous in other myths. Agave married Echion, one of the Spartoi, and their son was Pentheus, the opponent of Dionysos. The other Spartoi more or less disappear from surviving myth, though the seer Teiresias was descended from Oudaios (*Library* 3.6.7). Some sources suggest that the Thebans (or perhaps just the noble families) were descended from the Spartoi, but this claim does not seem to have the same importance in Theban thought that autochthony has in Athenian thought.[11] In any case, the Theban story combines several ideas. Kadmos as founder was an immigrant from Phoenicia, but he was also Greek, since he was the descendant of Io. The Thebans themselves were in a sense autochthonous, in so far as they were the descendants of the Spartoi.

The last of the famous immigrants is Danaos. He and his brother Aigyptos were the sons of Belos, who was the son of Libya and the brother of Agenor, the father of Kadmos. Danaos and Aigyptos were thus also descendants of Io. By a remarkable coincidence Danaos had 50 daughters and Aigyptos had 50 sons. The sons of Aigyptos wanted to marry the daughters of Danaos, and initially Danaos agreed. Apollodorus gives the names of all these children and tells who was supposed to marry whom (*Library* 2.1.5). Aeschylus wrote a tragic trilogy based on this myth, but we have only one play, *The Suppliant Maidens*, probably the first of

Figure 7.2   Kadmos killing the serpent before the founding of Thebes. Attributed to the Python Painter (ca. 340 BCE). Detail of a red-figure calyx krater. Produced in Paestum, found in Sant'Agata de' Goti (Campania). H. 57 cm. Louvre, Paris, France. Inv. N 3157. Photo: Hervé Lewandowski. Copyright © Réunion des Musées Nationaux/Art Resource, NY

the three plays. According to Aeschylus, the daughters rejected the idea of marrying their cousins, and they fled to Argos, where they appealed to the king for protection.[12] The people of Argos voted to take in the suppliants, and the play ends with the arrival of the 50 brothers in pursuit of their cousins.

Exactly how Aeschylus continued the story of the Danaids cannot be recovered, but the basic outline of the story is clear from other sources. For some reason the Danaids agree or they are forced to marry their cousins, perhaps after the death of king Pelasgos. But on the wedding night they all kill their husbands, except for the oldest, Hypermnestra, who spares her husband Lynkeus. According to some sources, Danaos himself ordered his daughters to kill their husbands, and since Hypermnestra disobeyed he imprisoned her or put her on trial (*Guide* 2.19.6). The idea that Hypermnestra disobeyed her father must go back to Aeschylus, since Aphrodite defends her in a surviving fragment from the *Danaides*, the lost third play in the trilogy (see Gantz 1993: 205). At any rate, Lynkeus becomes the king of Argos (perhaps following Danaos himself), and a new royal dynasty is founded.

The grandson of Hypermnestra and Lynkeus, king Akrisios of Argos, heard a prophecy that he would be killed by his grandson, so he hid his daughter Danaë in an underground

Danaë and Perseus in Art

There are many paintings of this famous scene, including an Attic red-figure krater dated around 480 BCE, and another red-figure vase dated 450–425 BCE now in the Louvre (fig. 144 in Carpenter 1991). Modern interpretations of the shower of gold include paintings by Correggio, Artemisia Gentileschi, Jan Gossaert, Titian, Rembrandt, François Boucher, and Gustav Klimt. The adventures of Perseus were a common theme in ancient Greek art (see Carpenter 1991, figs. 147–62) and in Roman art as well; a fresco now in Naples Museum shows Perseus releasing Andromeda from her chains, and another fresco from Pompeii shows Andromeda chained to a rock while Perseus flies towards her. There are modern interpretations of the adventures of Perseus by Antonio Canova, Benvenuto Cellini, and Pierre Mignard.

chamber made of bronze. Zeus, however, managed to gain access to Danaë by taking on the form of a shower of gold. The child of Danaë and Zeus was Perseus, whose many adventures included killing Medusa and rescuing Andromeda. Herakles and his cousin Eurystheus were both descended from Perseus and thus were part of the family of Danaos.

IV. MYTHS OF COLONIAL FOUNDATION

In the stories of Pelops, Kadmos, and Danaos, an immigrant becomes the founder of a Greek city or the founder of an important mythic family, though these stories make some efforts to show the Greek heritage of these foreigners. Conversely, other stories tell about Greeks who moved from their homes to found cities elsewhere, either within Greece or in various places around the Mediterranean coast. Stories of colonization sometimes combine the mythic and the historical. Many Greek cities did in fact send out colonies. This process of colonization began in the Bronze Age and extended into the Hellenistic period, with a high point perhaps in the Archaic period, on the edge of firm historical knowledge. Greek colonial narrative often links historical foundations to mythic events and mythic themes.

According to Herodotus, the island of Thera was settled by a colonist named Theras, who was the great-great-grandson of Polyneikes. Although Theras was Theban by ancestry, he was related to the Spartan royal family, and he had been made regent after the Spartan king Aristodemos died and while his two sons were children. When the children grew up, however, he decided to leave Sparta and settle in an island then known as Kalliste. Kadmos had landed on this island during his travels, and had left behind some of his followers, whose descendants had been living on the island for eight generations, so when Theras went there he was joining distant relatives.

When Theras left Sparta he took with him some Spartans and also some Minyans who had settled near Sparta. These were the grandsons of the Argonauts who had stopped at the island of Lemnos on their way to find the Golden Fleece. But these grandchildren of the Argonauts were driven away from Lemnos by a group of Pelasgians who in turn had been driven out of Attica. Initially the Spartans welcomed them and gave them land and intermarried with them, but eventually they began to become troublesome and the Spartans decided to execute them. While they were awaiting execution, the Spartan wives of these Minyans were allowed to visit them in prison. Inside the prison the wives changed clothes with their husbands, who then managed to escape and flee to nearby Mount Taygetus. Theras suggested that these Minyans join him in settling Kalliste, and the Spartans allowed them to go. The island was then renamed Thera after Theras (Herodotus, *Histories* 4.145–47).

This story sits in between the mythic period of the great heroes, such as Polyneikes, and the Archaic period, which can be called historical, more or less. (Hyrnetho, the Argive heroine discussed in Chapter Six, also belongs to this in-between period.) There may be some historical basis for the claim that Thera was settled from Sparta, but there is much less reason to think that a great-great-grandson of Polyneikes was the settler or that he took with him descendants of the Argonauts, and there is no way to establish any date for this supposed settlement.

In the seventh century BCE, the king of Thera, a descendant of Theras, happened to visit the Oracle at Delphi in the company of a young man named Battos, a descendant of the Minyan Euphemos. They received a command from the Oracle to found a city in Libya. The king replied that he was too old, and he suggested that the task would be more suitable for Battos. (Herodotus also gives another account. In this version, young Battos, who lisped and stammered, went to Delphi to ask how he could cure his speech impediment and the Oracle told him to found a settlement in Libya.)

The king and Battus returned to Thera and forgot about the command from the Oracle. Seven years of drought followed, and when the Therans consulted Delphi, they were told once again to send out a colony to Libya. Battos and a company of Therans set out for Libya and settled first on the island Platea and then later founded the city Kyrene on the coast, where Battos himself ruled as king for 40 years (Herodotus, *Histories* 4.150–55). Battos is thought to be an historical person and the foundation of Kyrene is thought to be an historical event, dated to approximately 630 BCE, though the details of the story are not likely to be true.

A generation before Herodotus told these stories about Thera and Kyrene, the lyric poet Pindar had dealt with them in three of his Victory Odes. His *Ninth Pythian Ode* was written for Telesikrates, who lived in Kyrene, and who had won the race in full armor at the Pythian games of 474 BCE. As he praises Telesikrates, he also praises Kyrene – the city, but also a woman, a maiden hunter, the daughter of Hypseus, the king of the Lapiths. Apollo saw Kyrene as she was wrestling with a lion, and he was captivated by her strength and courage. He took her off to Libya (again both a region and a goddess), where her son Aristaios was born. (Malkin 1994: 148 argues that the nymph Kyrene is the founder of the land of Libya rather than the political founder of Kyrene city, who was Battos.)

Twelve years later, in 462 BCE, Arkesilas IV, the king of Kyrene, won the chariot race at the Pythian games, and Pindar wrote two odes in honor of this victory. One of these, the *Fourth Pythian Ode*, is the longest of all Pindar's surviving poems, and one of the most complex, because of its interwoven chronology. When the events are put in order they tell the story of Jason and the Golden Fleece in some detail. Pindar emphasizes, however, a few points which are peripheral to this story as it is usually told.

When the Argonauts stop at the island of Lemnos, where the women had all killed their husbands, Pindar particularly picks out Euphemos of Tainaros, and notes that it was there that he begot the child who would found his lineage (in the twelfth triad of the ode). Whereas Herodotus speaks generally of the Lemnian children of the Argonauts, who eventually moved to Sparta and from there to Thera, Pindar focuses on one Argonaut in particular, the founder of the Euphemid line.

When the Argonauts reached North Africa, they crossed the desert, hauling their ship with them over the sands. When they reached Lake Tritonis, they were welcomed by

Eurypolos, the son of Poseidon, who offered them a clod of dirt as a gift. Euphemos accepted the gift, but he did not keep an eye on it and as they were passing Thera it was washed into the sea. This loss caused Medea to break into prophecy. If Euphemos had brought the clod back to Tainaros, she says, then his descendants in the fourth generation would have settled Libya, but since he lost the clod, Libya would be founded from Thera by his later descendant Battos, who would be called King of Kyrene when he came seeking a cure for his stammer.

As Herodotus explains the founding of Thera and Kyrene, the myth of the Argonauts lies in the background, but Pindar places the myth in the foreground; the importance of the myth, however, derives from the occasion of the ode, a victory song for the current king, a direct descendant of the founder Battos.[13]

Battos himself is at the center of another ode, the *Fifth Pythian Ode*, also written to commemorate Arkesilas' victory in 462 BCE. His story has the position almost always held by the myth in a Pindaric ode, and in a sense this positioning makes Battos into a mythic character, though historians accept him as historical. The poem makes it clear that Battos was heroized as the founder of the colony.[14]

The incident which brings Battos into the poem must have occurred early in the process of settling Kyrene. When Battos encountered wild lions they ran from him in fear of his strange accent, all because Apollo wanted to make sure that the oracle telling Battos to found the city would be fulfilled. (Apollo in this poem is Apollo Karneios, for whom the pan-Dorian Karneian festival was held. Tradition said it had been passed on from Sparta to Thera and from Thera to Kyrene. This shared festival thus signified the links of association among these three cities.) Pindar then describes two of Battos' actions in founding the city: building sanctuaries for the gods and roads where the ritual parades can pass. Now the parade passes by the tomb of Battos himself, so that Battos can hear the praises given to his descendant, Arkesilas, perhaps when this very ode was performed at the Karneian festival (see Malkin 1994: 145).

These three poems thus tie together three cities – Sparta, Thera, and Kyrene – and they tie the current generation, including the victors Telesikrates and King Arkesilas, to Battos, the founder of the city, to the age of heroes, through the gift of earth given to their mythic ancestor Euphemos, and to the union of Apollo and the nymph Kyrene. Time for Pindar – and for Herodotus – includes what we think of as myth and what we think of as history without any sharp break.

CONCLUSION

A few of these myths of founders became Panhellenic, but most were primarily of local interest. Those most concerned with the Athenian claim to autochthony were Athenians; those most interested in the details of Spartan king lists were Spartans. The details of genealogies could be contested for various reasons, and of course there were no archives against which the different versions could be judged. But these myths of foundation nonetheless served an important function for Greek thought, or for what some scholars would call the Greek imaginary. Such myths provided a connection to the landscape, as mountains and rivers and springs were named after mythical ancestors, or perhaps as mythical ancestors were given the names of these features of the landscape. These stories also showed how the various ethnic divisions of the Greeks were related to each other, though different genealogies explained these relationships in different ways. Other stories explained how the Greeks were related to other groups in the Mediterranean.

The myths of autochthony and myths of immigration seem almost diametrically opposed, but stories of both types served a role in Greek self-understanding. And the myths of colonial foundation added a historical narrative of emigration to the myths of autochthony and immigration. Moreover, these stories of founders and their descendants provided a link between the heroes of the past and the people who told the stories. It is characteristic of the Greek imagination to forge genealogies that begin in myth and end in history. The Greek myths remained great stories for later times, including our own, but it is important to see how they functioned in ancient Greek society.

FURTHER READING

Loraux 1993 includes a full analysis of the myths of the early kings and also of Euripides' *Ion*, while Loraux 2006 includes an analysis of the idea of autochthony in the Athenian funeral speeches. Parker 1988 gives a brief account of the myths of early Athens. Rhodes 1995 gives description, analysis, and photographs of the architecture on the Acropolis, including the Erechtheion. Burkert 2001: 37–63 interprets the Arrhephoria as a girls' initiation ritual. Calame 1988 gives a thorough account of the very complicated genealogy of Spartan mythology. Guthrie 1957 begins with Greek myths of creation and continues with a more philosophic discussion of the topic. The foundation stories of Kyrene have received much attention recently; see three different discussions in Dougherty 1993, Malkin 1994, and Calame 2003, the first concentrating on myth and poetry, the second on myth and history, and the third on myth and theory. On the festival of Apollo Karneios see Malkin 1994: 52–57, 143–58 and Ogden 2007: 193–96.

APPENDIX: GENEALOGIES OF ION

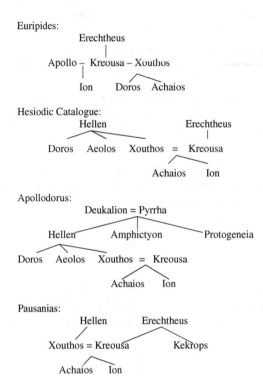

Euripides:

Erechtheus
|
Apollo – Kreousa – Xouthos
|
Ion   Doros   Achaios

Hesiodic Catalogue:

Hellen   Erechtheus
|
Doros   Aeolos   Xouthos = Kreousa

Achaios   Ion

Apollodorus:

Deukalion = Pyrrha

Hellen   Amphictyon   Protogeneia

Doros   Aeolos   Xouthos = Kreousa

Achaios   Ion

Pausanias:

Hellen   Erechtheus

Xouthos = Kreousa   Kekrops

Achaios   Ion

Chapter Eight

THE JUDGMENT OF PARIS
Comparative Myth

Many Greek myths show striking similarities to myths from other traditions. A variety of different scholarly approaches have attempted to interpret these similarities. The methods of comparative linguistics have been used to show that some Greek myths, such as the story of the Judgment of Paris or certain parts of the myth of Herakles, derive from and represent Indo-European myth and ideology. Other myths, however, such as the myth of the Flood and the Myth of Divine Succession, seem to have traveled from Near Eastern cultures to Greece in the process known as diffusion. Some scholars have argued that myths may reflect common or universal human concerns. Followers of Sigmund Freud and Carl Jung believe that myths can be interpreted in terms of universal features of human psychology; thus the study of myth is not only of scholarly interest but may also have benefits in psychotherapy. Students of comparative religion examine myths for expressions of universal religious themes, such as a concern with the sacred and the relation of human beings to divinity. All of these methods of interpretation tend to remove Greek myths from their immediate social and cultural context in order to place them in a wider context: Indo-European culture, or the various cultures of the Eastern Mediterranean, or universal features of religion or psychology.

I. GREEK MYTH AND THE INDO-EUROPEANS

The comparative study of myths derives its goals and methods from the comparative study of languages, particularly the study of the Indo-European languages, such as Greek, Latin, Sanskrit, German, English, Russian, and many others. During the nineteenth century scholars were able to show that these languages had all developed from a single language (or perhaps a small group of closely related dialects), now called Proto-Indo-European, which was spoken perhaps 6000 years ago, long before written records. As the speakers

Exploring Greek Myth. First Edition. Matthew Clark.
© 2012 Matthew Clark. Published 2012 by Blackwell Publishing Ltd.

of Proto-Indo-European gradually spread out in various directions from their homeland – the location of this homeland is a matter of some scholarly controversy – their ways of speaking changed and eventually became the various Indo-European languages, ancient and modern.

Scholars have been able to show that the historical changes in the sounds of these languages follow rather strict patterns. Thus, Proto-Indo-European words beginning with the sound "p" come into the Germanic languages with an initial "f", though Latin, Greek, and Sanskrit kept the Proto-Indo-European "p". Thus English "foot" corresponds to Latin "pes" and English "father" corresponds to Latin "pater". Similar arguments can be made about Indo-European morphology and syntax. The methods used to understand the history of the Indo-European languages have also been used to understand other language families, such as the Semitic languages, the Chinese languages, and so on.

The understanding of these linguistic relationships was one of the great intellectual achievements of the nineteenth century, and it led to the hope that the comparative method could be extended to other areas of culture, especially myth. As Gregory Nagy says, with specific reference to ancient Greece: "Just as the Greek *language* is cognate with other Indo-European languages, including Latin, Indic, and Old Norse, so also various Greek *institutions* are cognate with the corresponding institutions of other peoples speaking other Indo-European languages" (Nagy 1990a: 7).

Much of the work in comparative Indo-European myth is based on the researches of the French Indo-Europeanist Georges Dumézil, who was active from the 1930s until his death in 1986. Dumézil argued that the system of Indo-European myth ultimately derives from an ideology which thinks of society as made up of three divisions, each concerned with a particular social function. The first function was concerned with sovereignty, including religion, the second function was concerned with war, and the third function was concerned with abundance and fecundity (Dumézil 1969: ix). The extent to which this ideology reflects social reality is not clear. At first Dumézil argued that Proto-European society was divided into three classes according to this ideological scheme, but later he admitted that this claim could not be proved. On the other hand, he argued that a tripartite system was reflected in the caste structure of India, in the tribal structure of early Greece and Rome, and even in the three estates of early modern Europe (see Baldick 1994: 21–25). But many societies, even those which dropped the tripartite social divisions, still show the tripartite functions in myth.[1]

The three Roman pre-Capitoline gods, for example, represent the three functions. Jupiter represents the first function, sovereignty, Mars represents the second function, war, and Quirinus represents the third function, wealth or fecundity (Dumézil 1969: 5–6). Dumézil further argues that the early legends of Rome were historicized myth, and that these myths also show evidence of the tripartite functions (1969: 4). The first two kings of Rome, Romulus and Numa, represent two aspects of the first function, religion and law; the third king, Tullius Hostilius, represents the second function; and the fourth king, Ancus Marcius, represents the third function (1969: 7).[2] Dumézil finds similar patterns in Indic, Iranian, Germanic, and Celtic myth.

In Greek myth, the Indo-European tripartite ideology appears in the famous story of the Judgment of Paris. At the wedding of Thetis and Peleus (see Chapter Three), the goddess

Eris, whose name means "discord", caused an argument among the three goddesses Hera, Athena, and Aphrodite. She threw in front of them a golden apple inscribed with the words "For the most beautiful". Each of the goddesses claimed the apple, and they appealed to Zeus for a judgment. He wisely declined to adjudicate, so the goddesses instead went to Mount Ida, where the young Trojan prince Paris was living as a shepherd, and they asked him to judge among them. Each goddess tried to bribe Paris: Hera offered him royal power, Athena offered him victory in war, and Aphrodite offered him the most beautiful woman in the world, Helen, the wife of Menelaos. Paris, of course, chose Aphrodite, and thus the Trojan War was set in motion. In this story, the three goddesses seem to represent the three fundamental aspects of Indo-European ideology. Hera represents sovereignty, Athena represents war, and Aphrodite represents fertility (Dumézil 1969: 98).

The Judgment of Paris in literature and art

The story of the Judgment of Paris is one of the most popular of all Greek myths. Oddly enough, however, there is only a hint of the story in Homer's *Iliad* (24.28–30). Although Homer hardly mentions the story, it is told by several other Greek authors, more or less in the form given above. It was certainly narrated at some length in the *Kypria*, one of the poems in the post-Homeric Epic Cycle (the *Kypria* itself has been lost, but a late summary survives). Sophocles wrote a satyr play on the theme called the *Krisis* (*The Judgment*), but this has been lost. Euripides tells about the judgment and the bribes in *The Trojan Women* (924–37) and again in *Andromache* (274–92). Apollodorus includes the story in his *Library* (*Epit.* 3.2) and the satirist Lucian tells it at length in his dialogue *The Judgment of the Goddesses*.

The Judgment was a frequent theme in ancient art, and it continued to be popular in later art. The scene is shown on a Spartan comb from about 600 BCE, an Attic black-figure vase of about 540 BCE, an Attic red-figure vase of about 400 BCE (Carpenter 1991: figs. 290, 291, 292), an Etruscan amphora of about 530 BCE, an Attic white-ground pyxis of about 460 BCE, and a Roman mosaic from the second century CE (Woodford 2003: figs. 61, 62, 63). Among the later representations are paintings by Lucas Cranach, Albrecht Dürer, Peter-Paul Rubens, Antoine Watteau, Pierre-Auguste Renoir, Paul Cézanne, Salvador Dali, and many others.

Dumézil also finds the Indo-European trifunctional pattern in the myth of Herakles. A frequent Indo-European myth concerns a warrior who commits three sins, one against each of the three ideological functions. Dumézil finds this pattern in the Indic story of Indra, in the Scandinavian story of Starcatherus, and in the Greek story of Herakles, as told by Diodorus (Dumézil 1969: 53–104). "The career of Heracles is in fact divided into three and only three parts, each ended by a serious sin which demands an expiation.... The after effects of these sins bear heavily upon the hero, the first one in his mental health, the second in his physical health, and the third in his life itself. Finally, these sins correspond to the three functions, since they involve, in turn, a hesitation before an order of Zeus, the cowardly murder of a surprised enemy, and a guilty amorous passion" (Dumézil 1969: 97).

The first sin of Herakles occurred when he ignored Zeus' command to perform the labors in the service of Eurystheus. Hera sent madness upon him, and he murdered his children; but after his recovery he performed the labors (Diodorus 10.6–11.1). Dumézil interprets this episode as a sin against the first function, sovereignty, as represented by Zeus. The second sin of Herakles occurred when he killed Iphitos by throwing him off a tower, after which he was afflicted by a disease. The oracle of Apollo told him that he could be cured if he sold himself as a slave to Queen Omphale and gave the purchase price to the sons of Iphitos (Diodorus 31.1–4). Dumézil interprets the murder of Iphitos as an act of cowardice, since Iphitos was unarmed, and thus a sin against the second or military function. The third sin of Herakles occurred when he married Astydameia, even though he was already married to Deianeira. When Deianeira heard about her husband's new wife, she sent him a robe soaked in a potion given her by the centaur Nessus; he had told her falsely that it would work as a love charm, although in fact it was poison. When Herakles put on this robe he was attacked by a great agony, from which he was released only when he was cremated on the top of Mount Oeta (Diodorus 37.4–38.2). Dumézil interprets this episode as a sin against the third function, since it is a violation of the rules of proper sexual conduct. And so, according to Dumézil, the myth of Herakles exemplifies the Indo-European tripartite ideological system (1969: 96–101).

Dumézil's thesis that there is a common Indo-European tripartite ideology expressed in myth is based on a "fundamental assumption that basic social and religious ideas *tend* to be tied closely to the language of those who possess them, and that if the speakers of a language become separated from one another, such ideas *tend* to undergo the same sort of differential development that ultimately yields a set of related yet distinct languages" (Littleton 1966: 48).

This assumption has a certain plausibility, but its application is not simple. Comparative mythology is not fully comparable to comparative linguistics. The reconstruction of the Proto-Indo-European language and the systematic changes which have produced the later Indo-European languages are well established and widely accepted, but the analysis of Indo-European ideology remains controversial. Dumézil and his followers have been able to marshal an impressive range of research in a wide variety of mythic traditions, and while some of the parallels adduced are compelling, others sometimes seem to suggest that anything can be compared to anything.[3] Moreover, there is a distinction to be made between the general claim that Indo-European patterns of thought can be found in later myth and the more specific claim that the basis of Indo-European myth is trifunctionalism. A more flexible and inclusive interpretation of the Indo-European heritage may produce better results.

For the student of Greek myth, Dumézil's system presents a further problem. Dumézil himself has said that Greek myth provides rather poor evidence for the Indo-European tripartite ideology. "Greece, as a price no doubt of the 'Greek miracle', and also because the most ancient civilizations of the Aegean Sea very strongly marked the invaders from the north, contributes little to comparative study: even the most significant traits of the heritage there have been profoundly changed" (quoted in Littleton 1966: 54–55). The story of the Judgment of Paris certainly seems to fit the ideological pattern, and perhaps the sins of Herakles as well (though here the analysis may seem somewhat forced), but these are only two examples from an enormous body of Greek myth.

Scholars of Greek myth who accept Dumézil's assumptions and methods continue to search for additional trifunctional myths and for myths which show an Indo-European heritage in other ways, and with some success. Gregory Nagy argues, for example, that the theme of the parallelism of a hero and a god (as seen, for instance, in the relationship of Achilles and Apollo, or Odysseus and Poseidon) is part of an Indo-European pattern (Nagy 1990a: 11–12). Jean-Pierre Vernant argues that Hesiod's Myth of the Ages fits the trifunctional pattern (Vernant 2006: 25–51; see section II of this chapter for further discussion of the Myth of the Ages). And Allison Surtees suggests that representations of satyrs fall into the trifunctional pattern (Surtees, private communication).

Further research will no doubt lead to more instances of the Indo-European heritage in Greek myth. Still, there is a large group of myths, perhaps the larger part, which seem to be more closely related to Near Eastern traditions, and these are the topic of the next section.

II. GREEK MYTH AND THE NEAR EAST

After Jupiter observed the crime of Lykaon, Ovid tells us, he concluded that the whole of the human race was prone to violence and had to be eliminated. The other gods agreed, but they also wondered who would give them offerings and sacrifices if there were no human beings left. Zeus explained that he would provide a way for a new race, better than the one which had to be destroyed (*Met.* 1.163–252).

At first he considered burning the earth with his thunderbolts, but then he remembered a prophecy that one day the whole of the cosmos would be consumed by flames, and he decided to flood the earth instead. Ovid takes great pleasure in his description of the gathering clouds, the pouring rain, the swelling rivers, and the resulting destruction. He especially notes the paradoxes of trees and houses underwater, dolphins and seals in the treetops, and weary birds with nowhere to land (*Met.* 1.253–312).

The only survivors of the flood were Deukalion, the son of Prometheus, and Pyrrha, the daughter of Epimetheus, who came to land in a small boat on the summit of the mountain Parnasus in Phocis, near the temple which at that time belonged to the goddess Themis and would later belong to Apollo. No man had been better and more loving of justice than Deukalion and no woman had been more reverent of the gods than Pyrrha. When Jupiter saw that only these two had survived the flood, he scattered the clouds, calmed the seas, and dried the waters from the earth (*Met.* 1. 313–47).

Deukalion and Pyrrha realized that they were the only human beings left and that they were the total population of the world. They decided to ask Themis what they should do, and she told them to leave the temple, to veil their heads, to unbind their clothing, and to throw their mother's bones behind them. Deukalion was able to interpret the oracle: the bones of their mother were the stones of the earth. When they obeyed Themis' order, the stones turned into human beings. Those stones thrown by Deukalion turned into men and those thrown by Pyrrha turned into women. And so, Ovid says, we are a hard race, and the labors we endure give evidence of our origin. Then the rest of animal life is restored through a kind of spontaneous generation (*Met.* 1.348–421).

Ovid's Latin poem gives the most extensive surviving account of the myth of Deukalion's flood, but there are many references to the story in Greek literature and clearly the story was well known. The story is mentioned in more or less detail by Hesiod (*Catalogue of Women* frag. 234), Pindar (*Ninth Pythian Ode*), Plato (*Critias* 112a, *Timaeus* 22a, *Laws* 3.702a),

Pausanias (*Guide* 1.18.7; 1.40.1; 5.8.1; 10.6.1) and Apollodorus (*Library* 1.7.2). It is reasonable to suppose that Ovid learned the story from Greek sources, but in his version the flood is clearly a universal deluge, while in some of the Greek versions it is more localized.

The basic outlines of the story of Deukalion's flood are, of course, very much like the outlines of the Biblical story of Noah's flood in Genesis 6–8. In both stories, God (that is Jahweh or Zeus) decides that the human race has become evil and must be destroyed. In both stories he sends a great flood by releasing waters from above and below. In both stories he saves a reverent couple so that the human race can be renewed.

But the stories are also different. In the Biblical version, God warns Noah and tells him to build an ark. He tells Noah to take onto this ark his own family, his wife, his sons, and his sons' wives, and also breeding pairs of all the animals, so that the earth can be repopulated. In Ovid's version, there is no warning and only Deukalion and Pyrrha are saved (but according to Apollodorus Deukalion was warned by his father Prometheus). When the flood is over they create new human life not by reproducing themselves but by throwing stones behind their backs, and animals simply come to life from the hot mud left behind by the flood. The Biblical version includes the famous story of the birds sent out by Noah to see if the floodwaters had abated, but there is nothing like this in Ovid's version. After the flood, God promises Noah that he will not flood the earth again, and he sets the rainbow in the sky as a sign of his pledge, but Ovid's version does not include any pledge from Zeus. Despite these differences, the similarities are enough to show that the stories must be related.

Another ancient flood story can be found in the *Epic of Gilgamesh* (George 1999). This epic is a complex of stories composed in several languages – Sumerian, Akkadian, Hittite, Hurrian – over thousands of years, but all centered on the great hero Gilgamesh, the king of ancient Uruk, a city southwest of Babylon. The oldest surviving versions of the story are almost 4000 years old, but the origin of the story is still older. Gilgamesh himself may have been an historical figure from around 2800 BCE.

One of the central events of the epic is the death of Enkidu, the friend and companion of the hero Gilgamesh. When Enkidu dies, Gilgamesh realizes that he too is mortal. He has heard a story, however, about his ancestor Uta-napishti, who shared in the company of the gods and gained immortality. Gilgamesh decides to seek out Uta-napishti, who lives at the end of the world, in order to learn the secret of eternal life (Standard Version, Tablet IX). After many difficulties, Gilgamesh manages to find Uta-napishti, who tells him the story of the great flood, which came about when the gods decided to destroy the human race. Uta-napishti was warned by the god Ea and he built a boat, which is described in some detail. He loaded onto this boat his family, his wealth, craftsmen, and various animals. The flood lasted for seven days, and then the boat ran aground on the mountain Nimush. Uta-napishti sent out a swallow and a dove to see if the waters had abated, which returned because they could find no place to land, and then a raven, which did not return. Uta-napisthi makes offerings to the gods, and the mother goddess Belet-ili brings out her necklace of lapis lazuli and says that it will serve as a remembrance of the flood. The gods then make Uta-napishti and his wife immortal.

This story shares some features with the Biblical story which are missing from Ovid's version. Uta-napishti is warned about the flood, and he builds a boat, which he loads with his family and with animals; when his boat comes to ground, he sends out three birds to see if the flood is over; and the necklace of Belet-ili is no doubt the rainbow, a sign in the sky as a memorial of the flood.

These three stories must be related. Since the version in Gilgamesh is much older than the versions in the Bible and in Greek myth, it is reasonable to suppose that this version came first and diffused into the mythic systems of the ancient Hebrews and the ancient Greeks. Most likely the Hebrews learned the story during the Babylonian Captivity (586–537 BCE). When the story came into the Greek tradition is hard establish, but scholars note that there were extensive contacts between Greece and the Near East during the Bronze Age and then later in the eighth and seventh centuries BCE.

The story of the flood is by no means the only element of Greek myth that seems to have close counterparts in Near Eastern traditions. One of the most important is the Myth of Succession found in Hesiod's *Theogony*. That myth presents a series of kings of heaven – Ouranos, Kronos, Zeus – each deposed by the next, until Zeus manages to establish a permanent reign. This story has close analogues in several Near Eastern myths, including the Babylonian creation myth, the *Enuma elish*, and especially the Hittite myths titled *Kingship in Heaven*, the *Song of Ullikummi*, and the *Myth of Illuyanka* (Walcot 1966: 1–26). Although the Hittites spoke an Indo-European language, these myths seem to have been borrowed or at least influenced by Semitic cultures of the Hurrians and the Syrians (Walcot 1966: 19).

The Hittite succession myth features a succession of three kings of heaven, Anu, the sky god, Kumarbi, the corn god, and Teshub, the storm god. These correspond to Ouranos, the sky god, Kronos, probably a god of agriculture, and Zeus, who is associated with storms. In addition, certain episodes and actions appear in both the Greek and the Hittite stories: in particular, castration of a father by a son, and swallowing of children by a father, and the substitution of a stone for a child. Because these texts are fragmentary, it is not clear how closely the Greek myth resembles the Hittite myths. The Babylonian *Enuma elish* is better known, and Walcot argues that it is in some ways closer to Hesiod's Myth of Succession (Walcot 1966: 34–46). The scholarly debate about the relationship between Hesiod's Myth of Succession and these various Hittite and Babylonian myths is complex and by no means settled, but it does seem clear that there was a connection between the Greek and Near Eastern traditions.

Other myths in Hesiod have been seen to have roots in Near Eastern traditions. The Myth of the Five Ages, for example, seems to be related to a familiar story from the Biblical book of Daniel. The Babylonian king Nebuchadnezzar had a strange dream; he demanded that his wise men first tell him what the dream was and then interpret it, but they all failed. The king then called on Daniel, a young Hebrew who had been brought to Babylon when Nebuchadnezzar conquered the kingdom of Judah in 586 BCE. Daniel was able to tell the king that he had dreamed of a colossal statue, the head of which was gold, the chest and arms were silver, the belly and thighs were bronze, the legs were iron, and the feet iron mixed with clay. While the king was looking at the statue, a stone struck the feet of clay and shattered them (thus the phrase "feet of clay"). The statue fell into fragments and the fragments were blown away, while the stone which had struck the statue grew into a mountain which filled the earth. Daniel then proceeded to interpret the dream as a prophecy of a series of empires, each represented by one of the metals in the statue; the stone which shattered the statue represents the kingdom of God (Daniel 2).

The series of four metals in this story is exactly the same as the series in Hesiod's Myth of the Ages, though Hesiod adds a fifth age, the age of heroes, between the Age of Bronze and the Age of Iron. (Ovid's version of the myth – which he surely derived from Hesiod – leaves out the heroes, and so his series of metals is identical to the Biblical series.) It is difficult to imagine that this similarity is accidental. There must be some traditional pattern from which they both derive, though it is also clear that each author is using the pattern for his own purposes. One might suppose that this story is ultimately Babylonian, and that it was borrowed by the Biblical tradition and by the Greeks, just as both of these traditions borrowed the story of the Flood from Babylon.

Roger Woodard, however, notes that other versions of this pattern complicate the problem (Woodard 2007: 115–18). According to an Iranian story, the prophet Zardust (more commonly known by his Avestan name Zarathustra) dreamed of a tree with four branches, one of gold, one of silver, one of steel, and one of mixed iron; each branch represented an age. (A variant of the story lists seven branches: gold, silver, bronze, copper, tin, steel, and mixed iron.) And in Book Three of the great Sanskrit epic the *Mahabharata*, the hero Bhima, one of the sons of Pandu, is told by the ape-lord Hanuman about four ages of the world; each age is named by a throw of the dice and in each age the god Visnu takes on a different color, white (associated with the priestly class), red (associated with the warrior class), yellow (associated with the worker class), and black (associated with the slave class). These can easily be interpreted in a Dumézilian trifunctional scheme. Although there are no metals in this Indian version, it is easy to see that the basic structure of the story is the same.

A related story is found in the *Rig Veda* (10.90): when the gods sacrifice the giant Purusa, the priestly class is made from his mouth, the warrior class is made from his arms, the worker class is made from his legs, and the slave class is made from his feet. (A similar story is found in the *Laws of Manu* and also in the *Mahabharata*; see Woodard 2007: 130–31).

These Iranian and Indian stories are Indo-European, and so one might argue that the weight of evidence might suggest that the myth of four ages, or four metals, is Indo-European, and that it diffused from Indo-European traditions into the Biblical tradition (Woodard 2007: 131). Hesiod's version, then, might be a direct reflex of the Indo-European tradition. On the other hand, it may be better to relax the boundaries somewhat. The Near East, including Greece, can be seen as a complex culture area, in which several traditions, including some Indo-European traditions, came into contact and influenced each other. It is possible that an Indo-European story passed into other Near Eastern traditions and then passed into the Greek tradition through Hesiod.

Hesiod's version of the myth includes a fifth age, the age of heroes. Many scholars have argued that this addition is an ad hoc adjustment to the basic four-age system, designed simply to accommodate the heroes of Greek myth, including the heroes of the Trojan War, who could not simply be left out of Hesiod's system. But the French classicist Jean-Pierre Vernant offers an elegant interpretation of Hesiod's five ages which shows that it can be justified as a structural representation of Hesiod's thought in terms of Dumézilian trifunctionalism. According to Vernant, Hesiod's five ages divide into three aspects: the gold and silver ages represent two aspects of the first function, sovereignty, the bronze age and the age of heroes represent two aspects of the second function, military, and the age of iron represents the third function, fertility (Vernant 2006: 25–51).

Vernant's interpretation raises further questions about the place of Hesiod's story in the various mythic traditions. It might be argued that a trifunctional analysis of the myth brings it more firmly within the Indo-European tradition. It is notable, however, that the other Indo-European versions, Iranian and Sanskrit, cited by Woodard, have only four ages, not five, and that these four ages can also be understood in a trifunctional analysis. The trifunctional system seems to be able to accommodate systems of three, four, or five with equal ease. It could also be argued that Hesiod inherited a myth with four ages – either from the Indo-European tradition or from a common Near Eastern tradition – and adapted it in a way which just happens to fit the trifunctional scheme.

A number of other Greek myths seem to be closely related to Near Eastern stories. In Book Six of the *Iliad*, the Lykian Glaukos and the Greek Diomedes meet on the battlefield, and before they fight, each identifies himself. Glaukos says that he is the son of Hippolochos, who in turn was the son of Bellerophontes (who was the son of Glaukos, the son of Sisyphos). The gods gave Bellerophontes beauty and valor. Anteia, the wife of the Argive king Proitos, fell in love with Bellerophontes, but she was unable to convince him to sleep with her. She then went to her husband and accused Bellerophontes of attempted rape. Proitos was unwilling to kill Bellerophontes himself, so he sent Bellerophontes to the king of Lykia, Anteia's father, and he gave him a tablet with "baleful symbols" to give to the king, so that the king would kill him (*Iliad* 6.155–96). One interpretation of this detail suggests that these symbols were a kind of writing, unknown to Bellerophontes but known to the king of Lykia.

This story seems very similar to the Biblical story of Joseph and Potiphar's wife. When Joseph's brothers sold him into slavery, he was bought by an Egyptian named Potiphar, a captain in Pharaoh's guard, who made Joseph overseer of his house. Potiphar's wife desired Joseph, but he would not sleep with her. One day she caught him alone and tried to embrace him, and when he ran off he left part of his garment in her hand. She went to her husband, showed him the garment, and accused Joseph of attempted rape. Potiphar then threw Joseph into prison (Genesis 39.7–20).

The story of Hippolytos, as told in Euripides' *Hippolytos* and Seneca's *Phaedra*, is also related to these stories. Phaedra, the young wife of Theseus, falls in love with her stepson Hippolytos, who rejects her (in Seneca's version when he flees he leaves his sword behind). Phaedra accuses Hippolytos of attempted rape (in Euripides' version, she leaves a note which Theseus reads after she has killed herself), and Theseus curses his son. The sword in Seneca's version plays the same part as the garment in the Biblical story, but these are likely independent developments rather than evidence of direct influence.

Joseph occurs in another story which has a Greek analogue. When he is in prison, he successfully interprets dreams for two other prisoners. Later one of the prisoners, who is Pharaoh's butler, is released, and when Pharaoh has a dream, the famous dream of the seven fat cows and the seven lean cows, the butler tells him about Joseph's ability as an interpreter. When Joseph successfully interprets Pharaoh's dream, Pharaoh releases him from prison and makes him overseer of all Egypt (Genesis 40–41). The story of a prisoner who is a diviner is also found in the Greek tradition. Melampous, the brother of Bias, attempted to steal the cattle of Phylakos in order to help his brother, who wanted the cattle as the price for marrying Pero (see Chapter Three). Phylakos catches Melampous and throws him into prison. Melampous, who has the ability to understand the language of animals, hears woodworms saying that they have nearly eaten the beam in the ceiling. Melampous asks to be moved to a different cell, and when the roof collapses, Phylakos realizes that Melampous is a diviner and releases him (*Library* 1.9.12).

Other Biblical stories that seem to have Greek analogues include the story of Lot's wife, who turned into a pillar of salt when she looked back as she and her husband were fleeing from Sodom (Genesis 19). This story is often compared to the story of Orpheus and his wife Eurydike. When Eurydike died, Orpheus went to the Underworld and convinced Pluto to let him bring her back to earth. Pluto agreed, on the condition that Orpheus not look back at her as she followed him. But Orpheus was unable to restrain himself; he did look back, and Eurydike had to return to the Underworld (*Library* 1.3.2).

The story of the sacrifice of Isaac, when a ram is substituted for Isaac (Genesis 22), is in some ways similar to the story of the sacrifice of Iphigeneia, when a deer is substituted for Iphigeneia (as in Euripides' *Iphigeneia at Aulis*). The Bible also tells another story of a father – this time a military commander – who sacrifices his daughter. When the Israelite military leader Jephthah was fighting against the Ammonites, he made a vow that if he should defeat the Ammonites, he would sacrifice as a burnt offering whatever would first meet him on his return home. As it happened, the first person to greet him was his daughter, his only child. When she learned about his vow, she voluntarily agreed to be sacrificed, and afterwards the women of Israel lamented the daughter of Jephthah in an annual ritual (Judges 11).

It is not necessary to conclude that these stories show a direct connection between the Greek and the Biblical traditions, but taken all together they do suggest that there was a large common pool of Near Eastern folktales and folktale motifs.

III. GREEK MYTH, WORLD MYTH, AND PSYCHOANALYSIS

Greek myth can be studied not only in its relation to Indo-European or Near Eastern traditions, but also in the perspective of world myth. Myths often seem to address common questions, questions that are likely to arise in any human society such as: How did the cosmos come to be? How were human beings created? Why do we have to die? And some students of myth would ask a further question: What can we learn today of relevance to our own lives from ancient myth and from myths of ancient cultures? By and large, those who are asking these and related questions are less likely to be concerned with the kinds of issues discussed in the previous sections – issues of tradition, heritage, diffusion, and so on – and more likely be interested in whatever parallels and patterns they can discover in various mythic traditions, no matter how they might have come about. Two disciplines which discuss myth in the broader perspective of world myth are psychoanalysis, especially through the work of Sigmund Freud (1856–1939) and Carl Jung (1875–1961) and their followers, and comparative religion, especially through the work of the historian of religion Mircea Eliade (1907–86) and his followers.

Sigmund Freud is famous, of course, for introducing the idea of the Oedipus complex, which takes its name from Greek myth. Even so, Freud himself was not particularly interested in the study of myth and he did not write extensively about it. Some later scholars of myth, however have found his ideas useful. Richard Caldwell, for example, argues that the "most important and characteristic functions [of myth] are psychological":

1. Myths allow the expression of unconscious, usually repressed, ideas in a conventional and socially sanctioned form.
2. Myths use the emotional content attached to these ideas to energize other, non-emotional functions of myth.
3. Myths provide a societal response to psychological needs, whether universal or culture specific. (Caldwell 1990: 346)

It is easy to see Freudian themes in Greek myths, many of which do seem to involve the kinds of family conflicts that Freud finds psychologically important. But many attempts at Freudian interpretation seem to suffer from an impulse to force psychoanalytic interpretations onto stories which make better sense in other terms. For instance, many Greek myths are concerned with the question of sacrifice, its forms and justification; this theme fits poorly into a Freudian model.

Carl Jung was at first a follower of Freud but he later split from Freud and developed his own psychoanalytic theory and practice.[4] He often wrote about myth, and his interest in myth has been continued by his followers. Jung noted that certain ideas and symbols can be seen in large numbers of myths from various cultures (and, he claimed, in dreams as well). Some of these similarities can be explained as common inherited traditions or as borrowings, as discussed in the previous sections of this chapter, but other similarities are difficult to explain in these ways.

Jung argued that myths, as well as dreams and fantasies, were a manifestation of what he called archetypes of the collective unconscious. According to Jung, "elements often occur in a dream that are not individual and that cannot be derived from the dreamer's personal experience." These elements are "mental forms" which "seem to be aboriginal, innate, and inherited shapes of the human mind" (Jung 1968b: 56–57). These archetypes are found not only in the dreams of individuals, but also in myths. The archetypes are not specific representations, but general motifs. So a specific representation in a myth or in a dream is not itself an archetype, but the manifestation of an archetype.[5] Important archetypes include self, shadow, animus, anima, and persona, as well as more specific concepts, such as mother, father, child, maiden, trickster, hero, and sage. But Jung does not seem to say exactly how one decides what counts as an archetype, nor does he ever give a complete list.

By the definition of myth used in this book, archetypes do not count as myths in themselves, since they are not narratives. An archetypal figure, however, may play a role in a story; the myth of Herakles is a representation of the hero archetype, the myth of Demeter and Kore is a representation of the mother and daughter archetypes. Jungian

> **Further explorations**
>
> Caldwell 1989 presents an extensive Freudian interpretation of Hesiod's *Theogony*, in which the origin and succession of the divine figures of Greek myth are understood mostly in terms of variations of Oedipal conflict. Clay 2003, however, argues that in the *Theogony* Hesiod is reflecting on "the relationship between human beings and those powerful beings called gods. . . . Hesiod's cosmic vision offers the first systematic presentation of the nature of the divine and human cosmos, of Being and Becoming" (Clay 2003: 1–2). Write an essay comparing these two interpretations of Hesiod's *Theogony*. What questions does each interpretation seek to answer? To what extent do these interpretations conflict, and to what extent are they different but complementary?

analysis can show how myths fit into larger and perhaps universal patterns, but the danger of Jungian analysis is that it abstracts away important details of the myths in the service of archetypal analysis.[6]

The Romanian historian of religion Mircea Eliade was also interested in widespread patterns in world myth. In some ways his approach is compatible with Jungian theory; Eliade in fact often refers to Jung, and he uses the idea of the archetype, though perhaps not just the way Jung used it. Jung was primarily interested in myth as part of a therapeutic method: "myths of a religious nature can be interpreted as a sort of mental therapy for the sufferings and anxieties of mankind in general" (Jung 1968b: 68). Eliade, on the other hand, argued that the study of myth was part of the study of religion, and religion must be studied in his own terms: "To try to grasp the essence of such a phenomenon by means of physiology, psychology, sociology, economics, linguistics, art or any other study is false; it misses the one unique and irreducible element in it – the element of the sacred" (Eliade 1958: xiii). Although Eliade was an academic, and one of the most prominent figures in the academic study of religion, he was also a deeply religious person, and he saw a revitalization of religion as important to the health of the modern world.

Eliade was not primarily interested in Greek myth. He argued that the Greek myths had been "modified, adjusted, systematized" by the poets and the mythographers, and therefore they were not good evidence for the study of comparative myth. He preferred therefore to look at the myths of more traditional and archaic societies, both ancient and modern (Eliade 1963: 4). Some of his students, however, have included Greek myth in their comparative work.

Wendy Doniger O'Flaherty, for instance, places the Greek myth of Pentheus and Dionysos against the Hindu myth of Daksha.[7] Pentheus was the son of Agave, who was the sister of Semele, the mother of Dionysos. When Dionysos came to Thebes and demanded to be honored as a god, Pentheus, the young king, refused. Moreover, the women of Thebes, including Pentheus' mother Agave, had also refused to honor Dionysos, who made them insane and drove them out of the city and into the mountains. Dionysos (in disguise as a priest of his own cult) convinced Pentheus to dress as a woman and spy on the women in the mountains. The women saw him but believed that he was a lion cub; they tore him apart, and Agave carried his head in triumph back to Thebes, where her father Kadmos managed to get her to see what she had done. This, in a very abbreviated form, is the story told by Euripides in the *Bacchae*.

In the myth of Daksha, also much abbreviated, the god Shiva had married Daksha's daughter Sati against Daksha's will. When Daksha was sacrificing, he refused to invite Shiva or Sati. Sati went to the sacrifice and in her anger and humiliation she burned herself. Shiva then created a demon, which found Daksha, tore off his head, and threw the head into the sacrificial fire. The gods went to Shiva and promised him a share in the sacrifice if he would restore Daksha. Shiva restored Daksha but gave him the head of a goat. Daksha now praised Shiva, who allowed the completion of the sacrifice, in which he received a full share (based on O'Flaherty 1995: 98).

Clearly these are not the same myth. O'Flaherty does argue, however, that they have some shared features and that they are concerned with similar issues. Both Shiva and Dionysos are outsider gods; Pentheus, Dionysos' relative, refuses to acknowledge Dionysos, and Daksha refuses to acknowledge Shiva; and both Pentheus and Daksha themselves become sacrificial victims of a sort. Both female relatives – Sati and Semele – are destroyed by fire (though I think O'Flaherty does not make this point). Both myths, as O'Flaherty understands them, "teach us that, as we are animals, we are sacrificed to the gods; and as we are unbelievers, the gods draw us into their sacrificial rituals" (O'Flaherty 1995: 110). O'Flaherty does not argue that either myth is derived from the other, nor that they are both derived from a common source. She does argue that they (and other myths, including the myth of Jesus) are concerned with the same issues. In order to make this argument, she must find a general resemblance and ignore some specific details, the kinds of details that tie each myth to its own cultural context. For instance, Sati's death by burning, according to O'Flaherty, is an aetiology of the Hindu practice of *suttee* (O'Flaherty 1995: 20), but Semele's death by burning is not linked to any such practice.

CONCLUSION

There can be no methodological objection to generalization; without generalization scholarship could never move beyond the mere collection of facts. But each scholar has to decide when generalization will produce the most worthwhile results, and when attention to detail is more fruitful. There is no universal or permanent answer to this question. The approaches discussed in this chapter seek commonalities between Greek myth and other traditions. Some scholars use the methods of comparative linguistics to show that some Greek myths, such as the Judgment of Paris, derive from an Indo-European stock of stories, while others relate Greek myths to Near Eastern traditions, as in the Myth of the Flood or the Myth of Succession. Psychoanalytic interpretations argue that myth derives its themes and its emotional force from universal features of the human unconscious. Scholars of comparative religion seek general or universal religious themes, often in the service of personal growth (if not quite the kind of therapy which motivates psychoanalytic inter- pretations). For all these purposes, broad cross-cultural comparisons can lead to general and perhaps even universal spiritual lessons. Because these broad comparisons omit the kinds of details which tie Greek myths to ancient Greek culture and social practices, they do not give us much help in understanding the particular role of myth within ancient Greece. On the other hand, an exclusive attention to the details of Greek myth can lose sight of important general themes expressed in Greek myth.

FURTHER READING

Only a selection of Dumézil's many publications have appeared in English, but the basic themes of his system may be found in Dumézil 1969, and in many other publications. For a good summary and discussion of Dumézil's theories, see Littleton 1966. Nagy 1990a is largely concerned with various aspects of the Indo-European heritage in ancient Greek culture. Baldick 1994 includes a useful summary of recent comparative work as well as an extensive analysis of the *Iliad* and the *Odyssey* in trifunctional terms; his work demonstrates both the advantages and dangers of the approach. For an ideological critique of Dumézil's work, see Lincoln 1991: 231–68. On Near Eastern influences on Greek mythology, see Walcott 1966, Penglase 1994, and West 1997. For Freudian interpretations of various myths, see Slater 1968 and Caldwell 1989 and 1990. For a critique of the application of Freudian method to Greek myth, see Csapo 2005: 80–131. On Jungian analysis of myth see Jung 1968a and 1998, and von Franz 1972. Kerényi's archetypal studies of Greek myth include Kerényi 1967, 1973, 1975, 1976, and 1997; see also Jung and Kerényi 1963. On mythological analysis within comparative religion, see Eliade 1954, 1958, 1959, 1963, and 1977; also O'Flaherty 1995 and Doniger 1998. Ellwood 1999 is a critique of Jung and Eliade (and Joseph Campbell) in political terms.

Chapter Nine

BOYS IN DRESSES, BRIDES WITH BEARDS
Myth and Gender

Questions of gender are pervasive in Greek myth. One of the tasks of any culture is to teach its children how to become adults – how boys can become men and how girls can become women – and then to teach both men and women how to live with each other. Ancient Greek myths often reflected and perhaps formed Greek thought on these subjects, but not in any simple way. The roles of men and women in ancient Greek society were sharply distinguished, and Greek myth often reflects this division of roles. At times myth seems to confirm this division, but at other times myth seems to question or even destabilize the ancient Greek gender system.

This chapter begins by exploring myths and rituals connected to the maturation of young boys and girls. Initiation myths and rituals are common in most cultures around the world, and in many societies every young person must go through some sort of initiation ritual. Modern Western society is in general rather poor in such initiation myths and rituals. In ancient Greece various rites of passage for young people took place in various cities, but often these were carried out by only a few people, a selection from among the total population.[1] Some of these rituals involved practices which we would find odd or even disturbing today.

Other myths deal with the relationship between men and women in Greek society. Some of these are spectacular stories of violence, sometimes directed by men against women, and sometimes directed by women against men. These have been interpreted as evidence of a fundamental patriarchal oppression of women and of a deep-seated hostility between the sexes, but there are other stories that show a sincere affection between married couples.

Exploring Greek Myth. First Edition. Matthew Clark.
© 2012 Matthew Clark. Published 2012 by Blackwell Publishing Ltd.

I. BOYS AND MEN

Young boys in Crete, according to the geographer Strabo, ate in the community's men's house, a separate structure just for the use of men, but they sat on the ground wearing shabby clothing, and they waited on the adults. Older boys were organized in troops, which ran races and hunted; on set days the troops would fight each other. All the boys of the same age married at the same time, though they did not take their brides home until the girls were ready to manage a house (*Geography* 10.4.20).

Some boys were also abducted by older men in a formalized custom which amounted to a maturation ritual. An older man would inform the friends of his chosen youth beforehand, but it was forbidden for the friends to prevent the abduction. On the appointed day, provided that the older man was suitable, the boy's friends would hand the boy over. The older man would then give the boy presents and take him away to the country, accompanied by the others who were party to the abduction, and they would hunt and feast for two months. The older man would then give the boy military clothing, an ox, and a drinking cup,[2] and they would return to the city. The boy would sacrifice the ox and at the ceremony he would have the opportunity to express his displeasure and get rid of his lover. But Strabo adds that it was considered disgraceful for a handsome boy or for a boy with illustrious ancestors not to have a lover, and the boys who have gone through this abduction receive honors and wear special clothing (*Geography* 10.4.20–21). This custom has the general characteristics of a maturation ritual, but it was restricted to a small group within Cretan society.

This Cretan custom is somewhat like the story Pindar tells in his *First Olympian Ode* (see Chapter Four), in which the young Pelops is abducted by Poseidon and then returned to society with gifts (Vernant 1982: 20; Nagy 1990b: 129–30). The gift Pelops receives is the chariot team with which he wins Hippodameia, so the boy's relationship with an older man is not inconsistent with a later heterosexual marriage, either in the myth or in historical Cretan society. Pindar was not Cretan, and the story in the ode is not the myth of the Cretan custom, but it seems that the Cretan custom and Pindar's story of the abduction of Pelops draw on common Greek ideas.

Sparta also had a formalized maturation custom for boys, again probably restricted to a small group within the ruling class. The members of this class, called "Spartiates", were the only full citizens of Sparta, and they devoted their lives exclusively to military training and warfare. Those in the lowest class, called "helots", who had originally been free inhabitants of territories conquered by the Spartans, were slaves of the state; they were agricultural workers, and their service freed the Spartiates from any work except for warfare. Every year the chief magistrates of Sparta, the "ephors", officially declared war on the helots. (There was also a class called the "perioikoi", who were free but not citizens.)

In the Spartan custom called the "krypteia", a select group of boys from the Spartiate class was sent out into the countryside for a period, perhaps in the winter, armed only with daggers. They had no provisions and had to live on whatever they could find or steal. During the daytime they hid themselves, but at night they came out and killed any of the helots they came across. (Plutarch, *Lycurgus* 28; Plato, *Laws* 1.633).

Pierre Vidal-Naquet has argued that the situation of the boys in the krypteia was systematically opposed to the regular situation of an adult Spartan hoplite warrior: hoplites fought in an organized formation, the phalanx, while the boys went out alone or in small irregular groups; the hoplites were heavily armed, while the boys had only daggers; the hoplites fought in open fields, while the boys lived and fought in the countryside and in the mountains; the hoplites fought in the summer, while the boys (probably) were sent out in the winter; the hoplites fought during the day, while the boys hid during the day and came out at night; the hoplites dined together in a common mess called the "syssition", while the boys ate whatever they could find; the hoplites stayed near Sparta unless they were on campaign in a foreign territory, while the boys were in the frontier areas, in between Sparta and enemy territory (Vidal-Naquet 1986: 113). Thus the custom of the krypteia is an inversion of normal adult male life in Sparta; such inversions are common in rites of passage.

The Spartan custom has some similarities to the Arcadian myth of Lykaon and its associated rituals (see Chapter Four). According to some sources, select Arcadian boys would spend a period living in the bush as "wolves", but at the end of that time they would return and once again become part of society, just as the Spartan boys lived in the countryside and then returned to become Spartiates. The story of Lykaon includes elements of violence against other human beings, in the form of cannibalism, while the young Spartan boys are allowed to hunt and kill helots. The story of Arcadian Lykaon cannot be considered the myth of the Spartan krypteia, but both the myth and the historical practice involve initiation through temporary exclusion, violence, and inversion of normal patterns of life.

Young men of Athens, the ephebes, also spent some time in military training at the edges of Athenian territory. At the age of 18 they were first given a year of military training, and in the next year they were sent to the countryside where they served as *peripoloi*, that is, frontier guards. This service at the frontiers was quite unlike the standard adult service of hoplites in full armor fighting in open fields. While they were serving at the frontier, the young men were exempt from civic duties and excluded from civic rights, but at the end of this period the young men became full citizens. As in the Spartan krypteia, the young men went through a period of temporary exclusion, violence, and inversion. The formalization of this system, the Ephebia, came only in the mid-fourth century BCE, but it clearly has ancient roots in Athenian culture (see Vidal-Naquet 1986: 97).

Athenian boys were registered as citizens in kinship groups called phratries, and after the reforms of Kleisthenes in the late sixth century BCE, they were also registered in political groups called demes, though the details of these registrations are not completely known. A part of the boys' initiation and registration took place at a festival called the Apatouria, which lasted for three or four days during the month of Pyanepsion. (The Oschophoria also took place during Pyanepsion; see below.) Each phratry organized its own celebration of the Apatouria, but the various celebrations all had the same format. The first day of the festival, called Dorpia, probably consisted of a communal meal; the second day, called Anarrhysis, was a day of sacrifice; and the third day, called Koureotis, was the day on which boys were registered as members of the phratry. Evidently baby boys born since the last festival were registered, and boys aged 16 cut their hair and dedicated it as a symbol of reaching adulthood (Parke 1977: 89).

The name of the festival was understood by folk etymology to be connected to the Greek word *apate*, which means "deceit", and an aetiological myth about deceit was associated with the festival.[3] During a war between the Athenians and the Boiotians, the two sides agreed to settle their dispute through a duel. The Athenian king Thymoites was too old to fight, so an Athenian warrior named Melanthos or Melanthios ("the black one") volunteered to fight the Boiotian king, whose name was Xanthos or Xanthios or Xanthias ("the fair one"). During the fight, Melanthos suddenly shouted out that Xanthos was cheating, because he had someone fighting along side him. Xanthos looked around to see who was there, and Melanthos took the opportunity to kill him. Some ancient sources say that Melanthos was simply tricking Xanthos, but others say that the extra fighter was an apparition of Dionysos of the Black Goatskin. At any rate, Melanthos won the fight and became king of Athens, and the festival of the Apatouria was founded as a memorial of the event (Parke 1977: 90; Vidal-Naquet 1986: 110).

The Oscophoria, which was celebrated during Pyanepsion, has also been interpreted as a festival of initiation (see Chapter Six, section III). The festival was linked to events in the early life of Theseus, who was in many ways the prototypical Athenian ephebe, a boy who is an outsider, who performs great deeds, and who is then recognized as a citizen. The association of Theseus with the Oscophoria may be late, but the festival includes events which can be seen as typical of rites of initiation whether or not they are directly linked to Theseus.

The festival included a procession led by two boys dressed as girls. According to the aetiological myth, Theseus had included two boys dressed as girls in the group of young Athenians sent to feed the Minotaur in Crete, but this detail could be a story to justify an already existing custom. After the procession led by the boys reached the temple of Athena Skiras in Phaleron, there was a race of older boys back to Athens.

Thus the festival has several aspects typical of rites of initiation: first, the procession away from the city, led by boys in women's dress; second, a journey to a marginal area; and third, a display of masculine athleticism as the boys return to the city (Walker 1995: 100–01). Though Walker claims that the Oscophoria was "clearly a festival of initiation", no boys were actually initiated during it, so it may be better to think of it as a festival mimicking various features of initiation. Cross-dressing is a frequent feature of initiation rituals in Greece and elsewhere; the feminization of the boys marks them as opposite to adult men, so that their initiation as adult men is all the more dramatic.

Several other Greek myths include cross-dressing. Thetis, for instance, attempts to keep her young and still beardless son Achilles out of the Trojan War by hiding him among a group of girls on the island of Skyros; but when Odysseus displays weapons of war, Achilles cannot restrain his excitement, and so his identity is discovered (*Guide* 1.22.6; *Library* 3.13.8; Hyginus, *Fab.* 96; *Met.* 13.162–70). When Herakles was sold to Queen Omphale of Lydia as punishment for his murder of Iphitos, she made him dress in women's clothing and weave cloth, while she wore his lion's skin (Ovid, *Heroides* 9 and *Fasti* 2.303–58;). Both Achilles and Herakles managed to father children while they were disguised as women, so the cross-dressing did nothing to diminish their virility. A rather different story occurs in Euripides' *Bacchae*, where Dionysos tricks Pentheus into wearing women's clothing to go up into the mountains to spy on his mother and the other women of Thebes. The women see him but in their madness they think he is a lion cub and tear him apart.

Some myths tell about actual changes in gender, such as the story of Leukippos, who was born female and then became male; the moment when he took off the clothing of a girl and was revealed to be a man gave its name to a Cretan festival, the Ekdysia ("Undressing"). Dowden argues that this story of Leukippos originated as a story of initiation, as did the somewhat similar story of Kaineus (Dowden 1989: 65–67; cf. Delcourt 1961: 4, 33–34).[4] But the story of Teiresias, who was born male, became female, and then became male again, is "perhaps the Greek interpretation of the artificial androgyny of the shamans" (Delcourt 1961: 42).

Many Greek myths can be interpreted as myths of boys' initiation, including, for example, the myths of Chrysippus, Hyacinthus, Narcissus, Cyparissos, Philoctetes, Admetos, Kadmos, and Hippolytos (see Sergent 1986). Some of these seem to narrate successful transitions to adulthood, but others, such as the myth of Hippolytos and the myth of Pentheus, tell about a boy's death and consequent failure to become adult. (Though the death of the boy can be interpreted as his death *as* a boy and thus a successful initiation into adulthood, especially if there is some return to life, as in the story of Pelops.) A few of these myths can be linked to specific rituals, but others seem to use the symbolism of initiation without reference to any specific custom. Any story which gradually became detached from actual ritual, for example in the process of Panhellenization, at the same time became available for independent narrative evolution and elaboration, even though it may have retained the structure of an initiation ritual.

The proliferation of myths directly or indirectly connected to initiation suggests that the boy's transition to adulthood was an important theme in ancient Greek thought. These stories show that the image of the adult male in ancient Greece was closely linked to hunting and more particularly warfare. To be a man was to be a fighter, at least in the Greek imagination, whatever other tasks and duties faced men in daily life.

II. GIRLS AND WOMEN

Women's lives in ancient Greece were in general more restricted than men's lives, though how great these restrictions were remains somewhat controversial.[5] It is likely that different places and different times had different rules and practices, and some scholars believe that the best known society of ancient Greece – classical Athens – was among the most restrictive. According to the Athenian general and politician Pericles (as Thucydides reports), a woman's virtues consisted of two elements: a woman should not show more weakness than is natural to her sex, and she should not be talked about either for good or for evil among men. Much evidence from literature and the law courts shows that the wives and daughters of Athenian citizens did not move freely in the city and did not participate in public affairs, and though women in some other places may have had somewhat more freedom, never in ancient Greece was there anything close to equality of the sexes. Women's lives were domestic; if the ideal task for men was protecting the city in war, the ideal task for women was care of children and home.

In myth, however, women were by no means weak or silent. Helen, Penelope, Klytemnestra, Medea, Antigone are all strong characters with a lot to say, and they all contribute to the Greek image of women. Virtually all of the literary versions of the myths that we have were written by men. It is possible that women had some role in the creation and transmission of myth in the oral tradition, but what women thought about themselves is difficult to discover. What Greek men thought about women, however, is told in abundant (and contradictory) detail, and more can be learned from examining rituals involving women.

In Aristophanes' play *Lysistrata*, in which the women of Athens and Sparta go on a sex-strike in order to end the Peloponnesian War, the women of the chorus (using the collective singular pronoun "I" to represent the group) defend their right to take part in public affairs by recounting their service in various rituals: "at the age of seven, I carried the holy vessels as an *arrephoros*, at ten I ground grain as an *aletris* for the goddess, then I was a bear in a yellow dress at Brauron, and as a tall and pretty girl I carried the basket as *kanephoros*, wearing a necklace of figs" (*Lysistrata* 641–47). Here Aristophanes presents a list of four Athenian rituals in which young girls played a greater or lesser role.[6]

The *arrephoroi* were the four young girls who assisted in the weaving of the garment for the great statue of Athena and who also carried the baskets with secret contents down from the Acropolis, as described in Chapter Seven. An *aletris* ground grain for some ritual, probably for Demeter or Athena, but nothing more is known about this service (Parker 2005: 223). *Kanephoroi* carried special baskets containing a knife and barley grains for sacrificial rituals. Probably every sacrifice required *kanephoroi*, but the most notable were those in the Panathenaic procession. The *kanephoroi* were probably girls of marriageable age, perhaps 14 or so (Parker 2005: 223–26).

The best known of the rituals in Aristophanes' list was the service at Brauron (Parke 1977: 139–40; Dowden 1989; Parker 2005). Although the details of this ritual service are controversial, the basic outlines are reasonably clear. Evidently a number of Athenian girls, probably between the ages of five and ten years, spent a prolonged period at the sanctuary, perhaps as much as a year. During this period they were called "bears". Perhaps every year, and certainly every fourth year, there was a festival, the Arkteia, when the little girls put on some kind of performance, perhaps including a dance or a race or both. (Related rituals were held on the Acropolis, at Munychia –citadel of Peiraeus, the port of Athens – and also at Halai, not far from Brauron.)

Some ancient sources say that all Athenian girls were expected to participate in this ritual before they married, but other sources suggest that only a few girls participated; the archeology of the site does not provide enough room for large numbers of residents. Perhaps all girls dedicated little pottery offerings to Artemis, and this offering constituted their participation in the ritual (Dowden 1989: 27–28).

According to a myth recorded in the Byzantine encyclopedia called the *Souda*, once upon a time a tame bear lived near the sanctuary at Brauron. One day it scratched the face of a young girl who was playing with it, and the girl's brothers killed the bear. The Athenians thereupon suffered from a plague, and they were told by an oracle that their daughters had to perform service as bears (Dowden 1989: 21).

This myth is similar to another myth, also recorded in the *Souda*. According to this myth, a bear which appeared in the shrine at Munychia was killed by some Athenians. A famine followed, and an oracle said that the famine would end if someone would sacrifice his daughter to Artemis. An Athenian named Embaros agreed, on the condition that the priesthood of Artemis would thereafter remain in his family. But when the time came for the sacrifice, Embaros hid his daughter inside the temple and substituted a goat dressed up as a girl (Dowden 1989: 21; Parke 1977: 138).

These two stories are clearly related to the story of Agamemnon's sacrifice of Iphigeneia at Aulis and her last-minute replacement by a deer. According to Euripides, Iphigeneia was a priestess at Brauron and her tomb was there (*Iphigeneia in Tauris* 1435–74). Moreover, an Athenian historian named Phanodemus claimed that the sacrifice of Iphigeneia actually took place at Brauron, and the animal substitute was a bear rather than a deer (Parker 2005: 238–39). This version could be merely an attempt to explain the connection between the myth of Iphigeneia and the ritual of playing the bear at Brauron. Bears, however, are frequently associated with Artemis; for example, after Kallisto has been seduced by Zeus, Artemis changes her into a bear.

But Artemis is also associated with deer, and the substitute victim for Iphigeneia is clearly a deer. Dowden notes that three ancient inscriptions from Thessaly use the obscure verb *nebeuo* in relation to Artemis; he suggests that the verb is related to the noun *nebros*, meaning "deer", so that the verb would mean "to play the deer", just as the verb *arkteuo*, related to the noun *arktos*, "bear", means "to play the bear" at Brauron. Perhaps, then, the sacrifice of Iphigeneia at Aulis was related to a ritual of "playing the deer for Artemis", just as the myths at Brauron and Munychia were related to a ritual of "playing the bear" (Dowden 1989: 41). Io's transformation into a cow might be part of a similar pattern (Dowden 1989: 134). These girls' rituals can be compared, for instance, to the ritual in which Arcadian boys "played the wolf". All of these myths and rituals take the form of a typical rite of passage, including seclusion, transformation, ritual death, and reintegration into society.

These stories of animal transformations are related to (and partly overlap) a set of myths designated by Burkert as "the girls' tragedy", which has five fundamental plot elements: (1) leaving home; (2) seclusion; (3) rape; (4) tribulation; and (5) rescue. He includes in this group the stories of Kallisto, Auge, Danaë, Io, Tyro, Melanippe, and Antiope (Burkert 1979: 6–7). Another common element in all these stories is childbearing: each of these girls is the mother of a son who is then the founder of a city or of an important mythic family. This pattern seems again to symbolize the maturation of a girl through the tribulation of an initiation ritual. The element of childbearing is in fact crucial, both in this mythic pattern and in society: girls mature in order to have children. This function is true for the heroines of myth, but it is no less true for any Greek girl.

Another ritual pattern of initiation for girls would turn them temporarily into boys or men, as other rituals temporarily turn boys into girls, either in behavior or in appearance. Girls in stories of this type typically reject marriage and childbearing, the fundamental roles of women in ancient Greece, and typically hunt in the wilds rather than stay at home to weave. This pattern is apparent, for instance, in the story of Kyrene, or Kallisto, or Daphne. All of these mythic women reject marriage and become hunters instead. But their attempts to take on a man's role end in failure. Kyrene is abducted by Apollo and becomes the founder of a royal dynasty. Kallisto is raped by Zeus and is turned into a bear; her son Arkas becomes the founder of the Arcadians. Daphne is pursued by Apollo and becomes a laurel tree.[7]

Atalanta, according to Apollodorus, was the daughter of Iasos and Klymene (in other sources her father's name was Schoineus or Mainalos) but her father wanted only male children and so he exposed her. She was found and suckled by a she-bear, and then eventually she was adopted and raised by hunters. When she grew up she rejected marriage and spent her time hunting. Two centaurs tried to rape her, but she killed them. She participated in the Calydonian Boar Hunt and the quest for the Golden Fleece; at the funeral games for Pelias she wrestled Peleus and defeated him.

Eventually Atalanta found her birth family. When her father Iasos wanted her to marry, she declared that she would marry any man who could beat her in a race. She would give any suitor a head start, and she would follow, fully armed; if she caught up with the suitor she would kill him. She had killed many suitors when her cousin Melanion challenged her. Aphrodite had given him three golden apples, and as Atalanta tried to catch up to him, he threw down the apples in succession. She stopped to pick them up, and Melanion won the race. Atalanta married Melanion (though other sources say she was married to Hippomenes), but she continued to hunt along with her husband. One day when they were hunting, they stopped to make love in a sanctuary of Zeus, and for this sacrilege Zeus turned them into lions (*Library* 3.9.2). Atalanta, unlike Daphne or Kallisto, manages to continue her career as a hunter after her marriage. Thus the tradition did not universally insist that a woman had to be tamed and domesticated.

This complex story may be a conflation of two different stories about two different mythic women named Atalanta (Gantz 1993: 335–39). Atalanta the daughter of Schoineus rejects marriage and sets up a race for her suitors; Atalanta the daughter of Iasos is exposed and raised as a hunter. The first Atalanta marries Hippomenes and the second marries Melanion. It is curious, however, that there should have been two different stories about two different women who both rejected marriage and became hunters and who both were named Atalanta.

The myths do not explicitly say that any of these women hunters dressed as men; perhaps one could assume that any hunter would have to wear hunter's clothing. Several illustrations of Atalanta clearly show her in men's clothing (Carpenter 1991: figs. 282, 284, 285). Fewer women than men cross-dress in ancient myth and ritual, probably because men's rites of passage were socially more important, but a few instances are known. According to Plutarch, in Sparta a bride's head was shaved and then she was dressed in men's sandals and cloak; she then went to bed on a pallet on a the floor in the dark; her husband ate dinner with the men and then came to her secretly (Plutarch, *Lycurgus* 15).

In Argos, according to Plutarch, women wore false beards when they went to bed with their husbands. He explains this custom with a story. When king Kleomenes of Sparta attacked Argos, the poetess Telesilla organized the women to take up arms and the city was saved. This victory is still marked by a "Festival of Daring", during which the women dress as men and the men dress as women. After the war, because of the scarcity of men, the women found husbands from neighboring subjects, but they showed them disrespect and indifference, and therefore the Argives made it a law that a bride has to wear a beard when she goes to bed with her husband (Plutarch, *Virtue of Women* 245).

This ritual had evidently lost its meaning by Plutarch's time, and thus he resorts to historical aetiology. The Spartan and Argive rituals of women's cross-dressing fit into the general pattern of maturation rituals, and no doubt there were more that have not been recorded.

III. WOMEN ONLY

Although Greek women did not freely participate in public life, they were allowed to participate in many religious festivals, and a few festivals were actually restricted to women. The festival for Demeter called the Thesmophoria was one of these; this was one of the most widely celebrated festivals in the ancient Greek world, but much of what we know concerns the Athenian festival. Part of the festival was a mystery, and men were not supposed to know about it, though, as Parker notes, men probably had a general idea of what went on (Parker 2005: 272).[8] There was a story that Battos, the founder of Kyrene, tried to find out about the festival, but he was discovered by the women and castrated (Aelian frag. 44). A group of Lakonian women who were celebrating a festival for Demeter, perhaps the Thesmophoria, attacked a group of men with the knives and spits they were using in the sacrifice (*Guide* 4.17.1).

The evidence suggests that only the wives of Athenian citizens participated in the Thesmophoria. Girls did not attend, nor did slaves or concubines. If a woman lost her status – for instance, if she were convicted of adultery – she would be excluded from the festival.

The festival took place over three days in the month of Pyanepsion, just after the Oschophoria and the Theseia and the Stenia, which was another festival for Demeter. The first day was called "Anodos", or "Going up"; the second day was called "Nesteia", or "Fasting", and the third day was called "Kalligeneia", or Fair Birth. On the first day of the festival, women left their homes and set up huts or tents in various places around Attica. On the second day they fasted and evidently sat on mats woven for the purpose out of plants that were supposed to reduce sexual urges. On the third day there was a feast, and some of the evidence suggests that the women performed the sacrifice for themselves, rather than calling on men to help. At some point in the festival the women made obscene jests and insults, perhaps in imitation of an incident in the story of Demeter and Persephone, when a woman named Iambe or Baubo got Demeter to laugh by doing something obscene. Or perhaps the story of Iambe was invented to explain the obscene jokes at the festival.[9]

At some time before this festival – though it is not known for certain when – piglets had been thrown into pits to die and rot, perhaps along with figurines made of dough in the shape of male genitals and snakes. During the festival, some of the women would climb down into these pits and gather the rotted material which was then placed on altars; anyone who used it as fertilizer was supposed to be assured of a good crop. This part of the ritual was linked to another incident in the story of Demeter and Persephone; when Pluto came to abduct Persephone, a swineherd named Eubolos was swallowed in the chasm along with his pigs. It is worth mentioning also that "pig" was the common slang term for female genitals (for details of the Thesmophoria, see Parke 1977: 82–88; Detienne and Vernant 1989: 129; Parker 2005).

The Story of Myrrha and Adonis

According to Ovid, Adonis was the son of Cinyras, who was in turn the grandson of Pygmalion, the sculptor who made a statue so beautiful he fell in love with it. Cinyras (or Theias) had a daughter named Myrrha (or Smyrna); Myrrha failed to honor Aphrodite, and Aphrodite punished her by making her lust after her own father. With the help of her nurse, she managed to sleep with her father for twelve nights before he recognized her. When he realized what had happened, he chased her with a sword, she appealed to the gods for help, and they changed her into a myrrh (or Smyrna) tree. Ten months later the tree burst open and the baby Adonis was born.

Aphrodite, charmed by his beauty, hid him in a chest which she gave to Persephone, but when Persephone saw him she refused to give him back. Zeus decreed that the year should be divided into three portions; one third of the year Adonis would spend with Aphrodite, one third with Persephone, and one third as he chose. He chose to spend that third with Aphrodite. But one day while he was hunting he was gored by a boar and died (*Met.* 10.243–738; see also *Library* 3.14.3–4).

No doubt there were more events over the three days of the festival, but what is known suggests that the festival was a ritual designed to promote fertility, both agricultural and also human. In addition the festival must have served to define the status of the wives of citizens and to provide them with a sense of themselves as a group.

Although the Thesmophoria was celebrated only by women, it was a civic festival and part of the official calendar of festivals. But another women's festival, the Adonia, celebrated in honor of Adonis, was quite informal, neither recognized nor supported by the city. Adonis was certainly imported – his name is derived from the Semitic word "adon", meaning "Lord" – but he was fully accepted into the Greek religious system at least as early as Sappho (Burkert 1985: 177). His status is somewhat ambiguous. He is a mortal, born of mortal parents, who dies, but in the Adonia he is honored as a god. The Adonia was celebrated throughout Greece, and similar festivals were celebrated elsewhere in the Mediterranean region.[10]

The festival for Adonis was centered on his sad death. Something of the emotional tone can be seen in one of Sappho's fragmentary poems: "He is dying, Aphrodite, luxuriant Adonis is dying. What should we do?" Aphrodite replies, "Beat your breasts, young maiden, and tear your garments in grief." And in a fragment from the Athenian comic dramatist Pherekrates, some two centuries after Sappho, some unidentified person says, "We are celebrating the Adonia and weeping for Adonis" (see Winkler 1990: 190). But other evidence suggests that the weeping was only one part of the festival, which could also include drinking and dancing and singing.

Some days before the festival, women would plant little gardens of leafy vegetables such as lettuce and fennel in ceramic pots. According to a late lexicographer, when Adonis died, Aphrodite laid him to rest in a patch of lettuce. During the festival, women in informal groups would take their little gardens onto the roofs where they would dance and sing. In a comedy by Aristophanes, one of the male characters remarks that during an Assembly meeting, when Demostratos was proposing to send a naval expedition to Sicily, his wife was on the rooftops dancing and singing "Woe for Adonis! Beat your breasts for Adonis!" (*Lysistrata* 387–96; cf. Menander, *Samia* 35–50).

At the end of the festival, the gardens for Adonis were discarded. Socrates, according to Plato, contrasts these eight-day summer gardens of Adonis to the sensible practices of the farmer, who plants in the correct season and waits eight months until his crop matures (Plato, *Phaedrus* 271b). Some sources suggest that the discarding of these sprouts was symbolic of the death of the young Adonis before his time. Winkler quotes an ancient proverb to this effect – "You are more fruitless than the gardens of Adonis" – and the comment by the ancient collector of proverbs that the gardens are grown only until they become green, and then they are thrown away "along with the dying god". Even the emperor Julian noted that these gardens were grown only for a short time and then allowed to wither (Winkler 1990: 192).

The meaning of the festivals for Adonis has been a matter of considerable scholarly debate. Sir James Frazer, the great comparativist of the late nineteenth and early twentieth century, interpreted Adonis as a god of vegetation and fertility, and made the myth of Adonis central to his theory of the myth of the Dying and Resurrected God (Frazer 1948: chapters 32 and 33).[11] Adonis may well represent a dying god, and most likely the dying gardens symbolized the dying Adonis, but it is harder to see that the dying god symbolized dying vegetation. As the French classicist Marcel Detienne remarks, "everything indicates that the Adonis of the Athenians cannot be a god of vegetation, but is even the exact opposite"; in Athens there is "[n]o whiff of an allusion to an Adonis coming back to life" (Detienne 1994: 135, 136).

Detienne's own interpretation is based on a comparison of the Adonia (which honors the relationship of Adonis and his lover Aphrodite) and the Thesmophoria (which honors Demeter and her daughter Persephone). The Adonia, he says, was celebrated by courtesans and concubines, while the Thesmophoria was celebrated by lawful wives; men were invited to the Adonia, but excluded from the Thesmophoria; the Adonia was a festival of seduction, while the Thesmophoria was a festival of sexual continence; the plants characteristic of the Adonia were frankincense and myrrh, while the women at the Thesmophoria sat on mats woven from anti-aphrodisiac plants; women at the Adonia feasted, but women at the Thesmophoria fasted; women at the Adonia were perfumed, but the women at the Thesmophoria gave off the unpleasant smell of fasting (Detienne 1994: 82). The Thesmophoria, for Detienne, symbolizes the fruitfulness of good agriculture and legitimate sexual activity, while the Adonia symbolizes the sterility of bad agriculture and illegitimate sexual activity (Detienne 1994: 128–29).[12] Good agriculture is masculine and bad agriculture is feminine (see Winkler 1990: 199).

Detienne's argument (of which this summary is only a small part) is erudite and ingenious, but he tends to shape his evidence for his purposes. The Adonia was not in fact celebrated only or primarily by courtesans and concubines, and though the women at the Thesmophoria fasted on the second day of the festival, they broke their fast on day three. Detienne is surely right to see the Adonia as part of a larger system of actions and meanings and right to compare the Adonia and the Thesmophoria, but "[t]he notion that women gathered for both festivals in order to express the excellence of male farmers and the tawdriness of pleasure-bent females seems counter-intuitive" (Winkler 1990: 199).

Winkler's interpretation is based on an analysis of a set of myths in which a goddess seduces a mortal man. Eos, the goddess of the dawn, seduced Orion, Kephalos, and Tithonos; Selene, the goddess of the moon, carried off Endymion; Aphrodite had some sort of relationship with the ferryman Phaon, though the details of this story are obscure. In all of these stories, as in the story of Adonis and Aphrodite, the mortal man comes to some bad end, dead, hidden away, but at any rate powerless.[13] The story of Adonis and Aphrodite and the festival of the Adonia gain their meaning from their membership in this set of stories. As

Winkler notes, "[l]ike Tithonos, Endymion, and Phaon, Adonis' essential fate is to be no longer erect, decisively and permanently so" (Winkler 1990: 204). The gardens of Adonis thus symbolize the relatively fleeting character of men's sexuality. The Thesmophoria, on the other hand, shows that the generation of crops takes time, as does human gestation. "If any contrast is to be drawn between the respective roles of the sexes in cultivating these natural processes, men must be placed squarely on the side of Adonis, Aphrodite's eager but not long enduring lover" (Winkler 1990: 205).[14]

IV. MEN AND WOMEN

Many myths recount incidents of violence between men and women. Women in myth are often subject to sexual violence from males both divine and mortal. Zeus has his way with many women, including Io, Kallisto, Semele, Danaë, Europa, Leda, Alkmene, and Antiope; and similar though shorter lists could be presented for other gods, especially Poseidon and Apollo. Some of these relationships perhaps would count as seductions, but others are clearly rapes.[15] Mortal men are sometimes no better; perhaps the most horrifying story of sexual violence in Greek myth is the story of Tereus, who raped Philomela, the sister of his wife Prokne, and then hid her away and cut out her tongue. Philomela wove the story into a robe which she managed to send to Prokne. Prokne rescued Philomela and then killed her son, Itys, and served him up to the boy's father. When Tereus tried to kill his wife and her sister, the gods turned Prokne into a nightingale and Philomela into a swallow; Tereus became a hoopoe (*Library* 3.14.8; *Met.* 6.412–674).

Other stories recount violence perpetrated by women against men. The 50 daughters of Danaos,[16] for instance, were engaged against their will to marry their cousins, the sons of Aigyptos. On the day of the marriage, Danaos gave each daughter a knife, and each then killed her new husband, except for Hypermnestra, who spared her husband Lynkeus because he had allowed her to remain a virgin (*Library* 2.1.5; Aeschylus, *Suppliant Maidens*). Lynkeus escaped to Lyrkeia; he lit a beacon to let Hypermnestra know that he was safe and

---

Further explorations

Doherty 2001 and Lefkowitz 2007 present two rather different approaches to the study of gender in Greek myth. Doherty organizes her discussion around theoretical models, dealing successively with myth and gender systems; psychological approaches; myth and ritual; myth as "charter"; structuralist and post-structuralist approaches; and myth, folklore, and popular culture. Moreover, Doherty discusses modern uses of myth and even cites modern retellings of myth which are in some respects quite different from the classical models. Lefkowitz, on the other hand, says that her treatment "was written without constant reference to the theoretical constructs into which so much recent writing about myth and literature has been set", and, rather than connecting classical myth to modern concerns, she has attempted "to get away from the modern world and its preoccupations" (Lefkowitz 2007: ix). Compare the strengths and weakness of these two approaches; you may wish to focus on their discussions of the myth of Demeter and Persephone or the myth of the Amazons.

she lit an answering beacon on Larisa, the citadel of Argos. Every year in memorial the Argives have a festival of beacons (*Guide* 2.25.4). Later on Danaos gave his 48 unmarried daughters as prizes in a race (see Chapter Three).

The story of the Lemnian women is another tale of mass murder. The women of the island of Lemnos failed to give honor to Aphrodite, and as a punishment Aphrodite inflicted the women with a terrible smell.[17] Their husbands refused to sleep with them and took mistresses from Thrace instead. The Lemnian women took revenge by killing the men, though the queen, Hypsipyle, saved her father Thoas and hid him or sent him off to sea. Some time later Jason and the Argonauts, on their way to fetch the Golden Fleece, stopped at Lemnos and stayed with the women, who presumably had lost their smell. Hypsipyle had two children by Jason, Euneos and Nebrophonos.

The story of the Lemnian women was widely told (see, for example, Homer, *Iliad* 7.468; Pindar, *Pythian* 4; Hyginus, *Fables* 15; Apollonius, *Jason and the Golden Fleece* 1.600ff.; *Met.* 13.399; Valerius Flaccus, *Argonautica* 2; *Library* 1.9.17). Aeschylus wrote two plays on the topic (*Hypsipyle* and *Lemniai*) but these are lost, and he refers to the story briefly in the *Libation-Bearers*. Both Sophocles and Euripides wrote plays on the topic, but these also are lost. Clearly this was a story that mattered to the ancient Greeks.

The myth of the Lemnian women was evidently linked to an annual ritual on the island, known only from two late and obscure sources. One of these is a dialogue titled *Heroikos* written in the early third century CE probably by Flavius Philostratus, a native of Lesbos, or by another member of his family. According to this, Lemnos was purified, probably each year, as a consequence of the crime of the Lemnian women. All fires were extinguished for nine days; new fire was brought from the island of Delos, but the ship was not allowed to come to land while gods from under the earth were being propitiated. Once the ship landed, fire was distributed, especially to craftsmen, and they said that they were starting a new life (Burkert 2001: 65).

Another aspect of the ritual is provided by Myrtilos of Lesbos, from the third century BCE; in his version of the story, Jason and his crew came to Lemnos on their way back from getting the Golden Fleece, and it was Medea who gave the women their foul odor. Myrtilos then adds that even in his time on a certain day women stayed away from their husbands and fathers because of an evil smell, presumably caused by eating garlic, as women at the Athenian festival of the Skira ate garlic and kept away from their husbands (Burkert 2001: 69–70; Parker 2005: 173–75).

The elements of the Lemnian new fire ritual, according to Burkert, can be matched to the myth of the Lemnian women. The myth and the ritual share "an identity of rhythm . . . first there begins a period of abnormal, barren, uncanny life, until, second, the advent of the ship brings about a new, joyous life – which is in fact the return to normal life" (2001: 69). The extinguishing of fires amounts to a dissolution of normal life, a cessation of normal cults to the gods and cooked meals. Families are dissolved, and perhaps the women chew garlic, as often occurs in rituals elsewhere in ancient Greece. Women may have performed sacrificial killings. "Thus the situation in the city closely reflects the situation described in the myth: disagreeable women rule the town, the men have disappeared" (Burkert 2001: 70).

Even the rescue of king Thoas from the massacre could have a ritual analogue. As Valerius Flaccus tells the story, Hypsipyle led her father to the temple of Dionysos, dressed him up with a wig and garlands, put him in a chariot and surrounded him with cymbals and drums, so that he would look like the god; she then dressed herself as a Bacchant and took him down to the shore and set him off to sea (Valerius Flaccus, *Arg.* 242–77). This episode could match a common ritual in which a straw dummy is led to a river or the sea and thrown in to drift away. The festival would end with athletic contests, like the Argonauts' games when they first came to the island.

Burkert's argument seems at first to mitigate some of the violence of the story of the Lemnian women. No one is actually killed in the Lemnian ritual; the two sexes simply separate for a time, and the murders in the story are only the symbolic expression of that separation. In Burkert's view, however, the symbols of the ritual express real social tensions. He argues that ritual is a way of dealing with problems of attraction and aggression; the myth of the Lemnian women is about "love, hatred, and their conflict, murderous instincts and piety, solidarity of women and family bonds, hateful separation and lustful reunion." The innocent actions of ritual are expressed in the extreme actions of mythic fantasy: "Thus it is ritual that avoids the catastrophe of society" (Burkert 2001: 78).

Lemnians may have understood this myth as a counterpart to their ritual of new fire, but as the myth became Panhellenic, it also became detached from any association with ritual. It remained available, however, as an expression of conflict between the genders. Aeschylus, for example, uses the myth in the *Libation-Bearers* (the second play in the *Oresteia* trilogy) as an extreme example of violence perpetrated by women. In this play Orestes has returned to Argos to kill his mother. Just after he has outlined his plan of revenge, the chorus sings an ode about "the stubborn hearts of women, the all-adventurous passions that couple with man's overthrow." The chorus sings about Althaea, who killed her son, Meleager, who had killed her brothers in a dispute after the hunt for the Calydonian Boar (see Chapter Three). Then they sing about Skylla, who connived in the death of her father Nisus out of love for his enemy Minos, the king of Crete. But the story of the Lemnian women, they say, is the worst of all, so bad that people call any hideous crime "Lemnian" in memory of the wickedness of these women (*Libation-Bearers* 595–635). Aeschylus makes no reference to any ritual of new fire, he says only that the Lemnian women committed mass murder against their husbands.

At times the catalogue of Greek myths seems like an almost unremitting series of rapes and murders, and ancient Greek society might therefore seem merely a cesspool of sexual violence. Certainly ancient Greece was patriarchal, and recent feminist scholarship has taught us an essential lesson by insisting that the study of women's lives find its rightful place in our understanding of ancient Greece. Myths can contribute to this understanding, but it is important to remember that narrative tends to seek out extreme situations. Our own most popular narrative forms, on television and in the movies, also are full of violence, but they are not an accurate reflection of the actual condition of our society. Nor is Greek myth an accurate reflection of ancient Greek society. Moreover, Greek myth also includes stories of sincere affection between men and women. As Odysseus tells the Phaiakian princess Nausicaä, "there is nothing better than when a husband and wife keep a harmonious household; this brings distress to their enemies, pleasure to their friends, and it gives them the best reputation (*Odyssey* 6.182–85).

CONCLUSION

Gender is a constant theme in Greek myth. It is difficult to think of a myth which does not in some way involve questions of gender. There is, however, no simple analysis of gender in Greek myth, nor any simple relationship of myths about gender to social reality. Some myths included elements found in initiation rituals or rites of passage for boys and girls, including such features as cross-dressing, abduction or some kind of separation from society, playing the part of an animal, such as a wolf or a bear, and reintegration into society. Other myths were related to rituals primarily or exclusively performed by women, such as the Thesmophoria and the Adonia. And some myths recounted acts of violence between men and women, including rapes and massacres, while other myths represented affectionate relationships.

These topics by no means exhaust the question of gender in Greek myth, which is surely one of the most active areas of current research. Other topics could include, for example, incest, marriage and sacrifice, Amazons, and homosexuality in myth. Discussion of these topics and others can be found in the works listed for further reading.

FURTHER READING

The classic study of rites of passage is van Gennep 1977, first published in 1909. On boys' rituals, see Vidal-Naquet 1986; Sergent 1986 is an extensive discussion of homosexuality in Greek myth and boys' initiation in general. For discussion of the cross-dressing of Herakles and Achilles, see Cyrino 1998. There are many recent works on women and gender in ancient Greece, including Keuls 1985; Halperin *et al.* 1990; Loraux 1995; Davidson 1997; Doherty 2001; Golden and Toohey 2003; and Davidson 2007. Goff 2004 discusses the role of women in ritual. The first section of Blundell 1995 is specifically about women in myth; see also Doherty 2001 and Lefkowitz 2007. Dowden 1989 has extensive discussion of girls' rituals and myth (and other topics as well). Delcourt 1961 is a concise but full discussion of cross-dressing and bisexuality in Greek myth, with several good illustrations of sculptures of the hermaphroditic gods. Detienne 1994 is a structuralist analysis of the myth of Adonis in the context of various cultural codes of ancient Greece.

Chapter Ten

AGAMEMNON'S MASK?
Myth and History

Myth and history might seem to be very different things, almost opposites. According to common understanding, or misunderstanding, history is what really happened in the past, at least in so far as we can establish what happened on the basis of our more or less subjective interpretations of not always reliable evidence. Myth, again in the common view, is what didn't happen. We can produce evidence to show that Abraham Lincoln was killed by John Wilkes Booth, but no evidence can be brought forward to show that Athena was born from the head of Zeus. (The existence of a myth, on the other hand, is itself a part of history. We appeal to historical evidence to demonstrate that the story of the birth of Athena was told in ancient Greece.)

The discussion of the nature of myth in the first chapter suggested, however, that myth should not be thought of as what didn't happen, but rather as those stories which hold a particular place in a society, stories which are regarded as both true and important by members of a society, even though outsiders may not accept them. The Biblical story of the flood, for example, once was and for some people still remains a myth of this sort. Myths like these are not quite the same as the stories told by historians, however, since they often stand above any historical evidence which might be brought to bear. In a sense, these stories are the background against which historical stories are told and judged, at least for those who believe them.

This chapter begins with an investigation of how myth and history were connected in the minds of ancient Greeks, including the historians Herodotus and Thucydides; mythographers, such as Apollodorus; and travel writers, such as Pausanias. The chapter then concludes with a discussion of what modern scholars might learn about history from reading Greek myth, using as case studies the myth of the ownership of the Oracle at Delphi and the myth of the Trojan War.

Exploring Greek Myth. First Edition. Matthew Clark.
© 2012 Matthew Clark. Published 2012 by Blackwell Publishing Ltd.

I. HERODOTUS AND MYTH

The earliest surviving book of Greek history is Herodotus' account of the Greek wars against the Persians, written sometime in the second half of the fifth century BCE. This wonderful book in fact covers considerably more than the events of the war itself. Herodotus includes an account of Greece and other peoples to the East before the wars, including long discussions of Egypt and Scythia. His book covers not just what modern scholars would think of as history (the Greek word "history" means "inquiry" in general) but also a lot of ethnography, some of which seems to be reliable, as well as some stories which Herodotus himself does not believe.[1]

Herodotus begins his history with myth. What was the reason, he asks, for the hostility between the Greeks and the peoples of the East that led to the Persian Wars? According to the Persians, he says, some Phoenician traders came to the Greek city of Argos; they put their wares out for sale, and after a few days of trading, a group of women came to inspect the goods. One of these women was Io, the daughter of the king, Inakhos. The Phoenicians grabbed Io and a few of the other women and took them to Egypt. "This", Herodotus says, "is the Persian story, but the Greeks tell a different version" (*Histories* 1.1–2).[2] It is actually very unlikely that Herodotus learned this version from the Persians; most probably he is simply removing the "supernatural" elements from the traditional Greek story, which is told, for example, by Aeschylus (*Prometheus Bound*). Io was the daughter of the river Inachos and also a priestess of Hera, but she was raped by Zeus, and then changed into a cow, and then harassed by a gadfly, until finally she arrived in Egypt, where she was returned to her human form. She was the ancestress of the Danaids. (Ovid's Latin version (*Met.* 1.583–750) more or less follows the Greek tradition.)

Herodotus continues his story with another reference to myth. A little later some Greeks – probably Cretans – came to Tyre, a Phoenician port, and kidnapped Europa, the daughter of the king. This, he says is the Persian version, but again, the traditional version is different. Europa was kidnapped by Zeus, in the form of a bull, and taken to Crete, where she founded the Cretan royal line.

Later on, Herodotus says, some Greeks sailed to Kolkhis, on the river Phasis in the eastern end of the Black Sea, and there they abducted Medea, the daughter of the king. The king asked for reparations, but the Greeks refused, since they had received no reparations for Io. Herodotus' account of the Persian story makes no mention of Jason or the Golden Fleece.

Next, according to Herodotus, the Trojan prince Paris decided to steal a woman from Greece, since he thought he could get away with the kidnapping without penalty. But this time the Greeks became annoyed, and they sent a great army against Troy. The Persians, Herodotus says, blamed the Greeks for this war. Sensible people don't get so upset about a little abduction of women, especially since the women probably went voluntarily. In any case, Herodotus explains, these abductions, and especially the Trojan War, were the cause of the hostility between the Greeks and the Asians, according to the Persians. But Herodotus refuses to say if he thinks all this is true or false; he will rely on what he himself knows. He then begins to tell about king Croesus of Lydia (ca. 595–547 BCE), who was certainly a figure of history.[3]

Exactly what Herodotus meant by all this is not entirely clear. Perhaps he wanted to show the difference between the kind of stories myth provides and the kind of story that he will tell, or perhaps he was attempting to show that the stories of myth could be linked to historical events if they were stripped of their supernatural elements; thus Io was a real person, but she was never turned into a cow. In any case, however, he shows that the beginning of Greek historical thought lies in the traditions of myth.

These are hardly the only references to myth found in Herodotus. He reports, for example, that Paris stopped in Egypt when he was taking Helen away from Argos. The Egyptian king Proteus let Paris go, but he kept Helen, arguing that she was stolen property. Then when the Greek army got to Troy and demanded Helen back, the Trojans truthfully said that they didn't have her. At the end of the war the Greeks found out that the Trojans had been telling the truth, and Menelaos went to Egypt and got Helen from king Proteus. Herodotus says that he learned this version from Egyptian priests, but adds that he is inclined to believe it (*Histories* 2.113–20). The idea that Helen did not go to Troy is also found in a fragment of the poet Stesichorus and in Euripides' play *Helen*.

Other myths mentioned by Herodotus include the stories of Orestes (1.67–68); Kadmos (2.50, 2.145, 4.147, 5.57, 5.59); Jason and the quest for the Golden Fleece (4.145, 4.179, 7.193); Melampous (2.49, 7.221, 9.34); Danaos (2.171, 2.182); Perseus (2.91, 6.53, 7.61); Europa (1.2, 1.173, 4.45, 4.147); Peleus and Thetis (7.191); and Herakles (2.42–44, 2.145–46, 5.43, 6.53, 7.193, 7.198). Sometimes the version told by Herodotus is different from the best-known Panhellenic stories; he says, for instance, that the god Pan is the son of Penelope and Hermes (2.145). Occasionally he seems less than convinced that a story is true. In Book Seven he mentions the river Dryas, which, "according to the story", sprang up from the ground to help Herakles when he was burning on the pyre. Herodotus probably accepts the story of the death of Herakles but doubts that a river sprang up to help him. But overall Herodotus simply refers to these myths as the background to his historical account. Recent events, such as the Persian Wars, are understood in the context of stories modern scholars would call myth.

II. THUCYDIDES AND MYTH

Thucydides, a generation later than Herodotus, was the second great historian of ancient Greece. Whereas Herodotus wrote about events of the recent past, Thucydides wrote about an event of his own time, the Peloponnesian War, in which he himself played a part. He did not write much about the distant past, let alone the past of myth, because he did not believe that secure knowledge about such times was possible (*Peloponnesian War* 1.1). He admits that the story he tells may be less pleasurable because it lacks a quality he calls "mythodes", the element of fables and romance, the kind of storytelling that is such a prominent feature of history as told by Herodotus.

Even so, Thucydides does not absolutely exclude the mythic background from his account. He begins his history with a quick summary of the early condition of Greece. He argues that before the Trojan War Greece as a whole was not called "Hellas"; this name, he says, was at first applied only to those cities connected to the family of Hellen, the son of Deukalion, and Homer, for example, uses it only for the followers of Achilles (1.3).

The first great navy, according to Thucydides, was built by Minos, who controlled most of the Aegean Sea. Thus Thucydides counts Minos as a figure of history, but he does not say that Minos was the son of Europa, nor does he say anything about the Minotaur (1.4). Agamemnon was able to mount the expedition against Troy not because of the oath of the suitors, but simply because he was the most powerful ruler in Greece in his day (1.9). Thucydides also discusses the aftermath of the Trojan War and the returns of the heroes (1.12, 2.68, 4.120, 6.2). He quotes at length from the *Homeric Hymn to Apollo* and uses it as evidence for the antiquity of the festival of Apollo on Delos (3.104). He reports a story that the earliest inhabitants of Sicily were the Cyclopes and the Laestrygonians, both mentioned by Homer in the *Odyssey*, but what kind of people they were he does not claim to know, and he says we have to be content with the stories told by the poets. He clearly believed that the Trojan War was a fact of history (as do many scholars still today; see section IV), and he talks about Pelops and some other figures of myth as if they were real people, but he has little or no interest in the stories of Greek myth, such as the Theban cycle or the stories about Herakles.

III. MYTHIC HISTORY IN ANCIENT GREEK THOUGHT

Herodotus was probably closer than Thucydides to the common Greek attitude towards myth. The usual assumption was that the heroic parts of myth, at least, especially including the heroic genealogies, were true, more or less, granting that the extent of time and the lack of records allowed for some disagreement about details. And these heroic genealogies extended in an unbroken succession down into the time after the Trojan War and beyond. Divine myth, on the other hand, was less often linked to human time: the events of the Myth of Succession, for instance, were not placed within human history, they simply came in the time before other things. Deukalion's flood, according to Apollodorus, occurred when Kranaos was king of Athens (*Library* 3.14.5), but this period of the early kings was still a time of origins, and not quite historical. In Greek myth, there is a gradual transition from the events in mythic time towards the events of history.

It is easy to find evidence that the ancient Greeks believed in the continuity of mythic and historical events. One of the most compelling is the Parian Marble, an inscription on stone, created in 264/3 BCE on the island of Paros. This stone records events from early Athenian mythic history down to the time when the stone was inscribed (though the period after 299 BCE is missing). The stone begins with Kekrops, who became king of Athens 1318 years before the stone was inscribed, that is, in 1582 BCE. Deukalion's flood is dated to 1529 BCE; Hellen the son of Deukalion became king of Phthiotis in 1521 BCE; Kadmos founded Thebes in 1519 BCE; Danaos arrived from Egypt in 1511 BCE; Minos became king of Crete in 1506 BCE; Theseus became king of Athens and united the cities of Attica in 1259 BCE; the Greeks sailed against Troy in 1218 BCE; Neleus founded Miletus and other cities in Ionia in 1077 BCE; Homer flourished in 907 BCE; Archias, a descendant of Temenos in the tenth generation, left Corinth and founded Syracuse sometime before 684 BCE (the part of the stone that would give the date is damaged); Lysiades became archon in Athens in 682 BCE; Alyattes became king of Lydia in 605 BCE; Pisistratos became tyrant of Athens in 561 BCE;

and so on down to 299 BCE, when the inscription gives out. Clearly whoever wrote this document did not distinguish between myth and history in the way that we do.

The ancient Greek trust in mythic history was not just a matter of belief, but also of action. According to Herodotus, for example, at the beginning of the Persian War the Athenians and the Spartans went to Syracuse to ask the tyrant Gelon for military assistance. He agreed, on condition that he be made overall commander. The Spartans refused, saying that Agamemnon would have been distressed if the Spartans were removed from command. Gelon said that in that case, he would be content to be commander of either the army or the navy, but the Athenians refused, saying that they had come to ask for an army, not for a general, and in any case according to Homer the best military leader at Troy came from Athens. Gelon sent them away empty-handed (*Histories* 7.59–61).[4]

Many modern handbooks of myth include genealogical tables, showing, for example, the family relationships of the gods, then the family relationships of the various heroic figures, many of them descended from gods, such as the descendants of Deukalion, the descendants of Inakhos, the descendants of Kadmos, the descendants of Tantalos, and so on. The sense of time represented by these genealogies is completely linear, rather than cyclical. These tables can be drawn today because the ancient Greeks went to great trouble to establish these genealogies. The ancient Greek authorities often disagreed, of course. Io was the daughter of either Iasos or Inachos (*Library* 2.1.3); according to most sources, Iphigeneia was the daughter of Agamemnon and Klytemnestra, but according to other sources, she was the daughter of Helen and Theseus (*Guide* 2.22.7).

The genealogical tables printed in the handbooks usually end with the generation after the Trojan War, the generation of Telemachos and Orestes, or at most one generation later, with Tisamenos, the son of Orestes. After this, the tables seem to suggest, myth ends. Even in ancient times there was some feeling that things changed after the generation of the returns of the heroes from Troy. The *Library* of Apollodoros fundamentally ends with the returns (though there is a brief account of the return of the Heraklids to the Peloponnese in the third generation after the Trojan War), and there are hardly any Greek tragedies dealing with later events, just three lost plays by Euripides also about the return of the Heraklids.

But the local histories, most of which have been lost, did record a continuous account from the age of the heroes down into historical time. Some of this information survives in fragments, and some has been preserved by later writers. Both Herodotus and Pausanias, for example, give continuous lists of the kings of Sparta beginning with figures of myth and extending to kings who were definitely historical.[5] Pausanias begins with Lelex, the autochthonous founder, and continues to down to Tisamenos, the son of Orestes, in 11 generations.[6] Tisamenos was then deposed by the three sons of Aristomachos, who was the great-grandson of Herakles. Of these sons, Kresphontes took Messene, Temenos took Argos, and since the third son, Aristodemos, had died, the rule of Sparta went to his twin sons, Eurysthenes and Prokles. This story, according to Pausanias, explains the double kingship of Sparta. Pausanias then continues with an extensive genealogy of the two royal lines in Sparta, the Agiads, who were the descendants of Eurysthenes, and the Eurypontids, who were the descendants of Prokles. There are 16 generations from Eurysthenes to Kleomenes, who was king just before the Persian wars, and 16 generations from Prokles to Leotychides (the genealogies continue, but they get very complicated).[7] Pausanias thus traces the succession of Spartan rulers in almost 30 generations from the autochthonous founder Lelex down to the Persian Wars and beyond. The king lists in Herodotus and Pausanias make no division between myth and history, and they do not suggest that there was ever a Dark Age in Greece.[8]

To what extent do these lists reflect actual history? The kings towards the end of the lists were certainly real people, and the kings at the beginning of the lists were just as certainly not real, but in the absence of early evidence it is not easy to know where to draw the line. Paul Cartledge argues that several of the early Eurypontid kings (Soos, Prytanis, and Eunomos) before Charillos are most likely inventions; the Agiad line was thus the earlier of the two houses, and the first kings in the dual monarchy might have been Archelaos and Charillos, both in the seventh generation after the lists begin (Cartledge 1979: 104–06). Cartledge seems willing to grant the historicity of Agis, the eponymous founder of the Agiad house, to whom he gives "a genealogically plausible modern dating" of 930 to 900 BCE, that is, the early geometric period, but it is hard to believe that traditions from this period are reliable. The evidence from other cultures without writing suggests that such lists change as they are told over time, according to various political interests. Most likely there is no evidence which can determine exactly where myth ends and history begins.

Historical events could also have an effect on the way a particular myth was told at a particular time and place, so that in a sense history was read back into myth. Thus the trial at the end of Aeschylus' *Oresteia* probably reflects changes in the status of the court of the Areopagus; the plague at the beginning of Sophocles' *Oedipus the King* was likely an allusion to the plague the Athenians had been suffering at the beginning of the Peloponnesian War – at least it is easy to image that the original audience would have made such a connection – and Euripides' *Trojan Women* seems to have been written with the ongoing Peloponnesian War in mind. Because myth is always changing, it is always available for a retelling that reflects the interests of the moment.

IV. MYTH AND THE HISTORY OF THE DELPHIC ORACLE

What value do myths have for modern historians? Can myth be used as a tool for recovering the history of ancient Greece? Or must the myths be regarded simply as fanciful creations of nurses and poets? The answer to these questions requires a distinction between two types of history, at least. Myths are clearly important for the history of ancient Greek thought, because they often concern problems central to Greek society and religion. Myths can change over time, depending on the circumstances in which they are told and the interests of the teller and the audience, and these changes can be an index to changes in thoughts and attitudes. And because myths have a certain distance from the realities of the present time of their telling, they may be able to represent ideas which might be controversial or painful if considered more directly.

Myth and the history of thought, however, will be discussed in the following two chapters. The rest of this chapter takes up the question of myth and its use in determining the events of history; what actually happened, not what was thought about what happened. Some scholars believe that many myths have a core of historical validity, that behind the events of the stories it is possible to see historical events, but other scholars doubt the connection between myth and history. These positions can be examined and tested through two myths, the myth of the original owner of the Delphic Oracle, and the myth of the Trojan War.

As early as Homer, the Delphic Oracle belonged to Apollo (*Iliad* 9.404, *Odyssey* 8.79–80). He was the presiding deity, and the oracular responses were supposedly derived from his prophetic power as it entered and took possession of the Pythian priestess (Burkert 1985: 117). But according to a number of ancient sources, Apollo was not the first deity at Delphi. At the very beginning of Aeschylus' *Eumenides*, for instance, the Pythian priestess herself comes on stage to say that she gives first place of honor to Earth (Gaia), who was the first divinity to prophesy at Delphi; the second presiding divinity was Themis, who took over from her mother Earth; and the third was Phoebe, who finally gave Delphi as a present to her brother, Phoebus (*Eumenides* 1–8). The idea that Apollo was not the first owner of Delphi but took it over from a previous owner can be found in Euripides (*Iphigeneia in Tauris* 1259–83, *Orestes* 163–65) and Ovid (*Met.* 1.320–21, 4.643). Pausanias says that the Oracle originally belonged to Earth, and the nymph Daphnis was the first prophetess; his sources are unspecified general reports ("they say"). He adds that in a poem titled *Eumolpia*, supposedly written by Mousaios, Poseidon shared the Oracle with Earth (*Guide* 10.5.6–7, 10.24.4). On the other hand, the earliest account of the foundation of the cult at Delphi, the *Homeric Hymn to Apollo*, does not include any myth of a divine owner before Apollo.

Some scholars have taken the mythic accounts of the transfer of the cult as a reflection of the history of the cult at Delplhi. H. W. Parke and D. E. W. Wormell, for example, argue that evidence of the myths is supported by archeological evidence of a continuity of cult from Minoan-Mycenaean times:

> Hence if Delphi was a cult centre before Hellenic times, an original worship of an earth goddess would be a natural supposition on our archeological evidence alone. But since all our literary tradition agrees in making Apollo a settler come from elsewhere, and most of the tradition (though not in the earliest poem) makes Earth his predecessor, we can take it that the agreement of archeology and tradition is right. (Parke and Wormell 1956: 5–6.)

Hugh Lloyd-Jones agrees that "[t]he Greeks well knew that Apollo was a late comer to Delphi" (Lloyd-Jones 1976: 60). Without much in the way of argument, Lloyd-Jones claims that Apollo took over the Oracle from a previous female divinity, an Earth Goddess; the speaker of the oracles, the Pythian priestess, is female because the original goddess of the Oracle was female (1976: 66). Thus the myth reflects historical fact. Joseph Fontenrose notes that many historians accept the story of the transfer of the cult as historical; he adds that there is no evidence except the myth for this idea, but he moves on without either accepting or rejecting the story (Fontenrose 1978: 1).

Christina Sourvinou-Inwood, however, argues that there is no reason to believe that this myth reflects any historical fact. There is no evidence outside the myth itself, she says, that the Oracle ever belonged to any divinity before Apollo, and no evidence that Apollo displaced any other divinity (1988: 215–16). The earliest accounts of the Oracle – including the Homeric *Hymn to Apollo* and Alkaios' *Hymn to Apollo* (as summarized by Himerius) – make no mention of any divinity at Delphi before Apollo (1988: 216–17). There is no archeological evidence for a Mycenaean cult of Gaia at Delphi, and most probably there was no cultic continuity from the Mycenaean period to the Iron Age (1988: 217–19). Although Apollo shared honors at Delphi with other divinities, including Gaia, Themis, and Poseidon, there is no reason to think that these divinities preceded Apollo, and archeology cannot place the cult of these divinities earlier than the fifth century. It is most likely that these divinities came to be honored at Delphi because of the myth (1988: 220–21). Sourvinou-Inwood also rejects the idea that some features of the cult at Delphi, such as the gender of the priestess, are incompatible with the mythic nature of Apollo (1988: 223–25). Since the historical interpretation of this myth rests on the assumption that myth is good evidence for history, this historical interpretation cannot be used to prove the assumption on which it is based.

The idea that Apollo supplanted one or more previous divinities at Delphi seems to fit a pattern found in other Greek myths, the pattern of the Myth of Succession. This pattern is found, for example, in Hesiod's story that Ouranos was supplanted by Kronos who in turn was supplanted by Zeus. Gaia's subordinate status at Delphi shows that the "chthonic, dangerous and disorderly aspects of the cosmos have been defeated by, and subordinated to, the celestial guide and lawgiver" – that is, Apollo, the representative of Zeus (Sourvinou-Inwood 1988: 226–27). Themis, who stands between Gaia and Apollo in Aeschylus' version, is a mediating figure, the daughter of the chthonic figure Gaia, but also a symbol of Olympian order, as her name shows, with its connotations of lawgiving (1988: 228–29). The subordinate presence of Poseidon in Delphic cult can be explained in a somewhat similar way: "Apollo belongs to the symbolic pole of culture, Poseidon to that of wild nature" (1988: 232). The myth in which Apollo supplants earlier divinities thus expresses "relationships between Apollo and the other Delphic deities, especially those symbolically antithetical to the order and civilization represented by Apollo" (1988: 232). But these relationships are structural rather than historical; in this myth, as often, an ideological hierarchy is expressed as a chronological order (1988: 233).

V. MYTH AND THE HISTORY OF THE TROJAN WAR

The ancient Greeks had no doubt that the Trojan War really happened. The Romans also accepted the story, and Julius Caesar famously counted the Trojan prince Aeneas as his ancestor. The Middle Ages also accepted the War as a fact of history; the English chronicler Geoffrey of Monmouth (ca. 1100–55) wrote that Brutus, the great-grandson of Aeneas, settled in England with a group of Trojan refugees (*History of the Kings of England*, Book 1).

In the seventeenth century, however, the French philosopher and mathematician Blaise Pascal (1623–62) declared that Homer wrote his epics simply as a diversion; since Homer lived long after the events his works should not be regarded as historical accounts (*Pensées* 436). The Italian philosopher Giambattista Vico (1668–1744) declared that the Trojan War never occurred, and the English writer Jacob Bryant, in a treatise published in 1796, argued the same point. The English historian George Grote (1794–1871) stated that Greek history properly begins with the founding of the Olympic Games in 776 BCE; all events before that date he considered legendary rather than historical, though he admitted that some of the legends may be true, and he included a long summary of Greek myth and legend in the first volume of his history (*A History of Greece*, Preface). On the other hand, in 1791 the French traveler Jean-Baptiste Lechevalier argued that the Trojan War was a fact of history, and in the early nineteenth century George Gordon, Lord Byron denounced Bryant in his diary. But if there had not been a fairly widespread skepticism, no defense of the story would have been necessary.[9]

Thus by the mid-nineteenth century the historicity of the Trojan War was an open question. Lurking behind this debate was a deeper debate about the historicity of the early events of the Bible. If the Trojan War could be doubted, then could the stories of Moses be doubted as well? It was in this atmosphere that the idea of Greek myth as Greek history achieved its greatest moment of success.

Doubting the historicity of the Trojan War was made easier by the complete disappearance of the site of the city itself. According to Homer, Troy was somewhere in northwestern Asia Minor, an area called the Troad, near the Hellespont, but there were no visible remains of the city, and several different sites had been proposed. Until the remains of the city could be found, the skeptics could point to this lack in support of their disbelief.

The traditions of the Troy Tale

The story of the Trojan War in Greek myth is much more than the *Iliad*, which takes place over just a few weeks in the final year of the war, or the *Odyssey*, which takes place after the war was over (though with some references to events during the war). Other events before, during, and after the war were told in oral traditions, and some of these traditions eventually were written down in epic poems which, together with the *Iliad* and the *Odyssey*, are known as the Epic Cycle. The other poems of the Epic Cycle are now lost, but short summaries and a few other fragments survive. According to the summaries, the *Kypria* told about the events leading up to the war, including the Judgment of Paris; the *Aithiopis* told about events after the death of Hektor, including the arrival of the Amazons and the death of the Amazon queen Penthesilea; the *Little Iliad* told about the events after the death of Achilles, including the building of the Trojan Horse; the *Iliou Persis* told about the fall of Troy; the *Nostoi* told about the returns of various Greek heroes; and the *Telegony* told about the later life of Odysseus, including his death at the hands of his illegitimate son Telegonos.

The writers of Athenian tragedy generally avoided stories that were told in the *Iliad* and the *Odyssey*, but they did write about other events connected to the war.[10]

A number of Latin poems also concern the Trojan War, most notably Vergil's *Aeneid*, and a fragment of an epic, the *Achilleis*, by Statius. A Greek epic poem, the *Posthomerica*, about events after the *Iliad*, was written by Quintus of Smyrna probably in the third century CE.

A short version of the *Iliad* appeared in a Latin poem known as the *Ilias Latina*, probably composed in the first century CE. Other Latin versions include the *Historia de Excidio Troiae* (*History of the Fall of Troy*), which claims to have been written by Dares, a Trojan priest and eyewitness, but which actually dates from the early sixth century CE, and a *Journal of the Trojan War*, which claims to be by Dictys of Crete, another eyewitness, but which was probably composed in the fourth century CE. After the collapse of the Western Roman Empire and the loss of knowledge of Greek in the West, these Latin versions became the primary source for knowledge of the Troy tale. Dante, for instance, knew who Homer was, but he did not read Greek and he did not have a Latin translation of the Homeric poems. He did know Vergil's *Aeneid*, however, and also the versions of the Troy story attributed to Dares and Dictys.

The twelfth-century French poet Benoit de Sainte-Maure wrote a long epic, *Le Roman de Troi*, in 24,500 lines, and in the thirteenth century the Sicilian writer Guido delle Colonne produced a Latin prose account, the *Historia Destructionis Troiae* (*History of the*

Destruction of Troy). William Caxton's *Recuyell of the Historyes of Troy*, which appeared around 1475, was the first book printed in English. Clearly the story of Troy was still very popular in the later Middle Ages.

Benoit's poem introduced a new episode to the Troy tale, the story of Troilus, a son of Priam, and his ill-fated love for Briseida. This story was taken up by Guido delle Colonne and then by the great Italian writer Boccaccio, whose *Filostrato* appeared sometime around 1340. Boccaccio's story in turn became the basis for Geoffrey Chaucer's English poem *Troilus and Criseyde*, which then provided the model for Shakespeare's play *Troilus and Cressida*.

With the fall of the Byzantine Empire in the mid-fifteenth century, Greek scholars and Greek books began to arrive once again in the West. The first printed Greek edition of Homer appeared in 1488, and George Chapman's English translations of the Homeric epics were published between 1598 and 1615. The French playwright Jean Racine produced two plays on Trojan subjects, *Andromache* in 1667 and *Iphigenia* in 1674.

The story of the Trojan War and its aftermath has continued to provide inspiration for artists and writers. Twentieth-century works more or less based on Trojan themes include James Joyce's *Ulysses*, Nikos Kazantzakis' *The Odyssey, A Modern Sequel*, John Erskine's *The Private Life of Helen of Troy* and *Penelope's Man*, Eugene O'Neill's *Mourning Becomes Electra*, Jean Giradoux's *La guerre de Troie n'aura pas lieu* (*The Trojan War Will Not Take Place*), Jean-Paul Sartre's *Les Mouches* (*The Flies*), and Derek Walcott's *Omeros*. Two books by the American psychoanalyst Jonathan Shay, *Achilles in Vietnam* (1995) and *Odysseus in America* (2003), used the story of the Trojan War to understand war trauma, and James Tatum's *The Mourner's Song* (2003) is a study of the memory and the memorials of war from the Trojan War to Vietnam.

In 1868, a German businessman turned scholar named Heinrich Schliemann arrived in the Troad looking for the site of Troy; he intended to find it and excavate in order to establish the truth of the story once and for all. At first he favored a site called Bunarbashi, which had been proposed by Lechevalier, among others. But while in the Troad, he met an Englishman, Frank Calvert, who lived nearby and owned land in the area.[11] In particular Calvert owned part of a large mound called Hisarlik, not far from the coast, and he believed that the remains of Troy lay under this mound. Schliemann, urged by Calvert, began to dig there in 1870, and over the course of several years' excavations he discovered extensive and complex ruins of a series of cities, one on top of another, buried under the mound.[12] He quickly became convinced that these were the ruins of Troy, though he changed his mind several times about which layer was the city destroyed in the Trojan War.

In 1873 Schliemann found a remarkable group of metal objects, including bowls, platters, lanceheads, and jewelry made from copper, bronze, silver, and gold. This group became known as the Treasure of Priam; a photograph shows Schliemann's wife Sophie wearing the diadem known as the Jewels of Helen. But archeologists today agree that the Treasure and the Jewels cannot in fact be dated to the period of the Trojan War. Most likely they belong either to Troy II or Troy III, as the layers are now designated, dating from the third millennium BCE, long before the usual date of the war, around 1200 BCE. Most archeologists would now identify the city of the Trojan War as the layer called Troy VIIa.

In 1876 Schliemann turned his attention to the ruins of Mycenae, the Peloponnesian Greek city where Homer's King Agamemnon ruled. The site of Mycenae had never been lost, but it had been in ruins since ancient times. Some impressive remains were visible above ground, including the Lion Gate and the tholos tomb known as the Treasury of

Agamemnon, but the site had never been excavated. Schliemann, following the description of the ruins given by Pausanias in the second century CE, dug inside the remains of the walls of Mycenae, and there he uncovered a set of stone markers arranged in a large circle and then below them five shaft graves. (Eventually a sixth was found as well.) Inside the graves he found the skeletal remains of 19 adults and two children, buried with a quantity of bronze and gold weapons and decorations. The remains of the men had golden masks hammered to represent faces, and when Schliemann saw these he was convinced that he had found the grave of Agamemnon himself (see Figure 10.1) As he wrote:

> For my part, I have always firmly believed in the Trojan War; my full faith in the tradition has never been shaken by mode and criticism, and to this faith of mine I am indebted for the discovery of Troy and its Treasure. . . . My firm faith in the traditions made me undertake my late excavations in the acropolis of [Mycenae] and led to the discovery of the five tombs with their immense treasures. . . . I have not the slightest objection to admitting that the tradition which assigns the tombs to Agamemnon and his companions may be perfectly correct. (Wood 1996: 69)

Figure 10.1   Death-mask known as the "Mask of Agamemnon". Gold repoussé (16th century BCE). Mycenean, from Grave V, Grave Circle A, in Mycenae. The gold mask was the exclusive funerary apparel of Mycenean males. This mask depicts a bearded man and two holes near the ears indicate that the mask was held in place over the deceased's face with twine. National Archaeological Museum, Athens, Greece. Copyright © Vanni/Art Resource, NY

Once again, however, his dating was wrong; archeologists now date these shaft graves to the sixteenth century BCE, some three or four centuries before the Trojan War.

Schliemann continued to dig and make discoveries in these and other sites. After his death in 1890 the excavation of Hisarlik was continued by Wilhelm Dörpfeld (1893–94) and in the twentieth century by Carl Blegen of the University of Cincinnati (1932–38) and Manfred Korfmann of the University of Tübingen (1988–2005). Hisarlik is now one of the best excavated of ancient sites. Blegen's excavation suggested that the layer called Troy VI was destroyed by an earthquake, but Troy VIIa showed persuasive evidence of warfare, including charred wood, burned mudbrick, skeletons which showed the marks of violent death, and an arrowhead (Wood 1996: 115–16). Korfmann found extensive evidence of Mycenaean Greek burials nearby which can be dated to the late thirteenth century, the time of Troy VI, and very close to Troy itself large quantities of Mycenean pottery of about the same period. This date is perhaps too early for the Trojan War itself, but the graves and pottery are clear evidence of Greek activity in the area (Wood 1996: 262–64).

Additional light has been cast on the Trojan problem by documents from the ancient Hittite civilization, a late Bronze Age civilization in central Asia Minor. Extensive documents written in Hittite have been found, and these have made it possible to reconstruct Hittite political history in some detail. During the second millennium BCE the Hittites controlled a loose empire, including a region or town called Wilusa or perhaps Taruisa; a treaty from the thirteenth century BCE names a Wilusan king Alaksandu. These names look very much like Ilion and Troy and Alexander (in the *Iliad*, Priam's son Paris is often called Alexander). Hittite documents also record a foreign people called Ahhiyawa, perhaps the Homeric Achaeans. And according to the Hittite documents, Wilusa seems to have been troubled by political disturbances and military action during the thirteenth century BCE, more or less the time of the Trojan War. Many scholars believe that these Hittite references, coupled with the archeology of Hisarlik itself, strongly support the theory that what we think of as Troy was a kingdom on the edge of the Hittite empire, and that the story of the Trojan War reflects probably a series of engagements over a long period between the Wilusans and the Ahhiyawans, that is, between the people from Ilion and the Achaeans (Bryce 2005: 359–61).

When we put all this together, we must then ask about the meaning of these various discoveries, beginning with Schliemann's excavations and the excavations of his successors, and now including the evidence from Hittite documents. What, finally, did Schliemann

Further explorations

The study of history is not limited to big events, such as wars, but should also include the examination of the structure of society and the patterns of behavior and belief that make up culture. Ancient historians have been particularly interested in the possibility that the Homeric epics might be an important source for the social and cultural history of early Greece, a period from which written documents are scare or entirely absent. After Schliemann's discovery of Troy, some scholars believed that the *Iliad* and the *Odyssey* represented the period of the Mycenaeans, from perhaps 1600 to 1200 BCE, but this view was generally discredited by further archeological work, including the discovery and eventual deciphering of the Linear B tablets. Finley 2002 (first published in 1954) argues that the period represented by the *Iliad* and the *Odyssey* must be the Dark Age, the tenth and ninth centuries BCE, but Morris 1986 argues that the epics represent the eighth century, the period when the poems took on more or less the form in which we read them today. Discuss the various aspects of Homeric society identified by Finley and Morris and explain which of the two presents the more convincing argument.

find? Can we now say that the Trojan War really happened? Much depends on what the question means. Certainly there was a city more or less where Homer placed Troy. This city probably stood in a location between the Hittite empire to the east and the Mycenaean Greek culture to the west. There is good evidence that the Mycenaean Greeks were active in the area. It is very likely that this city was destroyed by war around the time that the Trojan War is supposed to have occurred. It is certainly possible that the Mycenaean Greeks were involved in this war. On the other hand, there is no evidence that would link specific people – such as Achilles, Helen, or Odysseus – to this war, and no reason to think that Helen was kidnapped by Paris, the son of the king. Certainly the Diadem of Helen never belonged to Helen, and the Mask of Agamemnon is not a portrait of Agamemnon. On balance, then, if the question means was there a war at the place we now call Troy at around the time that the Trojan War was supposed to have occurred, then the answer is very likely yes. But if the question is, did the Trojan War happen just the way Homer tells the story, then the answer has to be probably not.

CONCLUSION

Some scholars have insisted on a sharp division between myth and history. Mythic time is often seen as fundamentally different from historical time. According to Mircea Eliade, for example, the stories of myth belong to a time before history begins, a time outside of historical events. Moreover, mythical time tends to be cyclical; the events of myth recur especially as they are recreated in ritual. Historical time, however, is linear and events do not repeat with any exactness. Myth and history, according to these scholars, simply never meet each other.

Greek myth, however, challenges these distinctions. Some Greek myths do occur in a time outside of history, and some Greek rituals repeat the events of myth, but the ancient Greeks themselves did not always clearly distinguish myth from history, and at times they used their mythic history as justification for arguments and actions in their own time. It is possible to argue, in fact, that the idea of history in ancient Greece has its roots in myth, and Greek historians in general continued to grant the historicity of at least some mythic stories. Moreover, the extensive heroic genealogies express a linear conception of time, as the various characters of myth are related to each other in elaborate family trees. These genealogies continue well into the historical period and serve to connect the figures of myth to historical people and events. Furthermore, many stories which are firmly part of the traditions of Greek myth seem to be closely attached to what modern scholars would want to call history.

The use of myth as a source for historical research, however, is inevitably complex and problematic. Some mythic stories may well have a basis in historical events, and some historical events may have been read back into myths. Thus the stories of the Trojan War may be based on a war that really happened, though it is very unlikely that the details of this or any other mythic story are accurate accounts of what really happened. But even if the myths are a problematic source for knowledge of specific historical events, they represent aspects of ancient Greek culture and society and thus can have great value for the student of history.

FURTHER READING

On Herodotus and Thucydides, see Hunter 1982. Brillante 1990 is a theoretical discussion of the relation of myth and history. For the Parian Marble, see the website of the Ashmolean Museum (www.ashmolean.org). On the Spartan king lists, see Cartledge 1979: 102–06 and 341–46. On the epic cycle see Burgess 2001 and Davies 1989. The myth of the previous owner of the Delphic Oracle is discussed by Sourvinou-Inwood 1988. For discussion of the archeology of Troy, Mycenae, and other sites related to the Trojan War, see Fitton 1996; Wood 1996 is a more popular account, with abundant illustrations. For Schliemann's biography, see Traill 1995, which is illuminating on his character but perhaps too hard on his faults. Moorehead 1996 tells about the recent recovery of Schliemann's Treasure of Priam in Russia. For the reception of Homer and Homeric Troy in later times, see Hunter 2004, Farrell 2004, and Porter 2004, all collected in Fowler 2004. On the Hittite evidence for the Trojan War, see Bryce 2005: 357–71.

Chapter Eleven

ORESTES ON TRIAL
Myth and Thought

The Greek myths were not just entertaining stories, they were also tools for exploring questions and problems in Greek thought. To borrow a phrase from the anthropologist Claude Lévi-Strauss, myths were "good to think with". Aeschylus' *Oresteia*, for example, can be read as an investigation in dramatic form of the nature of justice and the necessary transition from personal vendetta to civic rule of law; Sophocles' *Antigone* can be read as an exploration of the relation between the household and the state; and Euripides' *Hippolytos* can be read as a meditation on self-control and moderation. Any drama, however, is likely to involve a complex of meanings, rather than one necessary meaning; moreover, different treatments of a myth, as in the various treatments of the story of Orestes' revenge, show that different writers could find various meanings in the same myth.

Literary works, such as the Athenian dramas, in the first instance express the thought of a particular artist, though insofar as they appeal to a larger public they also express public ideas. The thought of myth, however, belongs in a sense always to the society as a whole. Groups of myths with similar or related themes can express a range of ideas and attitudes. There are, for example, many myths concerning the origin or the proper form of sacrifice, and from these it is possible to see a variety of different views about the place of human beings in the cosmos, our relation to the gods and to animals, and the proper structure of society.

Mythic thought and literary thought based on myths are not philosophy. Philosophy presents arguments in a more or less logical form and offers them for scrutiny and potential refutation. Myths present ideas in the form of narratives rather than argument; contradictions are fatal to philosophic thought but abound in myth. Myth and philosophy will be the topic of the next chapter; this chapter explores a number of myths as expressions of ancient Greek thought about such subjects as justice, divinity, and the difference between gods and mortals.

Exploring Greek Myth. First Edition. Matthew Clark.
© 2012 Matthew Clark. Published 2012 by Blackwell Publishing Ltd.

I. MYTH AND THOUGHT IN ATHENIAN TRAGEDY

The Athenian tragedies were first of all dramas, works of art, the creations of individual poets. As works of art, however, they were also produced within a particular society and must to some extent express the ideas, conscious and unconscious, of that society. As Jean-Pierre Vernant says, "the true material of tragedy is the social thought peculiar to the city state" (1988a: 25).

Although the plots of the tragedies were almost exclusively taken from myth, the plays were very much involved with the present. The use of ancient myth in current drama seems to have created a kind of doubled distancing effect. On the one hand, "tragedy establishes a distance between itself and the myths of the heroes that inspire it. . . . It confronts heroic values and ancient religious representations with the new modes of thought that characterize the advent of law within the city-state" (Vernant 1988a: 26).[1] On the other hand, "this legendary world constitutes the past – a past sufficiently distant for the contrasts . . . to be clearly visible; yet a past still close enough for the clash of values still to be a painful one" (Vernant 1988b: 33). This distancing effect produced "a debate with a past that is still alive" (Vernant 1988b: 33). Tragedy thus constitutes a kind of dramatic thought, clothed in mythic narratives, staged within Athenian society as a critique of the society which allowed it to be staged.

Probably every tragedy can be seen as an expression of thought in some way. Some plays, however, are obviously concerned with public issues. And in most plays various themes are interwoven, so that the attempt to disentangle and analyze these various themes runs the risk of separating problems that were inextricable in Athenian thought. The following two sections explore the use of myth in dramatic thought through the analysis of specific plays.

II. MYTH AND THOUGHT IN AESCHYLUS

The plot of Aeschylus' *Oresteia* can be read as a meditation on the nature of justice. In the *Agamemnon*, the first play of the trilogy, Klytemnestra and Aigisthos kill Agamemnon when he returns victorious from Troy (see Figure 11.1.) In the *Libation-Bearers*, the second play, Klytemnestra and Aigisthos are killed by Orestes when he returns from years in exile; at the end of the play Orestes is driven mad by the avenging Furies. The third play, the *Eumenides*, begins in Delphi, where the Furies have chased Orestes, but then the scene changes as Orestes goes to Athens, where he is put on trial for the murder of his mother. The Furies are his prosecutors, Apollo defends him, Athena presides over the trial, and the verdict to acquit is rendered by a jury of Athenians, though Athena herself casts the deciding vote. At the end of the play Athena placates the Furies, who change their name to the Eumenides, the "Kindly Ones", and take on a new role as defenders of Athens.

Justice in various forms thus runs through the trilogy from beginning to end.[2] The Greek word for justice, "dikê" (pronounced "dee-kay"), has a broad range of meanings, including plain revenge, an action at law or a trial, and also the abstract sense of justice. The goddess Dikê was also a personified divinity. The Greek word and its derivatives occur frequently in all three plays of the trilogy, in all of these meanings.[3] Although different contexts lead to

Figure 11.1   Aigisthos prepares to kill Agamemnon, caught in a net while bathing. The Dokimasia Painter (ca. 460 BCE). Attic red-figure calyx krater (mixing bowl). H. 51 cm; D. 51 cm. Museum of Fine Arts, Boston, MA, USA. William Francis Warden Fund. 63.1246. Copyright © Museum of Fine Arts, Boston

different English translations of the word "dikê", all these meanings are related in the Greek root. The close relationships among all these meanings makes their conflict only the more bitter. The characters disagree not only about which actions in the play are "just", they also disagree about the very meaning of "justice".

As early as line 41 of the *Agamemnon*, the chorus describe Menelaos and Agamemnon jointly as the "antidikos" of Priam, that is, his opponent in a lawsuit. The meaning here must be metaphorical. The Trojan War was not a Trojan Lawsuit, and Aeschylus does not imagine any appropriate legal procedure at this point of the story. This use of the root "dik-", however, introduces the idea of justice as legality at the beginning of the trilogy. Likewise, Klytemnestra has no legal alternative to the murder of Agamemnon in response to the sacrifice of Iphigeneia.[4] Only at the end of the trilogy does the sense of Justice as a legal process reveal itself as the culmination of all the other senses.

A more abstract sense of justice is found at lines 249–50 of the *Agamemnon*, when the chorus say that "Dikê" or Justice inclines against some people so that they learn through suffering. Here the word may even refer to the personified divinity. But at lines 810–14, when Agamemnon first appears on stage, he gives thanks to the gods of Argos, who were jointly responsible with him for his return home and for the "dikaia" he brought about against the city of Priam. Here the word probably means revenge, rather than a court case or abstract justice.

Agamemnon's justice exacted against Troy is simply the destruction of the city. When Klytemnestra displays the corpse of her husband, she says that his murder was an act of justice (*Agamemnon* 1404–06). For her, too, justice is an act of physical revenge, murder.[5] A few lines later, she speaks of the fulfilled justice of her child; here the idea of revenge is not absent, but perhaps there is also the hint of a more abstract sense of Justice, since the word "Dikê" here is linked to the words "Atê" and "Erinys", which are the divine forces of Delusion and Retribution. In the following ode, the chorus sees Dikê not as a particular act of revenge but as an ongoing process; they foresee other acts of Dikê, as Justice is sharpened on the whetstone of Destiny.

As the chorus says, the kind of Dikê that Klytemnestra has called upon is likely to rebound and strike her, and that, of course, is what happens in the second play of the trilogy. When Orestes returns to seek justice for the murder of his father, it is clear that his idea of justice is revenge, and his sister Elektra shares his desire for revenge. (See, for instance, lines 394–98, where Elektra prays that the strength of Zeus may smash the heads of Klytemnestra and Aigisthos as the fulfillment of dikê.) But at times she seems to have a somewhat wider idea of justice, as can be seen, for instance, in the distinction she draws between a "dikastes", a juror, and a "dikephoros", probably someone who brings revenge (*Libation-Bearers* 119–20). The "dikastes" is different from the "dikephoros", but both are concerned with "dikê" in one sense or another.

The contrast between Elektra's view of "dikê" and her brother's is seen in two lines of their dialogue (*Libation-Bearers* 461–62):

> Orestes: Ares will collide with Ares; Dikê with Dikê.
> Elektra: O gods, be just in your judgments.

Here Orestes still thinks of Dikê primarily as revenge, something almost equivalent to the violence of war, while Elektra seems to appeal to the gods for a kind of justice that stands above the pattern of revenge and repeated revenge.

Orestes' murder of Klytemnestra cannot end the cycle of punishment. At this point, however, the method of punishment must change. Agamemnon's killing of Iphigeneia was avenged by Klytemnestra, and Klytemnestra's killing of Agamemnon was avenged by Orestes, but there is no member of the family in a position to avenge the killing of Klytemnestra. At first the Furies take on the role of avengers, at the end of the *Libation-Bearers*, and more explicitly in the *Eumenides*. The Furies drive Orestes mad, and although they threaten him, they do not kill him, as he had killed Klytemnestra and as Klytemnestra had killed Agamemnon.

At the beginning of the *Eumenides*, Apollo appears to Orestes and tells him to go to Athens, where he will find judges ("dikastes") for his case; and when Orestes arrives in Athens he says to the statue of Athena that he will await the outcome of his trial ("dikê"). The large central portion of the play consists of this trial; what had been an act of revenge or an idea of justice is now dramatized as a civic institution. This trial is presented as the first murder trial on the Areopagus; justice is no longer in the hands of individuals, but under the authority of the city and its citizens acting as jurors (lines 681–82).[6] The trial is established with a flurry of words of justice, and the language of justice continues during the trial.

Each participant in a trial is likely to make a claim for justice, and the Furies tell Athena repeatedly that it is their divine duty to punish Orestes as a matricide. She replies that they are telling only one side of the argument, and that they wish to be called just rather than to perform justice (428, 430). Apollo also claims that his side is just (615, 619). The trial itself – the "dikê", as it is called at line 582 – is designed to find out where "dikê" lies. In a sense, justice lies in the trial itself, since the only way to end the cycle of revenge is to turn punishment over to the city.

The status of the court of the Areopagus was a controversial issue in Athens at the time of the play. The democratic reforms of Ephialtes in 462/1 had limited the jurisdiction of the formerly powerful Areopagus to cases of homicide. It is hard to imagine that this play, first presented in 458, does not in some way refer to these reforms, but scholars have not agreed about what position Aeschylus takes.[7] In any case, the debate about justice in the trilogy occurs within a specific political context.

Many scholars interpret the trilogy as a whole as a lesson that dikê as revenge must be replaced by legal procedures.[8] Thus "the Justice of the Gods could become efficacious for men in this world through the workings of Law" (Podlecki 1966: 63). Gagarin, however, argues that "the Areopagus does not represent a new or different *dikè*. . . . Rather the *dikè* that the Areopagus upholds is basically the same *dikè* as in the earlier plays and includes a strong element of punishment, though it also includes the sense of lawful and peaceful behavior." It is the Furies who "stand firmly on the side of *dikè* in all its various senses . . . and who support the Areopagus and its principles" (Gagarin 1976: 71–72).

Trials at the court of the Areopagus certainly could end in punishment; to that extent the new judicial process continues the pattern of dikê as revenge. But there is an important difference, since the punishment is no longer determined by individuals or families but by the city. The Furies do not in fact firmly uphold the Areopagus. In the long choral ode they sing before the trial, they fear that the acquittal of Orestes would allow everyone to commit similar crimes (*Eumenides* 490–565); when he is acquitted, they say that the younger gods have trampled on the ancient laws which they represent (778–79). At the end of the play Athena must convince the Furies to take a new role in the protection of the city.

But more to the point, the movement of the entire trilogy shows a movement away from dikê as revenge towards dikê as legal procedure. This movement can also be seen in the context of political and economic changes in Greece. Justice as revenge, in this analysis, is linked to the "aristocratic, monarchic, and tyrannical forms of government", while justice as a legal process "is intimately linked with the presentation of a specific image of Athenian democracy" (Rose 1992: 198).[9]

In this trilogy Aeschylus takes advantage of the myth of the murder of Agamemnon, the murder of Klytemnestra, and the trial of Orestes to make a point in narrative form about the nature of justice. The thought presented in this trilogy is not political philosophy. It does not take the form of abstract argument, and it is not subject to the laws of logic. The value of mythic and literary thought is its narrative concreteness, the flesh it puts on the bones of an idea.[10]

This myth can be told, however, in other ways and with other themes. Homer uses it as an analogue to the story of the *Odyssey*, as a model against which the events of his own epic can be judged: thus Agamemnon corresponds to Odysseus, Klytemnestra corresponds to Penelope, Aigisthos corresponds to the suitors, and Orestes corresponds to Telemachos. The story is told again and again by various characters within the epic, each time for a different purpose.[11] But the question of justice does not arise.

Athenian dramatists after Aeschylus also dealt with parts of this story. Sophocles' *Elektra* tells about Orestes' return and the murder of Klytemnestra; although there is some discussion of dikê, the nature of justice is not an important issue, and Sophocles seems most interested to use the myth in order to present a character analysis of Agamemnon's daughter, Elektra. Euripides also wrote an *Elektra*, which deals with the same events. In this version, Elektra is rather self-important, and Orestes is a coward, while Aigisthos is a friendly host, and Klytemnestra is presented almost sympathetically. Euripides' *Orestes* takes place after the murder of Klytemnestra; in this play, the two children of Agamemnon are not much better than pathological killers. All of these meanings and more are available as interpretations of the myth of Agamemnon, Klytemnestra, and Orestes. When Aeschylus decided to present the myth of Agamemnon, he was not forced to make Justice his theme; but if he wanted to think about Justice in mythic and dramatic terms, he could hardly have found a better story.

III. MYTH AND THOUGHT IN SOPHOCLES AND EURIPIDES

Sophocles' *Antigone* is certainly one of the most political of his tragedies, but the political issues are also domestic, since they occur within a family. In part this play is concerned with two conceptions of law – the laws of the state as opposed to the laws of the gods.[12] Some modern scholars – most famously the philosopher Hegel – have interpreted the play as the conflict of the private moral conscience against the requirements of the state.[13] Something of the same interpretation is implicit in Jean Anouilh's revision of the play, written during the German occupation of France. For an Athenian audience, however, the laws of the gods were not private in the modern sense of the word.

The Myth of Antigone

Eteokles and Polyneikes, the two sons of Oedipus, have fought to the death over the rule of Thebes; their uncle Kreon, who has assumed power, grants burial rites to Eteokles but orders that the body of Polyneikes be thrown outside the city to be eaten by the dogs and birds. Antigone, one of the daughters of Oedipus, buries Polyneikes against Kreon's orders. She is arrested and brought before the king, her uncle, where she declares that the written laws of men cannot override the un-written laws of the gods. Kreon's son Haimon, Anti-gone's fiancé, argues for her life, but Kreon sentences her to be buried alive in a cave, so that she will die but not by execution. The blind prophet Teiresias then tells Kreon that he has polluted the city, and Kreon rushes off to the cave, where he finds that Antigone has hanged herself. Haimon attacks his father and then kills himself, and when his mother hears the news she too kills herself. Kreon is left alone to reflect on his errors.

There is no evidence for the story of Antigone before this play, and it is possible that Sophocles invented it, but the battle between Eteokles and Polyneikes at least was known to Homer (*Iliad* 4.377–78).

The play is organized around a number of oppositions, including the family and the state, the living and the dead, friends and enemies, and also the concerns of women, such as burial, and those of men, such as politics. Antigone insists that the unwritten laws handed down by the gods, most especially the laws concerning burial, are more powerful than Kreon's edict forbidding Polyneikes' burial. On the one hand burial is a family concern, and a concern particularly for women, but this household concern conflicts with the public interest, which is primarily a matter for men. She insists that the bonds of *philia*, or friendship, belong within the family, while Kreon argues that friendship should be calculated within the city. The story of Antigone thus brings together a complex of intersecting issues.

The play, however, should not be reduced to a political tract. As Charles Segal says,

> as a result of Hegel's famous analysis, much discussion of the play has focused on the question of which of the two protagonists has more of the right on his [or her] side. . . . We must avoid seeing the protagonists as one-dimensional representatives of simple oppositions: right and wrong, reason and emotion, state and individual, or the like. . . . The characters, like the play itself, have many levels that fuse organically, sometimes indistinguishably, into a complex unity; and here the confrontations of the two protagonists create an ever-ramifying interplay between interlocking and expanding issues. (Segal 1986: 137–38)

Segal here reminds us of an important difference between mythic or literary thought and philosophic thought. Philosophic thought has a kind of logical clarity missing from myth and literature, but myth and literature are better at showing the complexity of thought as it is lived, even if only in the imagination. Athenian tragedy, because of its particular form, is particularly good at staging conflicts between two characters as they actively manifest certain ideas. The task of the poet was to find a myth which could form the basis for such a conflict.

Euripides' *Hippolytos* is probably based on a traditional story, but evidence for the story before the play is thin. Homer mentions Phaidra (*Odyssey* 11.321), but he tells nothing about her. Sophocles wrote a play titled *Phaidra*, but it is lost and its date is unknown. At the end of Euripides' *Hippolytos*, Artemis promises the dying Hippolytos that the brides of Troizen will cut their hair in his honor and girls will sing songs about him and Phaidra (1423–30); most likely Euripides is offering an aetiology for a traditional practice. Pausanias' *Guide* (1.18.5; 1.22.1–3; 10.29.2) also mentions stories and monuments related to Phaidra and Hippolytos, and these may predate Euripides, though it is impossible now to be sure.

The Story of Hippolytos and Phaidra

Theseus had a son, Hippolytos, by the Queen of the Amazons, but later he married Phaidra, the daughter of King Minos and the sister of Ariadne. Hippolytos was devoted to the virgin goddess Artemis and scorned Aphrodite, who determined to destroy him. She made Phaidra fall into passionate love for her stepson, but Phaidra resolved to die rather than give in to her passion. Phaidra's nurse discovered the source of Phaidra's distress, and in an effort to save Phaidra's life she revealed the truth to Hippolytos, who reacted with revulsion and outrage. Phaidra then killed herself and left a note charging Hippolytos with attempted rape. Theseus discovered the note and despite his son's protestations of innocence he cursed him. When Hippolytos left to go into exile, his horses were thrown into a panic by the appearance of a bull from the sea, and Hippolytos was mortally injured. When he was brought to Theseus, the goddess Artemis appeared and explained to Theseus what happened. Theseus is left alone to mourn his wife and his son and to regret his rash curse.

Euripides in fact wrote two versions of the story. In the first version, which is lost, Phaidra probably spoke with Hippolytos directly to declare her passion. Scholars generally agree that this version was considered scandalous, and so Euripides produced a second version, in which Phaidra resists her passion and never speaks to Hippolytos. The myth of Hippolytos, in whatever form it came to him, gave Euripides opportunity to consider a number of ideas, including the nature of divinity, the nature of moderation, and the relations between the sexes.[14]

At the beginning of the play, the goddess Aphrodite explains that she is angry at Hippolytos and is determined to destroy him because he refuses to give her the honor she requires; she is unconcerned that she will incidentally destroy Phaidra. In this prologue, as Desmond Conacher notes, "Aphrodite as a goddess is intentionally overdrawn and unconvincing" (Conacher 1967: 16; cf. 28). Then at the end of the play, the goddess Artemis explains (perhaps unconvincingly) why she was unable to help her favorite, Hippolytos: the gods are not allowed to interfere in each other's plans. She promises, however, to take revenge by punishing the next mortal man Aphrodite falls in love with. Neither goddess appears to best advantage.

In between these two divine appearances, however, no god appears in the play, and the story works out through the personalities of the characters almost as if no divine influence were necessary. The chorus, on the other hand, repeatedly sings about the power and the danger of Aphrodite as a divine force; and these are demonstrated by the events of the play. Aphrodite as represented in these songs is quite unlike the petty jealous goddess of the prologue. Perhaps Euripides means to critique the anthropomorphic view of the gods (Conacher 1967: 29). The critique of religion is a major theme in many of Euripides' plays; it is important, however, to distinguish the critique of certain religious beliefs and practices from disbelief.

The cause of all the trouble in the play is Hippolytos' refusal to honor Aphrodite, not only in ritual, but also in his actions. He takes this refusal to be "sophrosyne", which is usually translated as "moderation" or "self-control",[15] but which in his mouth seems more narrowly to mean "chastity" (as in 79–80, 667–68, 995, 1007, 1034–35, 1100, 1365), as it does also when others speak about him (Phaidra, 731; Theseus, 949; Artemis, 1403). But others in the play use the term in something closer to its fundamental sense. Thus Phaidra explains that she tried to control her passion for Hippolytos through sophrosyne, or self-control (399). A key moment comes when Phaidra resolves to die rather than face public dishonor; and by her death, she says, Hippolytos will learn to be moderate (730–31). In his own eyes, he is the model of sophrosyne,[16] but according to Phraidra, sophrosyne is the virtue that he needs to learn. The lesson seems to be that extremism in the pursuit of moderation leads to disaster.

Hippolytos' chastity seems to be based not on self-control, but on revulsion. It is not just the thought of sex that he finds repellent, but the whole female sex. When he finds out from the nurse that Phaidra is in love with him, he delivers a long and bitter speech, not just against her, but against all women (616–77). He asks why Zeus created them in the first place, and he fantasizes that men should have been able to have children by purchasing them at temples. As it is, women are simply a drain on the household where they are born and a curse on the household where they live after marriage. The best wife is a simple fool, and clever women are the worst. He will never have his fill of hating women, for they are always evil. Someone should teach them to be chaste (to be sophron), or he will always trample them underfoot. There was certainly an element of misogyny in ancient Greek society, but these opinions of Hippolytos are not necessarily to be taken as the opinions of Euripides. Hippolytos is an extremist, and the audience is not expected to agree with what he says.[17]

Euripides was perhaps the most obviously intellectual of the three Athenian tragic poets. In order to understand the mythic thought of his plays, however, it is necessary to move beyond Vernant's claim that "the true material of tragedy is the social thought peculiar to the city state", or at least beyond the idea that social thought is primarily political. Thought in all three tragic poets ranges from the occasional specific political reference, though the exploration of more general civic or social problems, to the consideration of more abstract questions. And always the drama must be effective as drama.

Mythic Thought in Modern Drama

The use of myth as social critique continues in modern times. During the Nazi occupation of France, the philosopher and writer Jean-Paul Sartre wrote *Les Mouches* (*The Flies*), a revision of the story of Orestes produced in 1943, and Jean Anouilh's *Antigone* was produced in February 1944. Both playwrights used the distancing effect of myth to write about the situation at the time in a way that would elude censorship. To speak somewhat simplistically, Kreon in *Antigone* and Aigisthos in *The Flies* both represent the government of occupied France, while Antigone and Orestes represent some kind of resistance to illegitimate authority, but neither play is simply propaganda, and both Kreon and Aigisthos are portrayed more sympathetically than one might have expected. In addition, each author uses myth in the service of larger philosophic questions. *The Flies*, with its emphasis on human freedom and choice, is clearly an expression of Sartre's existentialism. Anouilh, on the other hand, has created a proto-structuralist world in which people are forced to act out roles handed to them no matter what they may want to do.

IV. SACRIFICE AND MYTHIC THOUGHT

Myth as literature can be understood through the tools of literary analysis, such as character analysis and close reading of verbal patterns. These tools, however, are less appropriate to the study of myth as myth. The study of mythic thought requires its own method: the collection of all available related myths rather than close reading of one canonized literary version, and a comparison of all these versions to take note of similarities and differences. Where these myths are similar, then most likely the myth is expressing something generally felt within the society, but where the myths are different, the differences may reflect some conflict within ancient Greek thought.

This section examines a selection of myths concerned with sacrifice. Ritual sacrifice was one of the most pervasive social practices in ancient Greece, and a number of myths deal with the origin of sacrifice or its meaning and function. Myths are not required to be consistent with each other, and each of these myths expresses something particular about sacrifice in Greek thought. Because Greek thought about sacrifice was complex, it could not be expressed by any one story.

Sacrifice took various forms in ancient Greece. It could be an offering of fruits and grains, but it often involved the killing and eating of an animal, almost always a domestic animal.[18] Often sacrifice was public, but there were also private, household sacrifices. Sacrifice could be offered to the Olympian deities or to the chthonic gods or to the dead.[19] An essential feature of sacrifice is that something is given up, but in most animal sacrifice, the best parts of the animal were kept and cooked and eaten.

The origin of animal sacrifice is of course featured in one of the earliest and most famous of all Greek myths, Hesiod's story of the sacrifice at Mekone (*Theogony* 535–69). This story takes place in the time when the gods and mortals still associate with each other and still eat together. Prometheus divides the sacrificed animal into two portions, and he tries to trick Zeus into taking the inferior portion – the inedible bones – by making it look appetizing. Zeus is not fooled, but he takes the inferior portion anyway. And so, Hesiod tells us, mortals burn the bones of the sacrificial animals for the gods. Hesiod's account continues with the withholding of fire and the creation of woman, both of which are punishments for the trick of Prometheus (see Vernant 1989).

This Promethean division of the animal is the first sacrifice. This moment when sacrifice was invented was also the moment when the gods were separated from mortals (*Theogony* 535). When mortals still associated directly with the gods, there would be no need to sacrifice to them, but once they were separated, sacrificial ritual showed how they could remain in communication. Sacrifice also distinguishes human beings from animals, who eat uncooked food, but who serve as cooked food for mortals. The ritual of animal sacrifice thus marks the fundamental division of the world into divinities, mortals, and animals, separated but linked (Vernant 1980: 149, 195–99; 1989: 24–29).

A first reading of Hesiod's story seems to suggest that mortals got the better of the deal, since we get to eat the meat and the gods get only the smoke from the burning bones. But another reading suggests that our mortality is caused precisely from our eating of meat. The gods do not eat meat, they do not live on other living things, and therefore they do not die (Detienne 1989: 7).

Animal sacrifice creates a society among the participants. There is a fundamental division between the people who are allowed to be part of a particular ritual and those who are excluded, or who, like the followers of Pythagoras and Orpheus, exclude themselves (Burkert 1985: 58; Detienne 1989: 5–6). The ritual may mark certain divisions among the participants. The meat could be divided into different portions, and the choice parts would be given to those of high rank as a sign of status; or else the meat could be divided into equal portions, to be shared equally among a society of equals; or the two systems could be combined (Detienne 1989: 13). Thus the ritual reflects different views of social organization.

Sacrifice, according to Hesiod, was initiated by a divinity, but once instituted, it is a human practice. Ordinarily the gods have no reason to sacrifice, no one to sacrifice to. The *Homeric Hymn to Hermes*, however, oddly violates this principle. The hymn begins with the birth of Hermes, the last of the Olympians (in this version), the child of Zeus and the nymph Maia, who, according to the poet, lives in a cave and avoids the company of the gods (1–19).

As soon as Hermes is born, he begins to perform amazing deeds. He immediately jumps out of his cradle and goes off to steal the cattle of Apollo. On his way he comes across a tortoise and makes it into the first lyre (20–67). He then steals 50 of Apollo's cattle; he makes them walk backwards so that they cannot be traced, until they reach the river Alpheios (68–104). There Hermes makes a fire, evidently the first fire (111).[20] Once he has made a fire, he now turns two of the cows over on their backs and kills them. He cuts up the meat, which he roasts on spits, and he stretches the hide out on a rock. Then he divides the meat into twelve portions, making each a perfect "geras", or gift of honor (112–29). The smell of the meat tempts him, even though he is an immortal, but he does not allow himself to eat any of the sacrifice. He then burns the heads and feet and cleans up after the ritual.

Some scholars interpret this performance as the first sacrifice (see Vernant 1989b), and so it must be if Hermes has just invented fire. The text does not explicitly make this claim, however, and myth is not required to follow logic. If it is the first sacrifice, it has a number of odd characteristics: Hermes makes a trench, which would be appropriate for an offering to a chthonic god or a hero, rather than an altar, which would be appropriate for the Olympian gods; and whereas in a proper sacrifice the victims are supposed to show their willingness to be killed, here it is emphasized that the cows struggle and Hermes must use force to kill them.

Jenny Strauss Clay (1989: 119–27) argues that this performance should not be seen as primarily a sacrifice at all, but rather as a *dais*, a feast of equals. Hermes' great desire is to enter the company of the gods as an equal, and everything he does in the hymn is organized towards that goal. It would thus be against his interests to organize a proper sacrifice, in which he as sacrificer would eat the meat and the gods would enjoy only the odors. Instead, he sets out twelve portions for twelve participants, the number of the Olympian gods if he is included. But the gods fail to appear, because they do not eat meat. And Hermes proves (perhaps paradoxically) that he belongs among them when he abstains. "It is not, as Hermes intended, the communal consumption of the *dais* that establishes Hermes' membership in the company of the Olympians, but on the contrary, his *inability* to partake of it that confirms his divinity" (Clay 1989: 122). As yet, however, Hermes' entrance to Olympus is only symbolic, and the rest of the poem describes how he brings it about in reality.

The story of fire and sacrifice in the *Homeric Hymn* is not at all the same as the story in the *Theogony*, but the two stories use some of the same materials to make rather different points. Sacrifice in the *Theogony* ultimately divides the immortals, who do not eat meat, from mortals, who do, whereas the symbolic feast in the *Hymn* shows that Hermes, by refusing to eat the meat, belongs among the immortals. In both stories, sacrifice imitates the structure of the cosmos.

The meat in sacrificial ritual was prepared and consumed in a fixed order. First the innards – the heart and the liver – were roasted on spits and eaten immediately by those most directly involved in the ritual; second, the rest of the meat was roasted or boiled and distributed to the other participants or even to those not directly involved in the sacrifice

(Burkert 1985: 56–57). In the Orphic myth of the death and resurrection of Dionysos, however, the procedure is different. In this myth, Zeus proclaims that Dionysos will be the next divine king. The Titans then kidnap the baby and cut it up into pieces, which they first boil, then roast, and then eat. Athena, however, saves the heart, from which a new Dionysos is born. Zeus blasts the Titans with his thunderbolt, and a new race of mortals is created from the soot. When these mortals die they are resurrected in human or animal form (see Chapter Two).

This mythic sacrifice is problematic in several ways. First, sacrifice is ordinarily a human activity, and the Titans, though they are not Olympian gods, are certainly not human. This sacrifice cannot serve the usual function of linking the world of mortals to the world of immortals. Second, divinities, even Titans, do not ordinarily eat meat. Third, the sacrificial victim is not a domestic animal, and not even a human being, but a god. And fourth, the sequence of boiling and then roasting violates the usual sacrificial order.[21] Clearly this is a sacrifice gone wrong.

The Hesiodic myth of sacrifice establishes both the division between gods and mortals and the practice of animal sacrifice through which they relate to each other. In Orphism, however, these three realms are not strictly divided. There is something divine in the human, but there is something human in the animal as well. The Orphics generally removed themselves from society, which, they believed, was founded on murder, since the animals that are sacrificed and eaten are resurrected human souls. "The living devour each other; legal cannibalism reigns" (Detienne 1989: 7). The myth of the sacrifice of Dionysos, as compared to the myth of sacrifice in Hesiod, reflects the Orphic view of sacrifice and the position of mortals in the world (Vernant 1989: 50–51).[22]

The Greeks ordinarily sacrificed only domestic animals. There was a time, however, when no animals were sacrificed and only grains were offered to the gods, or so the myths said. The myth of the Bouphonia explains how animal sacrifice began, how it first happened that an ox was killed and how this killing of an ox became a ritual practice (see Chapter One). The story takes place in the time of Erechtheus, a time of origins, when people ate and sacrificed only grains. The first killing of an ox was an act of angry impulse, and it was performed by a foreigner, but it became an Athenian ritual at the orders of the Oracle at Delphi. Thus, if now we live by killing, and if we kill the animals closest to us, we are not really to blame, so the story says, and so the ritual of the Bouphonia demonstrates through its elaborate deferral of responsibility away from the human actors onto the instrument of the killing.

Human sacrifice was of course forbidden, as was cannibalism, but neither was unthinkable. Barbarians, people outside Greek society, were thought to engage in human sacrifice. Bousiris, the mythic king of Egypt, performed human sacrifice in obedience to an oracle, but when he tried to sacrifice Herakles, the great hero killed him and his son; but Herodotus explains that this story cannot be true, since the Egyptians do not even sacrifice animals (*Histories* 2.45).[23] The Taurians also practiced human sacrifice; it was fitting, therefore, that Iphigeneia became their priestess after Artemis saved her from being sacrificed at Aulis. But as this example shows, in Greek myth Greeks can sacrifice Greeks. Agamemnon's attempt to sacrifice his daughter puts him in the company of Tantalos and Lykaon. In each instance the perpetrator is doing something fundamentally wrong, something non-Greek, and the result is disastrous.

Human sacrifice was hinted at in a few actual rituals: at Halai, a man's throat was cut just enough to draw blood (Euripides, *Iphigeneia in Tauris* 1450–61); and in Lakonia boys were whipped at an altar (this ritual scourging supposedly replaced a ritual of human sacrifice, see *Guide* 3.16.9–11). Both these rituals were connected with Artemis, who must have had a bloodthirsty side to her character.

Further Explorations

The ancient Greeks tended to think in terms of polar oppositions, such as mortal/immortal or male/female (see Lloyd 1966 for extensive discussion of polarities in early Greek thought). It is not surprising, therefore, that modern structuralist thought, which also works with binary oppositions, has been fruitfully applied to Greek myth, for example in the work of Jean-Pierre Vernant, Pierre Vidal-Naquet, and Marcel Detienne, some of which has been noted in these explorations. Thought in Greek myth, however, can be considerably more complicated than a simple binary analysis can explain. Sacrifice, for instance, distinguishes at least three positions – divine, human, and animal – and perhaps more – domestic animals as opposed to wild animals, for instance, and civilized human beings, who sacrifice in the proper manner, as opposed to those who are uncivilized and do not carry out proper sacrifice. Use the various stories about Herakles as an example to investigate the complexities of thought in Greek myth.

The imagery of sacrifice, and particularly sacrifice gone wrong, is common in literary versions of myth. For example, Odysseus' shipmates sacrifice the cattle of the Sun, which are divine and should be inviolate, and as a punishment they are killed in a storm at sea (*Odyssey* 12.260–419). The murder of Agamemnon and Cassandra is described over and over as a kind of sacrifice (Aeschylus, *Agamemnon* 1056–58, 1277–78, 1295–98, 1309–10, 1433). Herakles is sacrificing when he wears the poisoned robe sent to him by Deianeira, and the heat from the fire causes the poison to work; the death of Herakles on the pyre on Mount Oeta can be seen as a culmination of that sacrifice (Sophocles, *Trachiniae* 749–812).[24] These are only three of many possible examples.

Animal sacrifice is thus a primary topic in several myths and it plays a role in many more. In the golden age, the time of origins, no animals were sacrificed, only grains, and so the invention of sacrifice marks a change in the human condition. The fundamental division between gods and immortals is explained by the division of foods at the sacrifice (though the Orphic myth rejects that explanation). Hermes takes his place in the company of the gods because he shares their aversion to meat. Animals may be sacrificed, but human sacrifice is forbidden, non-Greek, and when it occurs it marks a disastrous breakdown of Greek morality and behavior. Hunted animals, however, are usually not sacrificed; they are the enemies of the human community, not its servants. The community of those participating in the sacrifice is structured by their participation in the process of the sacrifice and their consumption of the meat. And sacrifice, especially sacrifice gone wrong, becomes a frequent event or image in Greek literature. No single myth shows all these ideas together, but taken together the Greek myths about sacrifice display a complex process of thought on a wide variety of topics.

CONCLUSION

A myth is a story, made of characters and events, rather than an argument. Still, even if a myth is not a completed thought in itself, it is nonetheless good to think with. Individual artists – poets, dramatists, painters, sculptors – can use a myth in order to express themes and ideas about justice, moderation, relationships with families, and so on; but because a myth is not an argument, different artists can find different meanings in the same myth (see Chapter Four). Literary interpretation of myth most often concentrates on a specific work of art in order to discover the ideas of a particular artist. Of course the ideas presented by a particular artist may then find a more general response if they speak to the concerns of a community.

The mythic tradition as a whole is also good to think with, but the tradition expresses the thought of a society rather than an individual. This kind of thought is most often found not in one work of art, but rather in groups of related stories, and often not in what is said directly, but what is implied by the structures and patterns of the narratives. Analysis of these structures and patterns in myth may reveal Greek ideas about the structure of the cosmos or about the structure of society. This kind of analysis may discover contradictions, which the myths may attempt to resolve, or ideas which were below the level of conscious expression. Thus, as the readings suggested below demonstrate, the study of myth can be a valuable aid for understanding a deep level of ancient Greek thought.

FURTHER READING

The scholarship on Athenian tragedy is vast. Only those works referenced in the text are noted here; the interested student will easily find further bibliography. On the social context of Athenian drama, see Winkler and Zeitlin 1990. On mythic thought in tragedy, see Vernant 1988a and 1988b; also Hall 1997 (as well as Hall 1989 for detailed discussion on Athenian representation of barbarians in tragedy). On Aeschylus' *Oresteia* see Podlecki 1966, Gagarin 1976, Goldhill 1986, Goldhill 1992, Rose 1992, and Carter 2007. On Sophocles' *Antigone*, see Segal 1981 and 1986 and Blundell 1989. Steiner 1984 discusses the story of Antigone in the Western tradition. On Euripides' *Hippolytos*, see Conacher 1967: 27–46, Segal 1986, Burian 1997, and Rabinowitz 1993. Detienne and Vernant 1989 includes a variety of essays on sacrifice in ancient Greece. For a structuralist analysis of the story of Prometheus, see Vernant 1980: 183–201, and for an elaboration and extension of this discussion see Vernant 1989.

Chapter Twelve

PLATO AND THE POETS
Philosophy and Myth

Just as myth and history seemed to be fundamentally opposed, but then turned out to be linked, so the seeming opposition between myth and philosophy conceals a deeper and more complex relationship. On the one hand, myth and philosophy are simply different kinds of mental activity: myth is a collection of fabulous stories, while philosophy aspires to be a system of true statements. But on the other hand, philosophy in a sense grows out of myth, or at least comes into being in the context of myth. Hesiod, in particular, presents pre-philosophic speculation about the nature of the cosmos, while some of the pre-Socratic philosophers present their ideas in a somewhat mythical guise. But philosophy gradually became a distinct way of thought partly by working to deny its origins in myth.

Myths could be saved, however, through allegory, in which the gods and events of myth were understood symbolically, or through rationalization, in which the divine or magical elements are removed and the stories are interpreted as misunderstandings of the events of history or of everyday life. Rationalization saves the myths by reducing their imaginative quality, while allegory saves them by extending the imagination beyond the literal events of the stories.

At times, however, myth was used as a basis for philosophic thought, as in the pre-Socratic philosophers Parmenides, Prodicus, and Protagoras. Plato is famous for his hostility to myth and to the poets who told the mythic stories, but he mentions myth frequently, and many of his dialogues include stories with a mythic quality. Moreover, he is perhaps the only philosopher who invented a story that has a claim to true mythic status – the myth of Atlantis.

I. SKEPTICISM, ALLEGORY, AND RATIONALIZATION

Although myth was pervasive in ancient Greek culture, not everyone simply believed in the myths. Some skepticism can be seen as early as the sixth century, in the writings of the

Exploring Greek Myth. First Edition. Matthew Clark.
© 2012 Matthew Clark. Published 2012 by Blackwell Publishing Ltd.

pre-Socratic philosopher Xenophanes of Colophon (ca. 570–480 BCE). His works have come down to us only in fragments, but it is possible even from these scraps to see that he does not accept the traditional view of religion and the gods. Homer and Hesiod, he says, attribute all sorts of crimes to the gods, including theft and adultery and deception (Fragment 11).

Xenophanes also mocks the anthropomorphic portraits of the gods, which imagined the gods as if they have bodies and wear clothes; he suggests that if horses or cows or lions could draw and paint, they would portray the gods as horses or cows or lions (Fragments 14, 15). In his view, there is one god who is greatest, and this god is not like human beings either physically or mentally (Fragment 23); this god is a unity, seeing and thinking and hearing as a unity; he never moves, but he keeps the cosmos moving through his thoughts (Fragments 23–26). Xenophanes also developed non-mythical ideas about the nature of the world; he said that everything derives from earth and water (Fragment 33). Iris, the goddess of the rainbow, who was sometimes thought of as the messenger of the gods, since the rainbow links the earth and the sky, was really some kind of colored cloud (Fragment 32).

Xenophanes represents a new tone of rationalism in Greek thought, but it is possible to see a link between his rationalism and myth. His statement that everything derives from earth and water, for instance, could be expressed in the language of myth: everything is born from Gaia and Okeanos. The thrust of his fragments, however, is clearly opposed to the mythic tradition.

Allegorical interpretations of myth, in which the characters and events of myth were thought to symbolize natural processes, could preserve the mythic tradition in a way that was compatible with rationalism. Allegorical interpretations of Homeric myth begin as early as the sixth century BCE, when Theagenes of Rhegium (fl. 525 BCE) seems to have argued that the names of the gods in Homer represented natural elements. Thus Homer's battle of the gods (*Iliad* 20.54–75) was an allegory for a natural process, the battle of physical forces, and thus Homer was protected from the indecency of saying that divinities could fight each other. Allegorical interpretations of Homer were continued, for example by Metrodorus of Lampsacus (the elder: d. 464 BCE), and by some later critics as well. In the third century CE, the Neoplatonic philosopher Porphyry (?234–?305 CE) wrote an elaborate allegorical interpretation of Homer's description of the Cave of the Nymphs (*Odyssey* 13.102–12). This kind of allegorical interpretation has little appeal for most readers of Homer today, but it was popular in the ancient world.

Myths could also be rationalized by removing their divine or magical aspects and interpreting them as accounts of historical events or of everyday occurrences which had somehow been misunderstood. Thus Herodotus began his history with rationalized versions of the stories of Io, Europa, Medea, and Helen of Troy (see Chapter Ten). In Euripides' *Bacchae*, Teiresias gives a rationalizing account of the new god, Dionysos. Whereas Demeter (or Earth, as he says, and he adds, call her whatever you like) provides dry foods, grain, Dionysos provides wet nourishment, wine. And the story that Dionysos was sewn into the thigh of Zeus he explains as a verbal misunderstanding, a kind of pun in Greek: in order to protect the infant Dionysos from Hera, Zeus gave her a hostage – "omeros" in Greek – but this was confused with the Greek word "meros", which means "thigh" (*Bacchae* 275–300). The rest of the play casts this kind of rationalizing in a very poor light, and one wonders if the weakness of the pun is intended as a signal that it should be disregarded immediately.

In the late fourth century BCE, Euhemerus, who worked at the court of Cassander, king of Macedon, wrote a travel narrative (now surviving only in fragments and in a later summary) in which he suggests that the Greek gods Ouranos, Kronos, and Zeus had originally been mortal kings who had been regarded as divine after their deaths. Because so little of the original work remains, it is hard to know exactly how Euhemerus intended this story, but the term Euhemerism is now used to mean the interpretation of mythic characters as real persons of history.

In the second half of the fourth century BCE, a writer known to us as Palaephatus, perhaps connected with Aristotle's school, produced a collection of rationalized myths, part of which survives under the title *On Unbelievable Tales*. His method of rationalization, however, should be distinguished from Euhemerism, which calls into question the existence of the gods themselves. Palaephatus leaves the gods alone, and critiques the more fantastic elements of myths involving human beings (Stern 1996: 8). For instance, he rejects the story that Aktaion was turned into a stag and then killed by his own dogs. He also rejects the idea that Kallisto turned into a bear. Instead, he says, Kallisto went into a grove of trees where she was eaten by a bear. When her companions saw that only a bear came out of the grove, and Kallisto had disappeared, they thought that Kallisto had turned into a bear. He rejects the idea that Daidalos made statues that could walk. Instead, he says, Daidalos was the first sculptor who made his statues with feet in a striding position rather than held closely together, so people said that his figures were walking rather than standing.

Palaephatus rejects the idea that Pasiphaë, wife of King Minos of Crete, had intercourse with a bull. He notes that animals with different sexual organs are unable to mate, and he argues that even if they could mate, they could not have offspring. What really happened was that Pasiphaë fell in love with a young man named Taurus, which means "bull" in Greek, just at the same time that her husband, King Minos, was suffering from a genital ailment. When Pasiphaë then had a child, Minos realized that the child could not be his, and he realized it was the child of Taurus, the bull. When the child, now grown up, proved to be unruly, Minos tried to restrain him, but he dug himself a tunnel where he hid. Minos executed criminals by throwing them into the tunnel, where the Minotaur would kill them.

Palaephatus' collection comprises 45 such rationalized myths (and seven brief mythic narratives written by someone else and added to the collection). None of them show any intelligence or imagination, but they do show a complex desire to keep something of the mythic tradition while depriving it of any mythic vitality.

Greek intellectual culture continued to display a complex attitude to myth, as can be seen in Plutarch's *Life of Theseus*, written in the late first or early second century CE. Here Plutarch was faced with a problem, which he readily acknowledges. He considers Theseus an historical figure, but he realizes that many of the stories told about Theseus cannot be true. He tries, therefore, to "purify the fables" so that the stories can "take on the appearance of history"; but some stories, even though incredible, are too good to leave out, and he begs his readers for indulgence (*Theseus* 1). Plutarch does include much of the traditional account of the life and deeds of Theseus. At times he includes several conflicting accounts from different sources.

Many of the episodes in the life of Theseus are fabulous, but not impossible, and most of these Plutarch simply tells without bothering with any rationalization. But the story of the

Minotaur required an explanation. Plutarch grants that Minos demanded a tribute of young men and women from the Athenians, but the Labyrinth, he says, was merely a prison, and the Minotaur was merely a man named Taurus, a general in the Cretan army. Plutarch includes the episode of Ariadne and the thread, but he also reports other versions. In one of these, the annual funeral games for Minos' son Androgeus were about to occur, and the general Taurus was expected to win. His prize would be the young men and women sent from Athens. But Taurus was unpopular, and there were rumors about his intimacy with Pasiphaë. (Here there is an echo from Palaephatus' version, though Plutarch does not mention him.) Theseus challenged Taurus and defeated him. Ariadne, who was in the audience, fell in love with Theseus, and Minos, who was pleased by the defeat of Taurus, released all the Athenians (*Theseus* 19).

Plutarch goes on to give an account of the political reforms which Theseus was supposed to have brought about, in which the various independent towns of Attica were joined together into one political entity (*Theseus* 24). He also discusses Theseus' encounters with the Amazons. There is no good evidence that the Amazons ever existed, and certainly no good evidence for the stories about Theseus and the Amazons, but Plutarch treats the Amazons as fully historical figures (*Theseus* 26–27). He briefly mentions the story of Phaidra and Hippolytos, and he says that since the literary and the historical accounts agree, then the story is probably true (*Theseus* 28). Plutarch also includes the story of the marriage of Pirithous and the battle of the Centaurs and Lapiths at the wedding feast; once again he gives no indication that he doubts the story, though it is hard to imagine that he believed in Centaurs (*Theseus* 30).

According to the mythic tradition, Theseus and his friend Pirithous kidnapped Helen and went on a journey to Hades; Plutarch includes these stories, but in a rationalized form. In this version, after Pirithous and Theseus stole Helen, they went to Epirus to find a wife for Pirithous. They approached the king of the Molossians, whose name was Aidoneus (or Hades), and whose wife's name was Persephone, for the hand of his daughter, Kore. King Aidoneus required prospective suitors to fight his dog, whose name was Cerberus. The dog killed Pirithous, and Aidoneus kept Theseus prisoner, until Herakles came and rescued him (*Theseus* 31, 35).

Plutarch's account taken as a whole is not really consistent. He clearly finds the traditional stories important, and equally clearly he realizes that they cannot be considered history. At times he presents rationalized versions of the stories, such as the story of the Minotaur or the story of the trip to Hades, but at other times he tells incredible stories, such as the story of the Centaurs, without any suggestion of doubt. Perhaps there is no point in trying to make sense of Plutarch's position; he is, however, a good example of the complex attitudes Greeks could have to their mythic tradition.

II. PARMENIDES, PRODICUS, AND PROTAGORAS

It is hardly surprising that some philosophers, such as Xenophanes, were skeptical about myth, but other philosophers found myth useful as a basis for their investigations and speculations. For example, the close connection between myth and philosophy can be seen clearly in the fragmentary poem *On Nature* written by the pre-Socratic philosopher Parmenides (b. ca. 510 BCE). On the one hand, Parmenides draws a distinction between belief and knowledge, and also enunciates something like the principle of the excluded middle – either a statement is true or its negation is true – and thus he has a claim to be one of the founders of logical philosophy.[1] On the other hand, he presents his philosophic account in the form of a quasi-mythical journey through the gate that leads from night to day; the key to the gate is held by Justice. Parmenides is attended by the daughters of the sun, and at the end of his journey he meets a goddess, whose philosophic discourse forms the bulk of the poem. Because Parmenides' poem is difficult and fragmentary, there is much scholarly debate about what it means. It seems, however, that he wanted to establish a way of thought that is philosophic in itself, but that he felt the need to ground this way of thought in a mythical form.

The philosopher Prodicus of Keos was a contemporary of Socrates, born in the first half of the fifth century BCE, though his exact dates are unknown. Very little of his writing has survived, but Xenophon, the Athenian soldier and writer, has preserved a story, now known as the Choice of Herakles, which he says was told by Prodicus. In this story, which Socrates tells to his friend Aristippus, Herakles is addressed by two women, one the personification of Vice, the other the personification of Virtue, and each attempts to persuade him to follow her path. The story itself is not traditional, but it is cast in a mythical form, with personified divinities and the greatest hero of Greek myth.

The Choice of Herakles

When Herakles was a young man, he went off by himself to decide whether to travel the path of virtue or the path of vice. As he debated, two women of great stature came towards him. (Great stature was a characteristic of divinities.) One of these women was beautiful and modestly dressed in white, with a modest and sober countenance. The other had a full and soft figure; she was wearing make-up, and she was dressed provocatively.

This second woman ran up to Herakles and shouted to him, "I see that you are pondering which path of life to take. Choose me as your friend, and I will lead you along the easiest and most pleasant road; you will have all the pleasures and none of the pains of life. And you will never have to earn money, but you can live off the work of others and take money in any way you can. My friends call me Happiness, but my enemies call me Vice."

The other woman now approached him and said, "I hope, Herakles, that you will take my road and that you will become a person who achieves great and noble deeds. But I will not deceive you. The gods give nothing without work and effort. If you want the favor of the gods, you must worship them; if you want the love of friends, you must act well towards them; if you want honor from a city, you must give it aid; and if you want the praise of all Greece for your virtue, you must benefit all of Greece. If you want your fields to yield crops, you must cultivate them; if you want your flock to flourish, you must care for it. If you want the power to free your friends and defeat your enemies, you must learn the arts of war, and if you want a strong body, you must train it to be the servant of your mind through effort and perspiration." This woman was named Virtue.

Vice then said to Herakles, "Do you see what a long and hard road this woman recommends? But my road is short and easy." Virtue answered her, "What good thing is really yours if you do nothing to earn it? You don't even wait for desire. You eat before you are hungry, you drink before you are thirsty. You long for sleep not because your work makes you tired, but because your tedium makes you bored. You party at night and sleep all the day. You are immortal, but the gods hate you. What sane man would join your company? When your followers are young, they are weak, when they are old they are withered and weary; they are ashamed of what they have done, and what they do brings them only distress. They spent their early years in pleasure and have only pain for their old age."

"But I," Virtue continued, "associate with the gods and with good men, and no good deeds are done without my help. My friends enjoy their food, which they eat only when they are hungry. They sleep soundly, and they wake up happy. The young strive to win praise from the old, and the old are glad to be honored by the young. When their lives end, they are not forgotten, but they live on in song. Herakles, if you will toil in this way, you will achieve for yourself the most blessed happiness." (Xenophon, *Memorabilia* 2.21–34)

According to Plato, the sophist Protagoras claimed to be able to teach the art of living in the city, that is, politics (Plato, *Protagoras* 318e–319a). Socrates challenged him, on the grounds that political virtue is not a kind of expertise, such as architecture or shipbuilding, and also that those who are the best politicians, such as Perikles, have not been able to pass on their skills to their sons (*Protagoras* 319b–d). Protagoras defended his position in part with a philosophical fable.[2]

When it became time for mortal animals to be created, Protagoras says, the gods formed them from earth and fire and then gave to Prometheus and his brother Epimetheus the task of apportioning the various powers to each animal. Epimetheus asked if he could be in charge of the initial apportioning, and then Prometheus would review his work. Epimetheus then handed out these various powers in a kind of pattern of balances – he gave strength to the slow animals, for example, and speed to the weak animals – so that no kind of animal would be destroyed. He also apportioned fur or tough skin against the cold, and also the various kinds of food. He made predators less fertile and their prey more fertile.

But when Epimetheus came to the end of his various gifts, he found that he had nothing left to give to human beings. When Prometheus came to review the work, he found human beings without resources to save themselves. So he stole from Athena and Hephaistos fire and the various crafts and gave these to the human race (and later on he had to stand trial for his thefts).

At first there were no cities and people lived scattered about. Their knowledge of fire and technical skills could provide them with food, but these were not sufficient to protect them from wild animals. When they gathered in cities for protection, they lacked political wisdom and so they fought against each other. So Zeus sent Hermes to give people mutual respect and a sense of justice. Hermes asked how he should distribute these gifts: just to a few, as the various kinds of expertise were distributed, or to all? Zeus explained that people could never live in cities if political wisdom were given only to experts. And so, Protagoras explains to Socrates, the Athenians listen to everyone's opinion in political matters, because they believe that everyone must have a share of political wisdom.

This fable, like Prodicus' fable of the Choice of Herakles, is not traditional, and therefore it is not really a myth in the strict sense of the term, but it uses traditional elements, such as Prometheus' theft of fire, and it uses these elements to make its own point.

These three philosophical fables – Parmenides' story of his journey to the goddess, Prodicus' story of the Choice of Herakles, and Protagoras' story of the apportioning of the powers to the animals – all suggest that for the generation of thinkers just before and contemporary with Socrates, myth was a part of the intellectual background they could assume and use for their own purposes. At this stage, at least, myth and philosophy were not incompatible.

III. PLATO AND MYTH

Plato himself, of course, is famous for his hostility to the mythic tradition. In Book Two of the Republic, when Socrates is describing the characteristics of his utopian city, he specifically argues that the education of the Guardians must not include false tales about the gods, such stories as the Myth of Succession, in which Kronos castrates his father Ouranos and Zeus then binds his father Kronos (*Republic* 377e–378a), or the story in which Hephaistos fettered his mother Hera, or the battle of the gods (378c–d). Even as allegory these should be avoided, because the young are not able to distinguish literal meaning from allegorical meaning, and whatever they hear when they are young will stay with them throughout their lives. Instead the young should hear only the true qualities of god: that god is good, and therefore never does harm, that god is the cause only of good things, and not of bad things (379b).

Socrates then rejects specific passages from the Homeric epics, passages which characterize Zeus as the bringer of evils to mortals, and similar passages from other poets (379e–380a). He also rejects stories in which a god changes form (380d–381c), or in which a god deceives mortals (381e–382e), and again he quotes specific passages from Homer and Aeschylus that must be banned.

Socrates also bans any passages that would make the Guardians fear death, and he quotes as examples seven passages from the Homeric epics (386a–387b). Likewise any passages in which men of repute wail and lament, such as the lamentation of Achilles after the death of Patroklos or the lamentations of Priam after the death of Hektor, and especially any passages in which a god laments, as Zeus laments the death of his son Sarpedon (388a–d). Socrates would also ban the passage in Book One of the *Iliad* in which the gods laugh, as well as the passage in Book Fourteen in which Zeus is overcome by desire for Hera (389a; 390b–c). Nor should the heroes be shown as disrespectful to the gods, nor should they be shown performing evil deeds (391a–e). Such restrictions would certainly eliminate most of the stories we think of as Greek myth.[3]

In Book Ten of the Republic, Socrates returns to this theme, in the context of a wider discussion of imitation and the forms, and although the admits to love of Homer (595b, 607d), he argues that Homer and the other poets have been of no benefit to the city, but especially because of the power of poetry they have the potential to cause great harm (598d–600e, 605c–606e), and so the poet of traditional myth must not be allowed entrance into the city (605b); only hymns to the gods and the praises of good men should be allowed.

The city Socrates describes is a utopia, and probably Plato never thought that such a city was possible in our world, and so his strictures do not have to be taken as practical suggestions. Nonetheless, they show a definite hostility towards most of the characteristic stories of Greek myth. Fundamentally this hostility is theological and moral. Poets should not tell stories which might suggest that the gods do wrong or cause harm or which show the heroes as immoral or cowardly. Here Plato seems to accept Xenophanes' critique of the Homeric conception of the gods and then to extend it into a full critique of myth.

Elsewhere, however, Plato shows the kind of linkage between myth and philosophy that we saw in Parmenides, Prodicus, and Protagoras. The dialogues are full of references to the myths.[4] Many of these references are brief, and some are critical, but even these critical references suggest that philosophy depends on myth, that philosophy comes into being as a critique of myth, and perhaps that without myth philosophy could never exist.

Some longer and more developed references show that the myths are more than a decorative background to the philosophic argument. In one dialogue, for example, Socrates falls into conversation with Euthyphro, an Athenian citizen who is taking his own father to court on a charge of murder. Socrates is shocked at what seems to be a violation of family piety, but Euthyphro defends his action partly by reference to Hesiod's Myth of Succession: if Zeus tied up his own father for unjustly swallowing his children, and if Kronos in turn had castrated his father, then it must be justifiable for Euthyphro to take his father to court. Socrates replies that he takes it ill whenever he hears such stories; here again he takes more or less the position of Xenophanes (*Euthyphro* 5e–6b). Socrates then leads the discussion to a general debate about the nature of piety. The philosophic question thus in part derives from myth, but the discussion shows the inadequacy of the myth from Socrates' philosophic perspective.

In another dialogue Socrates and his young friend Phaedrus take a walk in the country where they discuss the nature of love, among other topics. As they walk they pass the place where, so the story goes, Boreas, the god of the wind, seized the Athenian princess Oreithyia (*Phaedrus* 229b) (see Figure 12.1). Phaedrus asks if Socrates believes the story, and Socrates replies that he would be quite up to date if, like the sophists, he did not believe it. He could give a rationalizing – or sophistic – explanation in which the girl was simply blown off the cliff by the wind.

Boreas and Oreithyia

According to some stories, Oreithyia was one of the daughters of Erechtheus, the mythic king of Athens; Boreas, the personification of the northeast wind, took her off to Thrace where she became the mother of two sons, Kalais and Zetes, who participated in the quest for the Golden Fleece (Apollonius of Rhodes, *Argonautica* 1.211–23), and two daughters, Cleopatra and Chione (*Library* 3.15.2). Chione was the mother of Eumolpos, the priest of Demeter at Eleusis (*Guide* 1.38.3). According to Herodotus, during the Persian Wars the Athenians received an oracle that they should call on their son-in-law for assistance. When the invading Persians were sailing off the coast of Chalcis in Euboea the Athenians prayed to Boreas – their son-in-law since he had married Oreithyia – and the northeast wind destroyed much of the Persian fleet. The Athenians built a shrine by the river Ilissus (Herodotus, *Histories* 7.189; *Guide* 1.19.6). Aeschylus wrote a satyr play on the theme, but it has been lost. The story was illustrated on the chest of Kypselos (*Guide* 5.19.1) and there are several vase illustrations of the story as well.

Such rationalizations, Socrates says, have a certain attraction, but he does not envy the people who invent them, since they then have to go on to give explanations of Centaurs and the Khimaira and Gorgons and other such monsters. All this would take a lot of time, and

Figure 12.1   In the top band Peleus abducts Thetis, while in the bottom band Boreas abducts Oreithyia. The Niobid Painter (ca. 460–450 BCE). Attic red-figure calyx crater. H. 48 cm; D. 50 cm. Museum of Fine Arts, Boston, MA, USA. Mary S. and Edward Jackson Holmes Fund. 1972.850. Copyright © Museum of Fine Arts, Boston

Socrates would prefer to spend his time trying to understand himself. So he doesn't bother about such matters (*Phaedrus* 229c–230a).

Plato here shows that rationalizing accounts of the myths were common, and that they were particularly associated with the sophists. Socrates' general skepticism finds these rationalizations attractive, but they are not important to him, because his own philosophic project is quite different. He is not trying to give an account of nature, but of himself and his own character.

Elsewhere, however, Plato's Socrates uses the myths in a more positive way. In the *Apology*, for instance, Socrates takes the heroes of Troy as a model of correct behavior, and especially Achilles, who disregarded danger in order to maintain his honor. Just as at the battles of Amphipolis and Delium, Socrates, like many others, remained at his post in the face of danger, so he will not desert his post in the philosophic task assigned to him by the god (*Apology* 28c–e). Then, after the court has condemned him, he tells his supporters that he does not fear death, since perhaps in the other world, where the true judges are the demigods Minos and Rhadamanthys and Aiakos and Triptolemos, he may meet the great poets of the past – Orpheus, Musaeus, Homer, and Hesiod – and also the heroes, such as

Palamedes and Ajax, who, like Socrates, were condemned unjustly, and other heroes, such as Agamemnon, Odysseus, and Sisyphos. To converse with such people, he says, would be unimaginable happiness.

Socrates here shows no doubt about these mythic figures. They are, however, mostly figures of heroic legend, rather than divine myth, and their stories can be understood without casting the gods in an unfavorable light, so Socrates may not have felt the need to reject them. In any case, all these references to myth in the various dialogues show that the philosopher Plato could not avoid the myths, whatever he might have thought about them, because the myths were the basic cultural language in which he spoke.

Plato was also at times a fabricator of mythic stories. These show an interesting aspect of the Platonic project of philosophy, particularly those that are told by Socrates himself. On the one hand, Plato's Socrates often demands from his interlocutors a coherent logical argument; on the other hand, when Socrates presents an argument sometimes the logic gives out at a certain point, and then he resorts to a story. Evidently Plato's Socrates did not reject the idea that stories have a place, and perhaps an important place, in philosophic discussion.

Further Explorations

Plato presents a powerful argument against the poets, on the grounds that the stories they tell are not only lies, but harmful lies. Therefore he would exclude poets from the city, and a book like this would presumably be banned in the city as well. Carefully read Plato's arguments in Books Two and Ten of the *Republic*, and write an essay in which you examine Plato's critique; you may defend the mythic tradition from Plato's critique or support his view that myth should be banned. Some questions you might consider: Is there a sense in which myth is true, or even if not true, beneficial rather than harmful? Is it necessarily wrong to present the gods and heroes in an unflattering light? Is there any good for the city in presenting the myths in epic or in tragic drama? Are people likely to take the myths as models or justifications for their own behavior? Are the ancient Greek myths still harmful for a society which does not believe in the Greek gods? Are there modern myths which should be banned, or should all arguments be allowed to compete in the free market of ideas? Is logic superior to narrative as a form of thought? Does myth become obsolete with the advent of philosophy and science?

Since these Platonic myths were the creations of a particular author and not traditional stories, they are essentially different from the myths that are the primary subject of this book. Plato certainly knew the difference between the traditional myths and his own stories. Most likely he intended his stories as a challenge to the traditional accounts, and perhaps he even wanted his stories to replace the traditional myths.

In the *Symposium*, the various participants at a dinner party, including Socrates, decide to spend the evening giving speeches in praise of Love. In a sense, the whole dialogue is connected to mythic themes, since the praise of Love is the praise of a god. Moreover, some of the speeches include references to myth, and two are in the form of invented mythic stories. The first speaker, Phaedrus, begins with a quotation from Hesiod's *Theogony*, and continues with references to famous couples in myth – Alkestis and Admetos, Orpheus and Euridike, Achilles and Patroklos (*Symposium* 178a–180b). The second speaker, Pausanias, argues that there are two kinds of Love, just as there are two goddesses named Aphrodite: one is the heavenly or Ouranian Aphrodite, and the other is the daughter of Zeus and Dione. This distinction takes advantage of rival genealogies in the mythic tradition (*Symposium* 180c–d).

The fourth speaker is the comic playwright Aristophanes, and Plato puts in his mouth an elaborate story about the origins of human beings. Originally, he says, people were spherical, each with four arms and legs, and two heads on a single neck, with four eyes, and two sets of private parts. Some of these doubled creatures were male and male, some were female and female, and some were male and female. The males were descended from the Sun, the females were descended from the Earth, and the mixed creatures were descended from the Moon. These creatures tried to scale the heights of heaven, and so gods decided to divide them, and thus our present form came into being. But each person now seeks to find its other half. Those that were part of a male and male seek male lovers, those that were part of a female and female seek female lovers, and those that were part of a male and female seek a lover of the opposite sex (*Symposium* 189d–193a).

The final speaker is Socrates. The center of his speech is a lesson he was taught, so he says, by a wise woman from Mantinea, named Diotima. The day that Aphrodite was born, according to Diotima, Necessity (a deified abstraction) came to beg at the birthday party, and while there managed to seduce Resource, the son of Craft (more deified abstractions). The son of this union was Eros. Eros, then, is a follower of Aphrodite, because he was conceived on her birthday. He is greedy because his mother was Necessity and he is resourceful because his father was Resource. He is neither mortal nor immortal, but both ignorant and wise. Love is not himself beautiful, but rather the lover of what is beautiful. And in his search for the beautiful and the good he ascends a ladder of desires from the love of a particular beautiful body to the love of beautiful bodies in general, to the love of the beautiful souls, beautiful laws and institutions, knowledge, and finally the love of the Beautiful in itself – as we would say, the Platonic form of the Beautiful. So Diotima's myth, as told by Socrates, ends at the height of Platonic philosophy (*Symposium* 201d–212a).

There are two famous Platonic myths in the *Republic*. The first of these is the Allegory of the Cave. In this story, Socrates imagines a group of people living in a cave, fettered so that they can only look further into the cave. Behind them, closer to the entrance, a fire is burning. Other men in between the fire and the prisoners in the cave have puppets in various shapes, so that the shadows of these puppets are cast on the inner wall of the cave, where the prisoners can see them. The prisoners would think that these shadows were reality. This situation, he explains, is an allegory of our own situation, as we are able to see only the shadows of the true forms. Now if one of the prisoners were to be released and dragged outside the cave, so that he could see the real situation, at first he would be dazzled by the light of the sun and he would not be able to perceive the real objects in the natural light. Eventually, however, he would adjust to the light and he would come to pity the prisoners in the cave. But if he were to return to the cave, his eyes would have difficulty adjusting to the darkness, he would not be able to see the shadows, and the other prisoners would think that his vision had been harmed by his trip into the light. This story, then is an allegory for the soul's ascent to the intelligible region, where it looks upon the forms (*Republic* 514a–517a).

The second great myth in the *Republic* is the story of Er, which comes at the very end of this long dialogue and serves as its culmination (*Republic* 614a–621d). Socrates here tells his interlocutor Glaucon the story of a Pamphylian warrior named Er who was killed in battle but then revived to recount his experiences in the afterlife. Er found that the dead were judged for their actions during their lives. Those who had been evil were punished in the Underworld, while those who had been virtuous ascended to their rewards in the heavens.

After a time, Er and many other souls, both virtuous and evil, traveled to a place where they saw a bright and pure light in the form of a line extending down from heaven to earth. This light was the girdle of the heavens, the Spindle of Necessity. It is not easy to visualize exactly what Plato had in mind here, but it seems that around this Spindle the orbits of the planets were organized. Each of these orbits was attended by a Siren, and the various notes they sang produced a harmony. Also there were the daughters of Necessity, the three Fates Lachesis, Clotho, and Atropos. Lachesis sang the things that were, Clotho sang the things that are, and Atropos sang the things that will be.

Lachesis then announced that the souls would return to earth, and each soul would have the opportunity to choose its new life for itself. Here, Socrates tells Glaucon, is the great hazard of human existence, and this is the reason each of us should try to determine what distinguishes the good life from the bad. According to Er, Socrates continues, the first of the souls to choose a new life rashly chose the life of a tyrant. But when he then examined this life more closely he found that in this life he would do great wrongs, including eating his own children. (Perhaps Plato intends here a reference to the feast of Atreus.) Animals were also allowed to choose new lives, and while some human souls chose to become animals, some animal souls chose to become human. Orpheus, for example, chose to become a swan, Thamyras became a nightingale, Ajax became a lion, Agamemnon became an eagle, Thersites (the clownish figure who causes a disruption in Book Two of the *Iliad*) became an ape, and Odysseus, after a long search, chose the life of an ordinary person who minds his own business. All the souls then went through the Plain of Oblivion, where they drank from the River of Forgetfulness and lost all memory of their former lives. After this they were all sent off to earth. But Er was not allowed to drink from the River, and so when he returned to life he kept a memory of everything he had seen. This elaborate story serves to add a narrative justification to the logical argumentation which takes up most of the dialogue. Plato grants the role of narrative in philosophy, here even as the culmination to his argument, but he replaces the traditional myths, which are full of disgraceful stories about the gods, and instead he makes his own philosophic myths.

IV. PLATO AND ATLANTIS

Although Plato was hostile to much of traditional myth, the characters in his dialogues often refer to mythic figures and events, and Plato himself made up stories that derive from the mythic background, even as they change it. Plato's stories, however, are not traditional and anonymous myths. On the other hand, Plato is one of the few philosophers – perhaps the only one – who created a story that has a claim to have become a true myth, the story of Atlantis.

The story is told in the late dialogue the *Timaeus* by the Athenian politician Critias (probably one of the Athenian 30 tyrants at a time after the dramatic date of the dialogue) and then the story is continued in the incomplete companion dialogue, the *Critias* (*Timaeus* 24a–25d; *Critias*). Critias says that he heard the story from his grandfather, also named Critias, who in turn heard it from the great Athenian statesman Solon, who learned it from Egyptian priests. These Egyptian priests read about it in records that were 8,000 years old, but the events had occurred 1,000 years before that and had been remembered in an oral tradition (*Timaeus* 20c–24a). This overly elaborate chain of narrative transmission is a clue that Plato made up the story.

Atlantis as Critias describes it is a sort of double to the city of Athens, which (according to the story) was its rival in these ancient times (*Timaeus* 24b–25d. His description of ancient Athens is of course also a myth, and the two cities can be seen as two aspects of Athens (Vidal-Naquet 1986: 269). Athens in this story was founded by Athena, while the island of Atlantis was founded by Poseidon. The Athenian constitution matched Socrates' ideal constitution, while Atlantis was a tyranny. Athens has a simple economy based on the fertility of the land, whereas Atlantis is a land of luxury based on maritime trade. The Atlanteans undertook to enslave the Athenians, but the Athenians led an alliance of Greek states and defeated the Atlanteans. Shortly thereafter both Athens and Atlantis were destroyed by a great earthquake; Atlantis disappeared into the ocean. The detailed description of Atlantis is found in the second dialogue, the *Critias*. Plato did not intend Atlantis to be a utopia, but it is easy to be charmed by his luxuriant attention to the rich detail of the description. Sir Francis Bacon's *New Atlantis*, published in 1627, describes a utopian island he names Bensalem, located off the coast of Peru, and the idea of a utopian Atlantis has persisted in the later tradition.

Some ancient writers, including Strabo and Posidonius, thought that Atlantis had existed, but the modern belief in Atlantis dates from the publication in 1877 of *Isis Unveiled* by the theosophist Helena Blavatsky and the publication in 1882 of *Atlantis: The Antediluvian World* by the American politician and writer Ignatius Donnelly (who based his work partly on the theories of the French ethnographer Charles-Étienne Brasseur de Bourbourg). A small but energetic fringe community still maintains that there is an historical basis to Plato's account, though there is no agreement about the supposed location of the vanished island.

Atlantis also occurs more or less prominently in many works of fiction, including Jules Verne's *20,000 Leagues Under the Sea* (1870), Edith Nesbit's *The Story of the Amulet* (1906), Sir Arthur Conan Doyle's *The Marcot Deep* (1929), Marion Zimmer Bradley's *The Fall of Atlantis* (1987), and the Disney movie *Atlantis: The Lost Empire*, released in 2001.

Many people have heard about Atlantis, but few realize that it was invented by Plato. His original concept is only the germ for the later myth, which has taken on a life of its own, as every myth must. Plato might well be distressed to see what has happened to his invention, but those who believe in Atlantis and those who use it as a metaphor or an image agree that the story of Atlantis expresses a powerful dream: the dream of a lost or hidden people, perhaps with mystic knowledge or advanced technology, with a secret teaching still important if it could be recovered today. Although the story of Atlantis cannot be considered a Greek myth, it was created in the context of Greek myth and Greek philosophy, and in its way it continues those Greek traditions.

CONCLUSION

According to Plato, there is an ancient quarrel between poetry and philosophy (*Republic* 607b), but this chapter has argued that the relationship between the two is considerably more complex. At an early date – the period of Homer and Hesiod – there was no such thing as philosophy distinct from myth, and the kinds of questions philosophy claimed for itself about the nature of the cosmos or about ethics and society were considered in the form of mythic narratives.

The development of the logical and critical activity we call philosophy was one of the most important moments in the history of Western culture. Inevitably some of the philosophic critique was directed against the tradition of mythic narrative. This process may have been encouraged by the invention and spread of literacy, through which different and conflicting versions of myths could be compared. Thus myth and philosophy – which at one time had been undifferentiated – split into two distinct forms of thought. In large measure philosophy created itself through its reaction against myth, a reaction that took the form of rationalization, allegorization, and ultimately repudiation.

The mythic stories, of course, did not die, but continued to be presented in epic, drama, visual art, and through their connection to religious ritual (as can be seen, for example, in Pausanias' *Guide*, which was written in the second century CE, well after the rise of philosophy). The Greek mythic tradition was taken up by Latin writers and artists and then became one of the foundations of Western culture. Often myth and philosophy seem to run in parallel streams, each content to serve its own cultural function, but even some modern philosophers have turned to myth as a source of philosophic speculation, as, for example, Hegel used the story of Antigone in his *Phenomenology of the Spirit*, as Nietzsche used the contrast between Apollo and Dionysos in his *Birth of Tragedy*, or as Horkheimer and Adorno used the story of Odysseus in the their *Dialectic of the Enlightenment*. Myth and philosophy may have diverged and taken different courses, but both are concerned with fundamental questions, and it is not surprising that from time to time their streams flow together.

FURTHER READING

For a good general introduction to the topic of myth and philosophy, see Kirk 1974: 276–303. Hatab 1990 presents an extended philosophic defense of myth based on Nietzsche and Heidegger. On Parmenides and myth, see Gallop 1991 and Popper 2001: 105–45. The fragments of Xenophanes and other pre-Socratic philosophers may be found in Kirk *et al.* 1983. On allegorical interpretation of myth, see Lamberton 1989 and Brisson 2004. Porphyry's *On the Cave of the Nymphs* is translated in Lamberton 1983. On Palaephatus and on rationalization in general, see Stern 1996. On Plato and myth, see Vidal-Naquet 1986: 263–84, Brisson 1998, Clay 2007, and Vidal-Naquet 2007.

Chapter Thirteen
CONCLUSION

This exploration of Greek myth began with a rough definition: *a myth is a traditional story that speaks to important issues in the culture in which it is told.* A wide definition such as this allows consideration of the range of stories which have been counted as myths by scholars of various schools of thought. Other characteristics of Greek myth include the extensive interconnections among the myths, often expressed in terms of genealogies, and a complex sense of time, which includes both stories outside historical time, such as much of Hesiod's *Theogony*, and stories, such as the story of the Trojan War and its aftermath, which verge on the legendary.

The discussion throughout these explorations addressed an essential aspect of this definition of myth, that is, the kinds of important issues myth spoke to in ancient Greek culture (and the kinds of important issues myth continues to speak to in modern times). The Greek myths did not float freely above the rest of ancient Greek culture and society. On the contrary, they were closely integrated with Greek ideas and practices related to religion, hero cult, colonization and the foundations of cities, gender, and history, as well as to questions such as the nature of the cosmos and the structure of human society. Scholars of myth need to know about Greek history and Greek society in order to understand the myths, and likewise, students of all aspects of ancient Greece can benefit from knowledge of the myths.

Most of the myths studied in introductory courses are the great Panhellenic myths, the myths which were known to all or almost all Greeks. Most of these myths are still widely known today, though some Panhellenic myths, such as the myth of Melampous, now survive in fragments and can be only partly reconstructed by piecing together a variety of sources.

The tradition of Greek myth also included many local myths, which were of primary interest to a particular city or region. Many of these local myths were closely related to local ritual or to the local landscape. Thus the story of the Bouphonia was related to the performance of a particular ritual in Athens, while the story of Lykaon was probably linked to a rite of passage in Arcadia. The local circumstances related to the story of Hyrnetho are now obscure, but it is likely that the story was linked to some rivalry between Argos and Epidaurus, since both cities claimed to have her body, and it may have been linked to social divisions as well. When such local myths were known to a wider Greek audience, they might lose some of the detail which linked them to their original locales, or they could be reinterpreted, as Greeks outside Arcadia used the story of Lykaon to express what they took to be the primitive quality of Arcadia.

Panhellenic myths could also have local variants; thus according to an Arcadian story recorded by Pausanias, when Demeter was searching for Persephone, she was pursued by Poseidon; she turned herself into a mare, but Poseidon turned himself into a stallion and mated with her. This story is not part of the *Homeric Hymn to Demeter*, and it was probably not widely told outside Arcadia. In addition, several different places could claim to be the location of an important mythic event, such as the meadow where Persephone was abducted or the crack where the water from the flood ran back into the earth. Such localization of details allowed the residents of a particular region to feel their own relationship to the Panhellenic story.

The local myths and local variants of Panhellenic myths have been important for the scholarly study of Greek myth, as the references throughout these explorations have shown. The student of Greek myth therefore needs to know where to find evidence for myths beyond the familiar sources, such as epic and drama; interesting myths can be found in many places, including ancient encyclopedias, guide books, historical accounts, and philosophic debates. Often these less familiar sources preserve fascinating details which can be important in reconstructing the role of the stories in Greek society. These explorations have touched on a few local myths or local versions of Panhellenic myths, but there is much more material for students to discover in the sources referred to in the text.

The meaning of a myth generally depends on the way it is told on a particular occasion. This range of application and interpretation is part of what made the myths "good to think with". Thus the story of Aktaion could be used to represent curiosity, pathos, the justice or injustice of the gods, and so on. On the other hand, a number of different stories can relate to the same topic, as sacrifice is seen from various perspectives in the story of Prometheus in Hesiod's *Theogony*, the *Homeric Hymn to Hermes*, the story of the Bouphonia, and in many other stories. Myths present their meanings in the form of narratives rather than logical arguments, and those who believe that thought is essentially logical may reject mythic thought and turn instead to philosophy, though philosophy itself has roots in myth and returns to myth from time to time. Sometimes the thought expressed through myth can be attributed to the author of a particular version, so it is reasonable to ask about Aeschylus' view of justice in the *Oresteia* or Sophocles' view of the family and the state in *Antigone*. Sometimes, however, mythic thought is expressed through groups of stories, and this kind of thought is best approached through analysis of deep patterns and structures.

Comparative study has demonstrated that Greek myth belongs to a wider world of Indo-European myth and world myth. The ancestors of the Greeks were among the speakers of the Proto-Indo-European language, and it is reasonable to suppose that they derived not just their language but also some of their fundamental conceptions of the world from their Proto-Indo-European heritage. But Greece was also part of a general eastern Mediterranean culture area, and the Greeks notoriously borrowed technology, art, and ideas from their Mediterranean neighbors. Some scholars, however, have argued that the similarities among various traditions of myth reflect deep levels of psychology or spirituality, and so Greek myth, like myth in general, is important for the study of comparative religion and also psychoanalysis.

The various approaches to myth have been more or less formalized in a number of theories and methods; several of these have been presented during these explorations – including structuralist, comparative, psychoanalytic, historical, and ritual approaches – without favoring any one theory or method. Most likely different theories and methods are appropriate for different purposes. The student of myth should have some familiarity with all of these approaches in order to understand scholarship in the field.

The Greek myths have played a large role in shaping many of the basic ideas and images of Western culture. From the age of the Roman Empire to our own time, the myths have been and remain a treasury of stories, images, and ideas for writers, visual artists, psychologists, and philosophers. Modern students of literature and visual art especially need to know about the traditions of myth and the way myth has been used in art. These explorations have included brief references to many works of art and literature based on Greek myth, but this aspect of the study of myth is a major field of study on its own.

It has not been possible in these explorations either to discuss all topics in the study of myth or to exhaust any topic which has been discussed. Much more could be said about every topic touched on here, particularly in the area of gender and myth, or in the area of the use of ancient visual art in the interpretation of myth. The goal of these explorations has been to help students move beyond the introductory stage so that they can investigate scholarly discussions of Greek myth. This book, then, should be considered a gateway rather than an end in itself. The suggestions for further reading will provide a key for that gateway.

Notes

CHAPTER ONE

1. See, for example, Detienne 1986: 46–47.
2. There were a few exceptions: Phrynicus, who was active in the late sixth and early fifth centuries BCE, wrote two plays on historical themes, the *Phoenissae* and the *Taking of Miletus*, both about the Persian wars, and Aeschylus also wrote a play about the Persian wars, the *Persae*; of these only the *Persae* is extant. Out of several hundred whose subjects are known, these are the only tragedies from the fifth century BCE that were not on mythic themes. In the fourth century BCE Theodectes wrote a historical play, *Mausolus*, and probably in the third century BCE Moschion wrote two historical plays, *Men of Pherae* and *Themistocles*, but none of these has survived.
3. See Snodgrass 1981 and Nagy 1990a.
4. The first vase is in Naples (Naples H3091); the second is at the Metropolitan Museum in New York; the third is in London (London F277); the fourth is in New York (New York 28.57.23); and the fresco is in Macedonia. All of these images may be found on the web. In addition, some images can be seen in Foley 1994 and some in Carpenter 1991.
5. For discussion of what is known today about the Eleusinian Mysteries, see Foley 1994: 65–75.
6. According to Burkert 1983: 137, Porphyry probably learned this story from Theophrastus, an Athenian philosopher of the fourth century BCE, who wrote about animal sacrifice in his book *On Piety*, now lost.
7. This story is not mentioned in Robert Graves' collection of Greek myths (not listed in References as it is widely available in various editions); none of the three standard introductory textbooks refers to it, and it is not mentioned in Ken Dowden's *The Uses of Greek Mythology* or Fritz Graf's *Greek Mythology*. It is discussed, however, in some scholarly sources, such as *Homo Necans* (Burkert 1983: 136–43), and *Athenian Myths and Institutions* (Tyrell and Brown 1991: 83–89).

CHAPTER TWO

1. Some scholars believe that these two poems, and perhaps some others which now exist only in fragments, were all composed by a single poet, Hesiod, but other scholars believe that these different poems were composed by different poets. There are good arguments on both sides. For the purposes of this discussion it is not necessary to settle this question.
2. In this passage, Herodotus may think of Homer as the author of the *Homeric Hymns* and parts of the *Epic Cycle* as well as the *Iliad* and the *Odyssey*, and of Hesiod as the author of the *Catalogue of Women*, the *Shield of Herakles*, and other poems as well as the *Theogony* and the *Works and Days*.
3. For details on many Greek cults, see Larson 2007.
4. For discussion of Hestia in relation to Hermes, see Vernant 2006: 127–75.
5. Orpheus is also a character in the *Argonautica*, an epic poem written by Apollonius of Rhodes in the third century BCE, and there he sings a brief theogony to his shipmates on the Argo (496ff.) with some details perhaps related to the Orphic theogonies (see West 1983: 127–28).

Exploring Greek Myth. First Edition. Matthew Clark.
© 2012 Matthew Clark. Published 2012 by Blackwell Publishing Ltd.

6. We cannot claim, however, that every myth had a ritual or that every ritual had a myth; nor is it clear that the myth associated with a ritual or festival was necessarily told during the festival. For discussion of the so-called Myth and Ritual school of mythological explanation, see Edmunds 1990 and Csapo 2005.

7. But not always: in Canada, when the Minister of Finance is about to bring in a budget, he often buys a new pair of shoes, and this purchase is always reported widely. So far as I know there is no aetiological myth to explain this ritual.

8. In this version of the story, Artemis is angry because two eagles sent by Zeus have killed a pregnant hare – probably this event is a symbol for the death of innocent people in Troy. In the lost epic poem the *Kypria*, however, Artemis is angry because Agamemnon has boasted that he is a better hunter than the goddess; and in Euripides' *Iphigeneia in Tauris*, Agamemnon has long failed to keep his vow that he would sacrifice the most beautiful thing to be born in a certain year – as it happened, his own daughter.

9. For further discussion of the *Oresteia* see Chapter Ten (Myth and History) and Chapter Eleven (Myth and Thought).

CHAPTER THREE

1. Homer also knows about Hypsipyle, the queen of Lemnos, with whom Jason had an affair, and he mentions their son Euenos (Il.7.468), but he does not mention Medea. Homer mentions the great hero Herakles several times in both the *Iliad* and the *Odyssey*. Theseus is mentioned once in the *Iliad* (1.265), though this line has been questioned, and also in the *Odyssey* (11.322; 11.631).

2. Homer does not explain why Sisyphos and Tantalos deserve punishment; according to later sources when Zeus abducted Aigina, Sisyphos told her father who the culprit was; later he managed to tie up Thanatos (Death), and still later he managed to scheme his way out of the Underworld. Tantalos, according to some sources, tried to feed his son Pelops to the gods, or else he tried to give away the food of the gods.

3. Other myths told in detail by a character within the epic include the myth of Lykourgos (Il.6.130–40), told by Diomedes to explain why he would not fight against a god, and the myth of Bellerophon (Il.6.155–202), told by Glaukos to identify himself and his family.

4. The *Catalogue* is sometimes called the *Ehoiai*, from a phrase in Greek which means "or such as she"; this phrase begins many lines in the poem, when one heroine is compared to another.

5. I use the numbering of the fragments in Glenn Most's Loeb edition of Hesiod; he includes a concordance to the other editions of the fragments.

CHAPTER FOUR

1. Ovid uses the Latin spelling "Lycaon", but I have changed this to "Lykaon" for the sake of consistency.

2. Both Pliny (*Natural History* 8.81–82) and Augustine (*City of God*, 18.17) mention a related story (derived evidently from Varro, who got it from Euanthes) in which a young Arcadian man is chosen by lot (in Pliny's account from a specific family). He hangs his clothing on an oak tree, swims across a lake, and spends nine years as a wolf. If he refrains from eating human flesh during that time he returns to the tree, changes back into a man, and puts his clothing back on. Augustine also mentions an Olympic athlete named Demainetos, who is presumably the same as the Damarchos mentioned by Pausanias.

3. The myth of Niobe is directly followed by a story about Latona, or Leto in Greek (*Met.* 6.313–81), and the myth of Marsyas (*Met.* 6.382–400), and then Ovid returns to Niobe in order to make a transition to Pelops.

4. Göttingen University J22; see Shapiro 1994: 81; Arezzo, Museo Nazionale Archeologico 1460.

5. In Pausanias' day this chest was kept in the temple to Hera at Elis, near Olympia, and it was said to be the chest in which the baby Kypselos was hidden by his mother when the Bacchiads were searching for him. Kypselos grew up to become the tyrant of Corinth from about 657 to 625 BCE, but the chest Pausanias saw probably dates from about 100 years later.

6. There were several stories about the foundation of the Olympic Games; some gave the credit to Herakles, and some said the games began with the wrestling match between Zeus and Kronos (see *Guide*

5.7.10–5.8.3). Hippodameia is supposed to have founded games for girls (*Guide* 5.16.2–4).

CHAPTER FIVE

1. Ovid uses the spellings "Actaeon", "Daedalus", and "Icarus", but for the sake of consistency I have used transliterations of the Greek spellings.
2. In other myths, mortal men do have affairs with goddesses (Anchises and Aphrodite, Tithonos and Eos, Demeter and Iasion), but Ovid does not tell these stories in the *Metamorphoses*.
3. Artists who have represented Aktaion include Lucas Cranach (1472–1553); Titian (1473–1576); Paolo Veronese (1528–88); Cavaliere d'Arpino (1568–1640); Hendrik van Balen (1575–1632); Francesco Albani (1578–1660); Rembrandt (1606–69); Marcantonio Franceschini (1648–1729); Giovanni Battista Tiepolo (1696–1770); Luigi Vanvitelli (1700–73); François Boucher (1703–70); Thomas Gainsborough (1727–88); Camille Corot (1796–1875); Eugène Delacroix (1798–1863); Paul Manship (1885–1966); and Calum Colvin (b. 1961).
4. Curiosity can also be a good quality; the Renaissance philosopher Giordano Bruno, in *The Heroic Frenzies* (1585), developed a complex allegory in which Aktaion is the symbol of intellect searching for divine wisdom, his dogs are his cognitive faculties, Apollo is full revelation, and Diana is the shadow of divine wisdom.
5. In this play Shakespeare also refers to Phaethon (1.4.33–34 and 2.6.11–12) and to Diana (4.8.22): this last reference may refer specifically to the story of Aktaion.
6. In addition there are paintings and sculptures by Sir Anthony Van Dyke (1599–1641), Peter Paul Rubens (1577–1640), Antonio Canova (1757–1822), Carlo Saraceni (1585–1620), Frederick Leighton (1830–96), Henri Matisse (1869–1954), and Pablo Picasso (1881–1973), among others.

CHAPTER SIX

1. This ship, according to Plutarch, was preserved down to the time of Demetrius of Phaleron, governor of Athens 317–307 BCE. Theseus dates from a generation before the Trojan War, so the Athenians must have regarded this ship as very old indeed. In fact it became something of a philosophic puzzle. Since it was so old, the planks making up the ship had gradually been replaced, one by one, until eventually not a single plank from the original ship was left. The philosophers asked if this ship could still be called Theseus' ship, and if not, at what point it changed (Plutarch, *Theseus* 23.1).
2. The following summary is closely based on the translation of W. H. S. Jones, found in the Loeb edition of Pausanias' *Description of Greece*.
3. Hyrnetho is mentioned in an epigram by Dioscorides (Gow and Page 1965: 1691–96) as if everyone would know who she was, and Apollodorus (*Library* 2.8.5) says that Hyrnetho's brothers killed their father and that the army gave the city – presumably Argos – to her and her husband Deiphontes.

CHAPTER SEVEN

1. See plate 5 in Loraux 1993 and her discussion pp. 40–41; other illustrations of the birth of Erichthonios are shown in her plates 1, 2, 3, and 4.
2. According to the genealogy presented by Apollodorus, Eumolpos was the son of Chione, the daughter of Oreithyia, the daughter of Erechtheus. By this account, Erechtheus takes the field against his own great-grandson.
3. In 508/7 the reforms of the politician Cleisthenes changed the Athenian political structure from a system of four tribes (based on families) to ten tribes (based on the location of residence). Each of the new tribes was named after a hero, and these as a group were known as the Eponymous Heroes. Statues of these heroes were set up in the Athenian Agora. The Eponymous Heroes were Erechtheus, Aigeus, Pandion, Leos, Akamas, Oineus, Kekrops, Hippothoon, Aias, and Antiochos.
4. Loraux notes that there were no female autochthons; in Athenian thought, Pandora took on the role of the first Athenian woman (1993: 78–79, 117).
5. Other mythic figures born from the earth or from rivers include Aras (*Guide* 2.12.4, 2.14.3), Koresos (*Guide* 7.2.4), and Aigina (*Library* 3.12.6). But other

Greek cities claimed mythic founders who were not autochthonous: Endymion, who was loved by Selene, the goddess of the moon, founded Elis; Neleus, the son of Poseidon and Tyro, founded Pylos; and Pheres, the father of Admetos, founded Pherae (*Library* 1.7.5; 1.9.9; 1.9.14). People other than Greeks also claimed that they were autochthonous. The Carians, for example, who lived on the mainland of Asia Minor just below the Lydians, claimed to be aboriginal, though the Cretans said that they were originally islanders subject to Minos (Herodotus, *Histories* 1.178).

6. Lelex, or another character of the same name, is mentioned in many different stories about the early period of Greek settlement. According to Herodotus, he was the true ancestor of the Carians (*Histories* 1.178). Pausanias says that someone named Lelex, the son of Poseidon and Libya, came from Egypt to Megara in Boiotia (*Guide* 1.39.5, 1.44.3), but he also says that the Carians were Leleges (*Guide* 7.2.3). Dowden suggests that the word "leleges" is, like the word "barbaroi," an "onomatopoeic word to describe those who speak unintelligibly" (1992: 81); if so it could be widely applied to pre-Greek or non-Greek peoples.

7. The Spartan genealogies vary from source to source, and these variations were discussed by Greek writers; Herodotus, for example, who notes that the genealogies claimed by the Spartans themselves were different from those in the poets (*Histories* 6.52–55, 7.204, 8.131).

8. According to Euripides (*Suppliant Maidens* 291), Io was a priestess of Hera; Ovid, in his well-known version of the story (*Met.* 1.590ff.), leaves out this detail. It is worth noting, however, because it fits an important pattern in which heroes and heroines are placed in an antagonistic mythic relation to divinities they are close to in ritual.

9. The myths of the foundation of Thebes are found in more or less detail in many sources, including Apollodorus' *Library*, as well as in plays, such as Euripides' *Bacchae*; for a full account, see Gantz 1993: 467–73.

10. But other names can be found; a clan with branches in Thebes, Sparta, and Thera claimed to be descended from one of the Spartoi named Aigeus. See Pindar, *Fifth Pythian Ode* 75 and *Seventh Isthmian Ode* 15.

11. The word "Spartoi" is occasionally used to mean "Theban", as in Pindar's *First Isthmian Ode* 30, or his *Ninth Pythian Ode* 80.

12. In this play the king of Argos is named Pelasgos; he is not earthborn, but he is the son of the earthborn Palaichthon, whose name means "old earth". But according to Pausanias (*Guide* 2.18.3) the king was named Gelanor.

13. The story of Euphemos and the clod of earth is also told rather differently by Apollonius of Rhodes in his version of the story of Jason (4.1725ff.); Callimachus also treats the foundation of Kyrene in his *Hymn II to Apollo*.

14. The poem also includes a brief reference to Helen and the sons of Antenor, who supposedly beached in Libya after the fall of Troy.

CHAPTER EIGHT

1. Dumézil's system is not limited to the analysis of the tripartite functions, but it is fair to say that these functions lie at the core of his work.

2. The tripartite functions are also seen in the three Roman tribes (Littleton 1966: 71). The battle of the three Horatii and the three Curiatii represents another related Indo-European theme, the contest of the hero against a triple enemy (Dumézil 1969: 9–10).

3. See Littleton 1966: 176–92 for discussion of Dumézil's critics.

4. Freudian theorists often show little respect for Jungian approaches to myth. Caldwell, for instance, characterizes Jung's theories as "mystical and mystifying theory" and he calls the concepts of archetypes and the collective unconscious "notorious" (Caldwell 1990: 386). Jungian theorists are often no more complimentary about Freudian approaches.

5. It is not altogether easy to find a clear and consistent definition of the term archetype in Jungian theory. On two consecutive pages, for instance, Jung himself says that archetypes are "archaic remnants" and also "the tendency to form ... representations of a motif", though it seems odd to say that a remnant could be a tendency (Jung 1968b: 56–57).

6. Perhaps the best application of Jungian ideas to Greek myth is found in a series of books on various archetypes by the Hungarian classicist Karl Kerényi

(1897–1973). Kerényi and Jung also collaborated (1963) on *Essays on a Science of Mythology*.

7. Wendy Doniger publishes also under the name Wendy O'Flaherty; her works are listed under the name used for each particular publication.

CHAPTER NINE

1. For some scholars, including Sergent 1986, Dowden 1989, and Walker 1995, the rituals described in this section count as initiations, but other scholars argue that these rituals should not be considered true initiation rituals, since they did not mark a definite change of status; Parker, for example, says that these rituals were rites of passage, but not initiations (Parker 2005: 209–10).

2. Sergent 1986: 20–26 considers these three gifts symbols of the three functions of Indo-European society, as discussed in Chapter Eight.

3. Most likely the real explanation, found in some ancient sources, is that the name of this festival means "of the same father", with an initial copulative alpha, because the members of each phratry were supposedly descended from a common ancestor (Vidal-Naquet 1986: 110). It may seem odd that a myth about deceit was linked to this initiation festival, but cheating is also a feature of the aetiological myth of Pelops' race associated with the founding of the Olympic Games.

4. There are a number of related stories about a figure named Leukippos or Leukippe; see Delcourt 1961: 3–4.

5. Keuls 1985 presents abundant evidence in an argument that Athenian men hated women and that Athenian women were little better than slaves; Lefkowitz 2007 does not deny that Greek society was patriarchal, but she argues that "Greek men may not have been so much concerned with repressing women as with protecting them, in a world where women from a physical point of view were far more vulnerable than they are today" (187).

6. Girls took part in some other Athenian festivals as well. For example, girls assisted in the elaborate festival called the Plynteria, in which the statue of Athena Polias was taken from its temple (the "Old Temple") on the Acropolis down to the sea where it was washed along with its clothing (Parke 1977: 152–55; Parker 2005: 478).

7. In another story, Leukippos, the son of Oinomaos, fell in love with Daphne and dressed as a woman to get near her – as Zeus, in some stories, disguised himself as a woman to approach Kallisto. When Daphne and her friends go swimming, Leukippos refuses to disrobe, and when the girls forcibly remove his clothing the deceit is revealed and the girls kill him (*Guide* 8.20.2).

8. Some of our knowledge of what went on at the Thesmophoria comes from a scholion to the satirical writer Lucian; this can be found complete in Winkler 1990: 194–95 and in Parker 2005: 273.

9. Obscene jokes were a probably a feature of two other women's festivals, the Haloa, which was celebrated in Athens on the twenty-sixth of the month Poseideon, and the Stenia, which was celebrated on the ninth of Pyanepsion, just before the Thesmophoria (Parke 1977: 88 and 98–100; Winkler 1990: 194–96).

10. See, for example, Ezekiel 8: 14–15: "Then he brought me to the door of the gate of the Lord's house which was towards the north; and, behold, there sat women weeping for Tammuz."

11. Frazer's theories as presented in *The Golden Bough* are now generally discounted; according to Robert Ackerman, "It seems safe to say that today literally no student of Roman religion in particular nor of primitive religion in general is sympathetic to the basic contention or method of *The Golden Bough*" (1987: 105).

12. The myth of the Lemnian women is the third item in Detienne's comparison; for this myth, see the next section.

13. One might add here the concern Peleus expresses in the *Homeric Hymn to Aphrodite* (163–293) when he realizes that he has slept with a goddess, and for a cross-cultural comparison, note Gilgamesh's accusation when Ishtar proposes to him that she has injured her previous lovers (*Epic of Gilgamesh*, Standard Version, Tablet VI).

14. Eva Keuls also attempts to recover the meaning of the Adonia from a woman's point of view. She argues that the festival "had unique counter-cultural, even rebellious aspects", and "everything in the cult of Adonis

spelled protest against the existing order". "In bemoaning the death of Adonis, Athenian women lamented their own, loveless lives" (Keuls 1985: 23, 24, 28). Her discussion, however, is fundamentally limited to Athens at the time of the Sicilian expedition in 415 BCE, and it is hard to see how it could be generalized to a wider context of ancient Greek culture.

15. Lefkowitz challenges "the common assumption that Greek mythology effectively validates the practice of rape and approves of the violent mistreatment of women, by ancient Greek standards as well as by ours cruel and unlawful acts. ... in the case of unions of gods and goddesses with mortal men and women, we should talk about abduction or seduction rather than rape, because the gods see to it that the experience, however transient, is pleasant for the mortals" (2007: 54). It is not necessary to believe that myth validates the practice of rape or on the other hand to accept Lefkowitz's rather benign view of these acts of divine violence.

16. Or 49; one, named Amymone, had been seduced by Poseidon.

17. It is this smell which in Detienne's analysis links the Lemnian women to the Adonia, where the women are perfumed, and the Thesmophoria, where the women have a slightly unpleasant smell due to fasting (Detienne 1994: 90–96).

CHAPTER TEN

1. See, for example, Herodotus' comment, "Anyone can believe these Egyptian stories if he wants to" (*Histories* 2.122–23).

2. A few sections later Herodotus gives the "Phoenician" version: Io slept with the captain of the Phoenician ship, and when she discovered that she was pregnant, she decided to flee with the Phoenicians rather than face the anger of her parents.

3. But not all the stories Herodotus tells about Croesus can be taken as historical. The tale of the death of Croesus' son Atys (*Histories* 1.34–45), for example, looks very much like a traditional story, and some scholars think that it is related to the Near Eastern story of Attis, which is also related to the Greek story of Adonis (see Chapter Nine).

4. For this and other instances when arguments about public life were based on mythic precedents, see Higbie 1997.

5. Herodotus, *Histories* 7.204, 8.131.2; *Guide* 3.1–3, 3.7.

6. The list is as follows, omitting a few complications: Lelex, his son Myles, his son Eurotas, his daughter Sparta (who married Lakedaimon), her son Amyklas, his son Kynortas, his son Oibalos (who married Gorgophone, the daughter of Perseus), his son Tyndareus, his daughter Klytemnestra (who married Agamemnon), her son Orestes (who married Hermione, the daughter of Menelaos and Helen), his son Tisamenos (*Guide* 3.1.1–5).

7. The lists are as follows: Eurysthenes, Agis, Echestratos, Labotas, Doryssos, Agesilaos, Archelaos, Teleklos, Alkamenes, Polydorus, Eurykrates I, Anaxander, Eurykrates II, Leo, Anaxandrides, Kleomenes (*Guide* 3.2–3, 3.4.7); Prokles, Soos, Eurypon, Prytanis, Eunomos, Polydektes, Charillos, Nikander, Theopompos, Zeuxidamos, Anaxidamos, Agesikles, Ariston, Demaratos, Leotychides (*Guide* 3.7.1–8).

8. Individuals could also claim that they were descended from the heroes of myth. The controversial Athenian politician Alcibiades, for example, claimed that he was descended from the hero Eurysakes, son of Aias, the hero of the Trojan War. And of course Julius Caesar claimed that he was descended from Aeneas, and through him from Venus herself.

9. See Wood 1996 for Grote (p. 28), Geoffrey of Monmouth (p. 33), and Lechevalier (pp. 40–41); see Porter 2004 for Vico (p. 329); see Fitton 1996 for Bryant and Byron (p. 52).

10. The extant tragedies on Trojan themes are Aeschylus' *Oresteia* trilogy, Sophocles' *Ajax*, *Elektra*, and *Philoktetes*, Euripides' *Iphigeneia at Aulis*, *Trojan Women*, *Andromache*, *Hekabe*, *Orestes*, *Elektra*, and *Iphigeneia in Tauris*.

11. The story of Schliemann (and Frank Calvert) is told in varying detail by Fitton 1996, Wood 1996, and Traill 1995.

12. Schliemann's methods of excavation, though reasonably good for his time, unfortunately destroyed much important material. Schliemann was unquestionably one of the great archeologists, but his standards of veracity were far from impeccable, and this fact has unfortunately damaged his reputation and even called

some of his finds into question. For a full discussion, see Traill 1995.

CHAPTER ELEVEN

1. Vernant here agrees with Rose: "The thrust of art, like myth, is to seek imaginary resolutions of real contradictions; but to the extent that art is more self-conscious than myth, it is capable of presenting solutions that do not simply validate the status quo but negate it, transcend it by projecting a utopian vision and inviting society to embrace that vision" (Rose 1992: 257–58). In my opinion, both Vernant and Rose exaggerate the conservatism of pre-tragic myth and underestimate, for instance, the use of myth as critique in Homer and Hesiod.

2. As Podlecki 1966: 63 says, "It is not going too far to say that the major theme of the *Oresteia* is that of Dikê, the cosmic principle of order which governs the dealings of gods and mortals and whose dictates man ignores to his cost."

3. In the *Agamemnon*, the word "dikê" or its forms and compounds occur at least 20 times; in the *Libation-Bearers* at least 18 times; in the *Eumenides* about 40 times. The theme of justice is expressed not just by the word "dikê" but also by other words, and also by the actions and structure of the trilogy.

4. In Euripides' *Orestes*, however, Klytemnestra's father Tyndareus admits that she should have taken Agamemnon to court.

5. This is the same kind of justice as revenge that Aigisthos appeals to as a justification for his role in Agamemnon's murder, for instance at lines 1607 and 1611; but at 1615 the chorus tell him that justice will turn against him, too.

6. In other traditions, however, the first murder trial was the trial of Ares for the murder of Halirrhothios, one of Poseidon's sons (*Library* 14.2).

7. For various opinions on the political views of expressed in the play, see Podlecki (1966: 83–100), Gagarin (1976: 105, 116–17), Macleod (1983), Rose (1992: 247), and Carter (2007: 61–63). Overall I am persuaded that Aeschylus favored the reforms, but perhaps not more radical democratic reforms.

8. But according to Lloyd-Jones (1971: 94), "the cliché we have heard repeated all our lives, that the *Eumen-*

ides depicts the transition from the vendetta to the rule of law, is utterly misleading."

9. Rose thus agrees that the overall movement of the play is a transition from revenge to legal process: at the end of the process, which Rose calls "Aeschylean dialectic", "human social and political institutions are changed and the issue of individual responsibility is subsumed in the concern for internalizing ethical behavior in the society as a whole" (Rose 1992: 217).

10. The mythic discussion of justice begins as early as Homer's depiction of adjudication on the shield of Achilles (*Iliad* 18.497–508). On Dikê as cosmic principle of balance in Hesiod and Heraclitus, see Gagarin 1976: 67. Justice is of course the major theme of Plato's *Republic*; Plato's use of myth is discussed in the following chapter.

11. The story is told by Zeus (*Odyssey* 1.32–43), Athena (*Odyssey* 1.298–300), Nestor (*Odyssey*, 3.247–316), and Agamemnon himself (*Odyssey* 11.385–461).

12. As Vernant says, "in *Antigone*, the word *nomos* may be used with precisely different connotations by different protagonists" (1988a: 26, see also pp. 41–42). See Blundell 1989: 106–15 on the word *philia* ("friendship") in the play.

13. For Hegel's interpretation of *Antigone*, see Steiner 1984: 27–42.

14. This list is certainly not exhaustive; one might also mention, for instance, the power of persuasion and the Athenian attitude towards slaves (Hall 1997: 116–18), and also the problems of speech and silence (Knox 1979: 205–30).

15. "Sophrosyne" was an important but contested term in Athenian ethical thought; see Dover 1974 and Rademaker 2005.

16. When he defends himself against his father's accusation, he says that there is no man more "sophron" than he (995; see also 1007, 1100, and 1366): more moderate? Or more chaste? He charges that Phaidra was chaste in action, though she lacked chastity in her character; he, however, was chaste in character, but he used his chastity to his own harm (1034–35).

17. But Rabinowitz takes this speech to be representative: "We can see that Hippolytos is in agreement with many of the values of his day" (1993: 156–59).

18. "The city wages war on wild animals but sacrifices and consumes only domestic species. The Greeks divide the animal world in two: animals that are hunted for

the harm that they can cause, and those that are protected because of the services that men have come to expect from them" (Detienne 1989: 8).

19. For basic details about Greek animal sacrifice, see Burkert 1985: 55–60, but (as Burkert notes) there were some variations in ritual practice. For an example of a ritual that does not fit Burkert's scheme, see *Guide* 2.35.4.

20. According to Clay 1989: 116, Hermes here invents only the specific manner of making fire with fire-sticks. The Greek, however, says that Hermes was the first to make both firesticks and fire. The obscure Argive figure Phoroneus is also supposed to have discovered fire (*Guide* 2.19.5).

21. "The rule dictating that the boiled follows the roasted is so compelling that by reversing it, the Orphic account of Dionysos (who was boiled and then roasted) undertakes to contest a cultural history, explicit elsewhere, that states that humanity, on the road from 'the worse to the better', must have eaten grilled meat before learning the art of stewed dishes" (Detienne 1989: 10–11).

22. Dionysiac ritual, however, violated ordinary practice in the opposite way, since meat was eaten unsacrificed and raw; see Detienne 1989: 8.

23. For illustrations of Herakles and Bousiris, see Carpenter 1991: nos. 207, 208, and 270.

24. "The pyre on Oeta that completes Heracles' destiny answers the perverted sacrifice that celebrated his impure victory early in the play. ... The flames at the altars of Cenaeum are the reverse of a true sacrificial fire" (Segal 1995: 55).

CHAPTER TWELVE

1. Although the Law of the Excluded Middle, also known as the Law of Non-Contradiction, was important in the development of logic, it applies only in certain situations; it does not apply well to blends or graded qualities, such as "This drink is sweet". Recent logic has been much interested in fuzzy or ambiguous concepts.

2. Some scholars believe that this story was made up by Plato and put into the mouth of Protagoras, but others believe that it must reflect, more or less closely, something said or written by Protagoras. In the absence of decisive evidence no final decision is possible, but the latter position seems more likely.

3. Plato's critique extends beyond myth to "imitation" in general, such as playing a part in a play (395b–396b), and he concludes that a poet who can imitate various characters would be honored by the city but then expelled. Only the austere poet, the poet who would imitate only the diction of the good man, would be allowed to stay in the city (398a–b). He also would ban certain musical modes and musical instruments, as well as disorderly poetic rhythms (398c–400c), and so on.

4. Mythical figures named by Plato include Admetos and Alkestis, Amphion, Daidalos, Deukalion and Pyrrha, Erechtheus and Erichthonios, Eriphyle, Ganymede, Herakles, Hippolytos, Kadmos, Marsyas, Medea, Melampous, Oedipus, Pelops, Phaethon, Theseus, and Teiresias; the gods Zeus, Hera, Athena, Aphrodite, Apollo, Artemis, Ares, Demeter, Dionysos, Hephaistos, Ouranos, Kronos, Poseidon, Pluto; and many of the Trojan heroes, including Agamemnon, Ajax, Hektor and Andromache, Priam and Hekabe, Menelaos, Helen, Nestor, Odysseus, and Patroklos. Brisson 1998: 153–55 lists 260 proper names of mythical characters in the Platonic dialogues, though some of these, such as Er, appear in stories made up by Plato rather than in traditional myths.

References

Ackerman, Robert. 1987. *J. G. Frazer: His Life and Work*. Cambridge: Cambridge University Press.

Aeschylus. 2009. *Fragments*. Trans. by Alan H. Sommerstein. Cambridge, MA: Harvard University Press.

Andersen, Oe. 1999 [1987]. "Myth, Paradigm, and 'Spatial Form' in the *Iliad*." In de Jong 1999, III, pp. 472–85. Originally published in Bremer *et al.* 1987, pp. 1–13.

Austin, J. N. H. 1999 [1966]. "The Function of Digressions in the *Iliad*." In de Jong 1999, III, pp. 403–18. Originally published in *Greek, Roman and Byzantine Studies*, 7/4, 1966, pp. 295–312.

Austin, Norman. 1994. *Helen of Troy and Her Shameless Phantom*. Ithaca, NY: Cornell University Press.

Bacon, Francis. 1864. *Works*. Vol. XIII, *De Sapientia Veterum* [On the Wisdom of the Ancients]. Coll. and ed. by James Spedding, Robert Leslie Ellis, and Douglas Denon Heath. Boston, MA: Taggard & Thompson.

Baldick, Julian. 1994. *Homer and the Indo-Europeans: Comparing Mythologies*. London: I.B. Tauris.

Belli, Angela. 1969. *Ancient Greek Myths and Modern Drama: A Study in Continuity*. New York: New York University Press.

Blundell, Mary Whitlock. 1989. *Helping Friends and Harming Enemies: A Study in Sophocles and Greek Ethics*. Cambridge: Cambridge University Press.

Blundell, Sue. 1995. *Women in Ancient Greece*. Cambridge, MA: Harvard University Press.

Blundell, Sue and Margaret Williamson. 1988. *The Sacred and the Feminine in Ancient Greece*. London: Routledge.

Boardman, John. 1974. *Athenian Black Figure Vases*. New York: Oxford University Press.

Boardman, John. 2001. *The History of Greek Vases*. London: Thames & Hudson.

Boedeker, Deborah. 1993. "Hero Cult and Politics in Herodotus: The Bones of Orestes." In Dougherty and Kurke 1993, pp. 164–77.

Borgeaud, Philippe. 1988 [1979]. *The Cult of Pan in Ancient Greece*. Trans. by Kathleen Atlass and James Redfield. Chicago, IL: University of Chicago Press.

Bremer, J. M., I. J. F. de Jong, and J. Kalff, eds. 1987. *Homer: Beyond Oral Poetry*. Amsterdam: B. R. Grüner.

Bremmer, Jan, ed. 1988. *Interpretations of Greek Mythology*. London: Routledge.

Brillante, Carlo. 1990. "History and the Historical Interpretation of Myth." In Edmunds 1990, pp. 93–138.

Brisson, Luc. 1998. *Plato the Mythmaker*. Trans. and ed. by Gerard Naddaf. Chicago, IL: University of Chicago Press.

Brisson, Luc. 2004. *How Philosophers Saved Myth: Allegorical Interpretation and Classical Mythology*. Trans. by Catherine Tihanyi. Chicago, IL: University of Chicago Press.

Bruit Zaidman, Louise and Pauline Schmitt Pantel. 1992. *Religion in the Ancient Greek City*. Trans. by Paul Cartledge. Cambridge: Cambridge University Press.

Bryce, Trevor. 2005. *Kingdom of the Hittites*. Oxford: Oxford University Press.

Burgess, J. S. 2001. *The Tradition of the Trojan War in Homer and the Epic Cycle*. Baltimore, MD: Johns Hopkins University Press.

Burian, Peter. 1997. "Myth into Mythos: The Shaping of Tragic Plot." In Easterling 1997, pp. 178–208.

Burkert, Walter. 1979. *Structure and History in Greek Mythology and Ritual*. Berkeley, CA: University of California Press.

Exploring Greek Myth. First Edition. Matthew Clark.
© 2012 Matthew Clark. Published 2012 by Blackwell Publishing Ltd.

Burkert, Walter. 1983. *Homo Necans: The Anthropology of Ancient Greek Sacrificial Ritual and Myth*. Trans. by Peter Bing. Berkeley, CA: University of California Press.

Burkert, Walter. 1985. *Greek Religion*. Trans. by John Raffan. Cambridge, MA: Harvard University Press.

Burkert, Walter. 2001. *Savage Energies: Lessons of Myth and Ritual in Ancient Greece*. Trans. by Peter Bing. Chicago, IL: University of Chicago Press.

Buxton, Richard. 1994. *Imaginary Greece: The Contexts of Mythology*. Cambridge: Cambridge University Press.

Calame, Claude. 1988. "Spartan Genealogies: The Mythological Representation of a Spatial Organization." In Bremmer 1988a, pp. 153–86.

Calame, Claude. 2003 [1996]. *Myth and History in Ancient Greece: The Symbolic Creation of a Colony*. Trans. by Daniel W. Berman. Princeton, NJ: Princeton University Press.

Caldwell, Richard. 1989. *The Origin of the Gods: A Psychoanalytic Study of Greek Theogonic Myth*. New York: Oxford University Press.

Caldwell, Richard. 1990. "The Psychoanalytic Interpretation of Myth." In Edmunds 1990, pp. 344–89.

Carpenter, T. H. 1991. *Art and Myth in Ancient Greece: A Handbook*. London: Thames & Hudson.

Carter, D. M. 2007. *The Politics of Greek Tragedy*. Exeter, Devon: Bristol Phoenix Press.

Cartledge, Paul. 1979. *Sparta and Lakonia*. London: Routledge & Kegan Paul.

Caskey, L. D. and J. D. Beazley. 1931, 1954, 1963. *Attic Vase Paintings in the Museum of Fine Arts, Boston*. 3 vols. London: Oxford University Press.

Charbonneaux, Jean, Roland Martin, and François Villard. 1971. *Archaic Greek Art*. New York: George Braziller.

Clader, Linda Lee. 1976. *Helen: The Evolution from Divine to Heroic in Greek Epic Tradition*. Leiden: E. J. Brill.

Clark, Isabelle. 1998. "The Gamos of Hera: Myth and Ritual." In Blundell and Williamson 1998, pp. 13–26.

Clay, Diskin. 2007. "Plato Philomythos." In Woodard 2007a, pp. 210–36.

Clay, Jenny Strauss. 1989. *The Politics of Olympus: Form and Meaning in the Major Homeric Hymns*. Princeton, NJ: Princeton University Press.

Clay, Jenny Strauss. 2003. *Hesiod's Cosmos*. Cambridge: Cambridge University Press.

Conacher, Desmond. 1967. *Euripidean Drama*. Toronto: University of Toronto Press.

Csapo, Eric. 2005. *Theories of Mythology*. Malden, MA: Wiley-Blackwell.

Cyrino, Monica Silveira. 1998. "Heroes in D(u)ress: Transvestism and Power in the Myths of Herakles and Achilles." *Arethusa*, 31/2, pp. 207–41.

Davidson, James N. 1997. *Courtesans and Fishcakes: The Consuming Passions of Classical Athens*. New York: Harper.

Davidson, James N. 2007. *The Greeks and Greek Love: A Radical Reappraisal of Homosexuality in Ancient Greece*. London: Weidenfeld & Nicolson.

Davies, Malcolm. 1989. *The Greek Epic Cycle*. 2nd edn. London: Duckworth.

de Jong, Irene J. F., ed. 1999. *Homer: Critical Assessments*. 4 vols. London: Routledge.

Delcourt, Marie. 1961 [1956]. *Hermaphrodite: Myths and Rites of the Bisexual Figure in Classical Antiquity*. Trans. by Jennifer Nicholson. London: Studio Books.

Detienne, Marcel. 1979. *Dionysos Slain*. Trans. by Mireille Muellner and Leonard Muellner. Baltimore, MD: Johns Hopkins University Press.

Detienne, Marcel. 1986. *The Creation of Mythology*. Trans. by Margaret Cook. Chicago, IL: University of Chicago Press.

Detienne, Marcel. 1989. "Culinary Practices and the Spirit of Sacrifice." In Detienne and Vernant 1989, pp. 1–20.

Detienne, Marcel. 1994 [1972]. *The Gardens of Adonis: Spices in Greek Mythology.* Trans. by Janet Lloyd. Princeton, NJ: Princeton University Press.

Detienne, Marcel and Jean-Pierre Vernant. 1989. *The Cuisine of Sacrifice Among the Greeks*. Trans. by Paula Wissig. Chicago, IL: University of Chicago Press.

Doherty, Lillian E. 2001. *Gender and the Interpretation of Classical Myth*. London: Duckworth.

Doniger, Wendy [O'Flaherty]. 1998. *The Implied Spider: Politics & Theology in Myth*. New York: Columbia University Press.

Doniger, Wendy. See also O'Flaherty, Wendy Doniger.

Dougherty, Carol. 1993. *The Poetics of Colonization: From City to Text in Archaic Greece*. Oxford: Oxford University Press.

Dougherty, Carol. 2005. *Prometheus*. New York: Routledge.

Dougherty, Carol and Leslie Kurke, eds. 1993. *Cultural Poetics in Archaic Greece: Cult, Performance, Politics*. Cambridge: Cambridge University Press.

Dover, Kenneth. 1974. *Greek Popular Morality in the Time of Plato and Aristotle*. Berkeley, CA: University of California Press.

Dowden, Ken. 1989. *Death and the Maiden: Girls' Initiation Rites in Greek Mythology*. London: Routledge.

Dowden, Ken. 1992. *The Uses of Greek Mythology*. London: Routledge.

Dumézil, Georges. 1969. *The Destiny of the Warrior*. Trans. by Alf Hiltebeitel. Chicago, IL: University of Chicago Press.

Easterling, P. E. 1997. *The Cambridge Companion to Greek Tragedy*. Cambridge: Cambridge University Press.

Edmunds, Lowell, ed. 1990. *Approaches to Greek Myth*. Baltimore, MD: Johns Hopkins University Press.

Ekroth, Gunnel. 2007. "Heroes and Hero Cult." In Ogden 2007, pp. 100–14.

Eliade, Mircea. 1954. *The Myth of the Eternal Return*. Trans. by Willard R. Trask. New York: Pantheon Books.

Eliade, Mircea. 1958. *Patterns in Comparative Religion*. New York: World Publishing.

Eliade, Mircea. 1959. *The Sacred and the Profane: The Nature of Religion*. New York: Harcourt, Brace & World.

Eliade, Mircea. 1963. *Myth and Reality*. Trans. by Willard R. Trask. New York: Harper & Row.

Eliade, Mircea. 1977. *From Primitives to Zen: A Thematic Sourcebook of the History of Religions*. New York: Harper & Row.

Ellwood, Robert. 1999. *The Politics of Myth: A Study of C. G. Jung, Mircea Eliade, and Joseph Campbell*. Albany, NY: State University of New York Press.

Elsner, Jas. 2007. *Roman Eyes. Visuality and Subjectivity in Art and Text*. Princeton, NJ: Princeton University Press.

Euripides. 2008. *Fragments: Aegeus – Meleager*. Trans. by Christopher Collard and Martin Cropp. Cambridge, MA: Harvard University Press.

Euripides. 2009. *Fragments: Oedipus – Chrysippus and other Fragments*. Trans. by Christopher Collard and Martin Cropp. Cambridge, MA: Harvard University Press.

Farnell, Lewis Richard. 1921. *Greek Hero Cults and Ideas of Immortality*. Oxford: Clarendon Press.

Farrell, Joseph. 2004. "Roman Homer." In Fowler 2004, pp. 254–71.

Felton, D. 2007. "The Dead." In Ogden 2007, pp. 86–99.

Fitton, J. Leslie. 1996. *The Discovery of the Greek Bronze Age*. Cambridge, MA: Harvard University Press.

Finley, M. I. 2002 [1954]. *The World of Odysseus*. New York: New York Review Books.

Foley, Helene P., ed. 1994. *The Homeric Hymn to Demeter: Translation, Commentary, and Interpretive Essays*. Princeton, NJ: Princeton University Press.

Fontenrose, Joseph. 1978. *The Delphic Oracle*. Berkeley, CA: University of California Press.

Fontenrose, Joseph. 1981. *Orion: the Myth of the Hunter and the Huntress*. Berkeley, CA: University of California Press.

Fowler, Robert. 2000. *Early Greek Mythography*. New York: Oxford University Press.

Fowler, Robert, ed. 2004. *The Cambridge Companion to Homer*. Cambridge: Cambridge University Press.

Franklin, James L. 1990. *Pompeii: The Casa del Marinaio and its History*. Rome: 'L'Erma' di Bretschneider.

Frazer, Sir James George. 1948 [1922]. *The Golden Bough*. Abridged edn. New York: Macmillan.

Gagarin, Michael. 1976. *Aeschylean Drama*. Berkeley, CA: University of California Press.

Gallop, David. 1991. *Parmenides of Elea – Fragments*. Toronto: University of Toronto Press.

Gantz, Timothy. 1993. *Early Greek Myth*. Baltimore, MD: Johns Hopkins University Press.

George, Andrew, trans. 1999. *The Epic of Gilgamesh: The Babylonian Epic Poem and Other Texts in Akkadian and Sumerian*. London: Penguin.

Goff, Barbara. 2004. *Citizen Bacchae: Women's Ritual Practice in Ancient Greece*. Berkeley, CA: University of California Press.

Golden, Mark and Peter Toohey. 2003. *Sex and Difference in Ancient Greece and Rome*. Edinburgh: Edinburgh University Press.

Goldhill, Simon. 1986. *Reading Greek Tragedy*. Cambridge: Cambridge University Press.

Goldhill, Simon. 1992. *Aeschylus, the Oresteia*. Cambridge: Cambridge University Press.

Gow, A. S. F. and D. L. Page. 1965. *The Greek Anthology: Hellenistic Epigrams*. 2 vols. Cambridge: Cambridge University Press.

Graf, Fritz. 1993 [1987]. *Greek Mythology: An Introduction*. Trans. by Thomas Marier. Baltimore, MD: Johns Hopkins University Press.

Guthrie, W. K. C. 1957. *In the Beginning: Some Greek Views on the Origins of Life and the Early State of Man*. London: Methuen.

Hägg, Robin, ed. 1999. *Ancient Greek Hero Cult*. Stockholm: Svenska Institutet i Athen.

Hall, Edith. 1989. *Inventing the Barbarian: Greek Self-Definition through Tragedy*. Oxford: Clarendon Press.

Hall, Edith. 1997. "The Sociology of Athenian Tragedy." In Easterling 1997, pp. 93–126.

Hall, Jonathan. 2007. "Politics and Greek Myth." In Woodard 2007a, pp. 331–54.

Halperin, David M., John J. Winkler, and Froma Zeitlin, eds. 1990. *Before Sexuality: The Construction of Erotic Experience in the Ancient Greek World*. Princeton, NJ: Princeton University Press.

Harris, Stephen and Gloria Platzner. 2011. *Classical Mythology: Images and Insights*. 6th edn. Boston, MA: McGraw-Hill.

Hatab, Lawrence J. 1990. *Myth and Philosophy: A Contest of Truths*. La Salle, IL: Open Court Press.

Hayes, Elizabeth T., ed. 1994. *Images of Persephone: Feminist Readings in Western Literature*. Gainesville, FL: University Press of Florida.

Heath, John. 1992. *Actaeon, the Unmannerly Intruder: The Myth and its Meaning in Classical Literature*. New York: Peter Lang.

Hesiod. 2007. *Hesiod: The Shield, Catalogue of Women, Other Fragments*. Ed. and trans. by Glenn W. Most. Cambridge, MA: Harvard University Press.

Higbie, Carolyn. 1997. "The Bones of a Hero, the Ashes of a Politician: Athens, Salamis, and the Usable Past." *Classical Antiquity*, 16/2, pp. 278–307.

Hunter, Richard. 2004. "Homer and Greek Literature." In Fowler 2004, pp. 235–53.

Hunter, Virginia. 1982. *Past and Process in Herodotus and Thucydides*. Princeton, NJ: Princeton University Press.

Jung, Carl G., ed. 1968a. *Man and His Symbols*. New York: Dell.

Jung, Carl G. 1968b. "Approaching the Unconscious." In Jung 1968a, pp. 1–94.

Jung, Carl G. 1998. *Jung on Mythology*. Selected and introduced by Robert Alan Segal. Princeton, NJ: Princeton University Press.

Jung, Carl G. and Carl Kerényi. 1963. *Essays on a Science of Mythology: The Myths of the Divine Child and the Divine Maiden*. New York: Harper & Row.

Kearns, Emily. 1989. *The Heroes of Attica*. London: University of London, Institute of Classical Studies.

Kearns, Emily. 1998. "The Nature of Heroines." In Blundell and Williamson 1998, pp. 96–111.

Kerényi, Karl. 1967. *Eleusis: Archetypal Image of Mother and Daughter*. New York: Pantheon Books.

Kerényi, Karl. 1973. *Asklepios: Archetypal Image of the Physician's Existence*. Princeton, NJ: Princeton University Press.

Kerényi, Karl. 1975. *Zeus and Hera: Archetypal Image of Father, Husband, and Wife*. Princeton, NJ: Princeton University Press.

Kerényi, Karl. 1976. *Dionysos: Archetypal Image of Indestructible Life*. Princeton, NJ: Princeton University Press.

Kerényi, Karl. 1997. *Prometheus: Archetypal Image of Human Existence*. Princeton, NJ: Princeton University Press.

Keuls, Eva. 1985. *The Reign of the Phallus: Sexual Politics in Ancient Athens*. New York: Harper & Row.

Kirk, Geoffrey. 1970. *Myth: Its Meaning and Functions in Ancient and Other Cultures*. Berkeley, CA: University of California Press.

Kirk, Geoffrey. 1974. *The Nature of Greek Myths*. Harmondsworth: Penguin.

Kirk, Geoffrey, J. E. Raven, and M. Schofield. 1983. *The Presocratic Philosophers*. 2nd edn. Cambridge: Cambridge University Press.

Knox, Bernard. 1979. *Word and Action: Essays on the Ancient Theatre*. Baltimore, MD: Johns Hopkins University Press.

Lamberton, Robert, ed. 1983. *Porphyry: On the Cave of the Nymphs*. Barrytown, NY: Station Hill Press.

Lamberton, Robert. 1989. *Homer the Theologian: Neoplatonist Allegorical Reading and the Growth of the Epic Tradition*. Berkeley, CA: University of California Press.

Larson, Jennifer. 1995. *Greek Heroine Cults*. Madison, WI: University of Wisconsin Press.

Larson, Jennifer. 2007. *Ancient Greek Cults: A Guide*. New York: Routledge.

Lefkowitz, Mary R. 2007. *Women in Greek Myth*. 2nd edn. Baltimore, MD: Johns Hopkins University Press.

Lexicon Iconographicum Mythologiae Classicae (LIMC). 1981–97. 16 vols. + Supplement 2009. Zurich: Artemis.

Lincoln, Bruce. 1991. *Death, War, and Sacrifice: Studies in Ideology and Practice*. Chicago, IL: University of Chicago Press.

Lincoln, Bruce. 1999. *Theorizing Myth: Narrative, Ideology, and Scholarship*. Chicago, IL: University of Chicago Press.

Ling, Roger. 1991. *Roman Painting*. Cambridge: Cambridge University Press.

Lissarrague, François. 2001. *Greek Vases: The Athenians and Their Images*. New York: Riverside Book Company.

Littleton, C. Scott. 1966. *The New Comparative Mythology: An Anthropological Assessment of the Theories of Georges Dumézil*. Berkeley, CA: University of California Press.

Lloyd, G. E. R. 1966. *Polarity and Analogy: Two Types of Argumentation in Early Greek Thought*. Cambridge: Cambridge University Press.

Lloyd-Jones, Hugh. 1971. *The Justice of Zeus*. Berkeley, CA: University of California Press.

Lloyd-Jones, Hugh. 1976. "The Delphic Oracle." *Greece & Rome*, 2nd series, 23/1, pp. 60–73.

Loraux, Nicole. 1993. *The Children of Athena: Athenian Ideas about Citizenship and the Division between the Sexes*. Trans. by Caroline Levine. Princeton, NJ: Princeton University Press.

Loraux, Nicole. 1995. *The Experiences of Tiresias: The Feminine and the Greek Man*. Princeton, NJ: Princeton University Press.

Loraux, Nicole. 2006. *The Invention of Athens: The Funeral Oration in the Classical City*. Trans. by Alan Sheridan. New York: Zone Books.

Lyons, Deborah. 1997. *Gender and Immortality: Heroines in Greek Myth and Cult*. Princeton, NJ: Princeton University Press.

Macleod, Colin. 1983. "Politics in the Oresteia." In his *Collected Essays*, Oxford, Clarendon Press, pp. 20–40.

Malkin, Irad. 1994. *Myth and Territory in the Spartan Mediterranean*. Cambridge: Cambridge University Press.

McCauley, Barbara. 1999. "Heroes and Power: The Politics of Bone Transfer." In Hägg 1999, pp. 85–98.

Mikalson, Jon D. 2005. *Ancient Greek Religion*. Malden, MA: Blackwell.

Moorehead, Caroline. 1996. *Lost and Found: The 9000 Treasures of Troy: Heinrich Schliemann and the Gold that Got Away*. New York: Viking.

Morford, Mark P. O., Robert J. Lenardon, and Michael Sham. 2011. *Classical Mythology*. 9th edn. New York: Oxford University Press.

Morris, Ian. 1986. "The Use and Abuse of Homer." *Classical Antiquity*, 5/1, pp. 81–138.

Nagy, Gregory. 1979. *The Best of the Achaeans: Concepts of the Hero in Archaic Greek Poetry*. Baltimore, MD: Johns Hopkins University Press.

Nagy, Gregory. 1990a. *Greek Mythology and Poetics*. Ithaca, NY: Cornell University Press.

Nagy, Gregory. 1990b. *Pindar's Homer: The Lyric Possession of an Epic Past*. Baltimore, MD: Johns Hopkins University Press.

O'Brien, Joan. 1993. *The Transformation of Hera*. Lanham, MD: Rowman & Littlefield.

O'Flaherty, Wendy Doniger. 1995. *Other People's Myths: The Cave of Echoes*. Chicago, IL: University of Chicago Press.

O'Flaherty, Wendy Doniger. See also Doniger, Wendy.

Ogden, Daniel, ed. 2007. *A Companion to Greek Religion*. Malden, MA: Blackwell.

Osborne, Robin. 1998. *Archaic and Classical Greek Art*. Oxford: Oxford University Press.

Pache, Corinne. 2004. *Baby and Child Heroes in Ancient Greece*. Urbana, IL: University of Illinois Press.

Parke, H. W. 1977. *Festivals of the Athenians*. Ithaca, NY: Cornell University Press.

Parke, H. W. and D. E. W. Wormell. 1956. *The Delphic Oracle*. Oxford: Basil Blackwell.

Parker, Robert. 1988. "Myths of Early Athens." In Bremmer 1988a, pp. 187–214.

Parker, Robert. 1996. *Athenian Religion: A History*. Oxford: Clarendon Press.

Parker, Robert. 2005. *Polytheism and Society at Athens*. Oxford: Oxford University Press.

Penglase, Charles. 1994. *Greek Myths and Mesopotamia: Parallels and Influences in the Homeric Hymns and Hesiod*. London: Routledge.

Podlecki, Anthony. 1966. *The Political Background of Aeschylean Tragedy*. Ann Arbor, MI: University of Michigan Press.

Popper, Karl. 2001. *The World of Parmenides: Essays on the Presocratic Enlightenment*. Ed. by Arne F. Petersen, with the assistance of Jørgen Mejer. London: Routledge.

Porter, James. 2004. "Homer: The History of an Idea." In Fowler 2004, pp. 324–43.

Powell, Barry B. 2008. *Classical Myth*. 6th edn. Upper Saddle River, NJ: Prentice Hall.

Price, Simon. 1999. *Religions of the Ancient Greeks*. Cambridge: Cambridge University Press.

Rabinowitz, Nancy Sorkin. 1993. *Anxiety Veiled: Euripides and the Traffic in Women*. Ithaca, NY: Cornell University Press.

Rademaker, Adriaan. 2005. *Sophrosyne and the Rhetoric of Self-Restraint: Polysemy and Persuasive Use of an Ancient Greek Value Term*. Leiden: Brill.

Rhodes, Robin Francis. 1995. *Architecture and Meaning on the Athenian Acropolis*. Cambridge: Cambridge University Press.

Richardson, N. J., ed. 1974. *The Homeric Hymn to Demeter*. Oxford: Clarendon Press.

Rose, Peter. 1992. *Sons of the Gods, Children of the Earth: Ideology and Literary Form in Ancient Greece*. Ithaca, NY: Cornell University Press.

Segal, Charles. 1981. *Tragedy and Civilization: An Interpretation of Sophocles*. Cambridge, MA: Harvard University Press,

Segal, Charles. 1986. *Interpreting Greek Tragedy: Myth, Poetry, Text*. Ithaca, NY: Cornell University Press.

Segal, Charles. 1995. *Sophocles' Tragic World: Divinity, Nature, Society*. Cambridge, MA: Harvard University Press.

Sergent, Bernard. 1986. *Homosexuality in Greek Myth*. Trans. by Arthur Goldhammer, with a preface by Georges Dumézil. Boston: Beacon Press.

Shapiro, Alan. 1994. *Myth Into Art: Poet and Painter in Classical Greece*. London: Routledge.

Shay, Jonathan. 1995. *Achilles in Vietnam: Combat Trauma and the Undoing of Character*. New York: Atheneum.

Shay, Jonathan. 2003. *Odysseus in America: Combat Trauma and the Trials of Homecoming*. New York: Scribner.

Slater, Philip. 1968. *The Glory of Hera: Greek Mythology and the Greek Family*. Boston: Beacon Press.

Snell, Bruno, Richard Kannicht, and Stefan Radt. 1977–2004. *Tragicorum Graecorum Fragmenta*. 5 vols. Göttingen: Vandenhoeck & Ruprecht.

Snodgrass, Anthony. 1981. *Archaic Greece: The Age of Experiment*. Berkeley, CA: University of California Press.

Sophocles. 1996. *Fragments*. Trans. by Hugh Lloyd-Jones. Cambridge, MA: Harvard University Press.

Sourvinou-Inwood, Christiane. 1988. "Myth as History: The Previous Ownership of the Delphic Oracle." In Bremmer 1988a, pp. 215–41.

Sourvinou-Inwood, Christiane. 2003. *Tragedy and Athenian Religion*. Lanham, MD: Lexington.

Stafford, Emma. 2007. "Personification in Greek Religious Thought and Practice." In Ogden 2007, pp. 71–85.

Steiner, George. 1984. *Antigones*. New Haven, CT: Yale University Press.

Stern, Jacob. 1996. *Palaephatus: On Unbelievable Tales*. Translation, Introduction, and Commentary. Wauconda, IL: Bolchazy-Carducci Publishers.

Strenski, Ivan. 1987. *Four Theories of Myth in Twentieth Century History: Cassirer, Eliade, Lévi-Strauss and Malinowski*. Basingstoke: Macmillan.

Tatum, James. 2003. *The Mourner's Song: War and Remembrance from the Iliad to Vietnam*. Chicago, IL: University of Chicago Press.

Traill, David. 1995. *Schliemann of Troy: Treasure and Deceit*. New York: St. Martin's Press.

Trzaskoma, Stephen, R. Scott Smith, and Stephen Brunet. 2004. *Anthology of Classical Myth: Primary Sources in Translation*. Indianapolis, IN: Hackett.

Tyrell, William Blake and Frieda S. Brown. 1991. *Athenian Myths and Institutions: Words in Action*. New York: Oxford University Press.

van Gennep, Arnold. 1977 [1909]. *The Rites of Passage*. Trans. by Monika B. Vizedom and Gabrielle L. Caffee. London: Routledge & Kegan Paul.

Vernant, Jean-Pierre. 1980. *Myth and Society in Ancient Greece*. New York: Zone Books.

Vernant, Jean-Pierre. 1982 [1962]. *The Origins of Greek Thought*. Ithaca, NY: Cornell University Press.

Vernant, Jean-Pierre. 1988a. "The Historical Moment of Tragedy in Greece: Social and Psychological Conditions." In Vernant and Vidal-Naquet 1988, pp. 23–28.

Vernant, Jean-Pierre. 1988b. "Tensions and Ambiguities in Greek Tragedy." In Vernant and Vidal-Naquet 1988, pp. 29–48.

Vernant, Jean-Pierre. 1989. "At Man's Table." In Detienne and Vernant 1989, pp. 21–86.

Vernant, Jean-Pierre. 2006 [1965]. *Myth and Thought among the Greeks*. Trans. by Janet Lloyd with Jeff Fort. New York: Zone Books.

Vernant, Jean-Pierre and Pierre Vidal-Naquet. 1988 [1972]. *Myth and Tragedy in Ancient Greece*. Trans. by Janet Lloyd. New York: Zone Books.

Versnel, H. S. 1988. "Greek Myth and Ritual: The Case of Kronos." In Bremmer 1988a, pp. 121–52.

Vidal-Naquet, Pierre. 1986 [1981]. *The Black Hunter: Forms of Thought and Forms of Society in the Greek World*. Trans. by Andrew Szegedy-Maszak. Baltimore, MD: Johns Hopkins University Press.

Vidal-Naquet, Pierre. 2007 [2005]. *The Atlantis Story: A Short History of Plato's Myth*. Trans. by Janet Lloyd. Exeter: University of Exeter Press.

von Franz, Marie-Louise. 1972. *Creation Myths*. Rev. edn. Boston, MA: Shambhala Press.

Walcot, P. 1966. *Hesiod and the Near East*. Cardiff: University of Wales Press.

Walker, Henry J. 1995. *Theseus and Athens*. Oxford: Oxford University Press.

West, M. L. 1966. *Theogony*. Oxford: Clarendon Press.

West, M. L. 1983. *The Orphic Poems*. Oxford: Clarendon Press.

West, M. L. 1997. *The East Face of Helicon: West Asiatic Elements in Greek Poetry and Myth*. Oxford: Clarendon Press.

Willcock, M. M. 1999 [1964]. "Mythological Paradeigma in the *Iliad*." In de Jong 1999, III, pp. 385–402. Originally published in *Classical Quarterly*, 14, 1964, pp. 141–54.

Winkler, John and Froma Zeitlin, eds. 1990. *Nothing to Do with Dionysos? Athenian Drama in Its Social Context*. Princeton, NJ: Princeton University Press.

Winkler, John. 1990. *The Constraints of Desire: The Anthropology of Sex and Gender in Ancient Greece*. London: Routledge, Chapman and Hall.

Wood, Michael. 1996. *In Search of the Trojan War*. Berkeley, CA: University of California Press.

Woodard, Roger D., ed. 2007. *The Cambridge Companion to Greek Mythology*. Cambridge: Cambridge University Press.

Woodford, Susan. 2003. *Images of Myths in Classical Antiquity*. Cambridge: Cambridge University Press.

Index

Note: page numbers in italics refer to Figures.

Exploring Greek Myth. First Edition. Matthew Clark.
© 2012 Matthew Clark. Published 2012 by Blackwell Publishing Ltd.

CPSIA information can be obtained
at www.ICGtesting.com
Printed in the USA
BVHW051743021120
592333BV00006B/57